Social Integration and Narrative Structure

New York University Ottendorfer Series
Neue Folge Band 23

unter Mitarbeit von
Helmut Brackert (Frankfurt/M.),
Peter Demetz (Yale), Reinhold Grimm (Wisconsin),
Walter Hinderer (Princeton)

herausgegeben von
Volkmar Sander

PETER LANG
New York · Berne · Frankfurt am Main

Nancy A. Kaiser

Social Integration and Narrative Structure
Patterns of Realism in Auerbach, Freytag, Fontane, and Raabe

PETER LANG
New York · Berne · Frankfurt am Main

Library of Congress Cataloging in Publication Data

Kaiser, Nancy A.:
Social Integration and Narrative Structure.

(New York University Ottendorfer Series;
n. F., Bd. 23)
Bibliography: p.
1. German fiction – 19th century – History and criticism,   2. Realism in literature.   3. Social problems in literature.   4. Auerbach, Berthold, 1812–1882 – Criticism and interpretation.   5. Freytag, Gustav, 1816–1895 – Criticism and interpretation.   6. Fontane, Theodor, 1819–1898 – Criticism and interpretation.   7. Raabe, Wilhelm Karl, 1831–1910 – Criticism and interpretation.
I. Title. II. Series.
PT763.K34   1987   833'.8'091   86-44
ISBN 0-8204-0327-X
ISSN 0172-3529

CIP-Kurztitelaufnahme der Deutschen Bibliothek

Kaiser, Nancy A.:
Social Integration and Narrative Structure:
Patterns of Realism in Auerbach, Freytag, Fontane, and Raabe / Nancy A. Kaiser. – New York; Berne; Frankfurt am Main: Lang, 1986.
(New York University Ottendorfer Series; N.F., Bd. 23)
ISBN 0-8204-0327-X

NE: New York University: New York University . . .

© Peter Lang Publishing, Inc., New York 1986

All rights reserved.
Reprint or reproduction, even partially, in all forms such as microfilm, xerography, microfiche, microcard, offset strictly prohibited.

Printed by Lang Druck, Inc., Liebefeld/Berne (Switzerland)

PREFACE

The disparate complex of fictional texts and programmatic writings characterized as nineteenth-century German Realism remains problematic for literary scholars. Traditional analyses have dealt with the reflection of social reality in the texts, emphasizing the mimetic mode of realistic fiction. Attempts to do justice to the uniquely German quality have often pointed out the "poeticizing" aspects of the works. My interest in the critical debates and in the literary works themselves has led me to consider realism as a category of literary communication, in which the process of reading is of primary importance. The interaction of text and reader may be thought of as constructing the world which a "realistic" novel is often said to reflect or describe. In examining specific segments of nineteenth-century German prose fiction, I have established distinct patterns of reader experience. It is not my purpose to attempt comprehensive reinterpretations of the works which I have chosen for careful analysis but rather to delineate the communicative structure common to all of the texts within a given segment. My work is intended as a contribution to the continuing discussion of literary realism and to the investigation of nineteenth-century German prose fiction.

In developing the original impulses and analyses in this study I was encouraged by Professor Peter Demetz of Yale University, whose scholarly work and patient counsel have been invaluable. I am further grateful to Professor Jeffrey L. Sammons of Yale University for his sincere interest and enlightening critical suggestions. The generosity of the Whiting Foundation enabled me to devote a year solely to the project at an important stage, and the support was essential. In addition I extend my gratitude for making publication of this book possible to the Department of German at the University of Wisconsin-Madison and to Professor Volkmar Sander of New York University, editor of the Ottendorfer Series. To my colleagues Professor Max Baeumer and Professor Reinhold Grimm I am indebted for opportune assistance and support.

A portion of Chapter IV appeared in an earlier version in *Germanic Review*, 59, 1 (Winter, 1984) as "Reading Raabe's Realism: *Die Akten des Vogelsangs.*" The editorial board has given permission to reprint sections of the article.

Nancy A. Kaiser

Madison, Wisconsin
August, 1985

TABLE OF CONTENTS

I. The Altered Perspective:
   Readers, Realities, and Narrative Structure 9
   The Point of Departure 9
   Modes of Integration 21
   The Narrative System 29

II. Cohesion and Integration:
   Reading as Reaffirmation 35
   Soll und Haben and Auerbach's *Dorfgeschichte:*
   A Parallel Pattern 35
   The Cohesive Social Universe and the Integration
   of the Individual 48
   The Authority of the Narrative System 69

III. Convention and Narrative Refraction:
   Reading the Social Code 87
   Social Event and Individual Perspective:
   Schach von Wuthenow 91
   The Opacity of the Social System:
   Effi Briest 105
   The Social Dynamics in *Der Stechlin* 118

IV. The Elusive Center: Narration as Disorientation 133
   The Force of Narrative Inertia: *Stopfkuchen* 137
   Isolation, Integration, and Compromise:
   Die Akten des Vogelsangs 150

V. The Extended Perspective: Realism
and Reader Experience 167

VI. Notes 173

VII. Bibliography 211

I. THE ALTERED PERSPECTIVE:
READERS, REALITIES, AND NARRATIVE STRUCTURE

The Point of Departure

An appropriate perspective for German prose fiction in the latter half of the nineteenth century entails a focus on processes of integration. The pattern of social history providing the context for the literature of the period and the thematic content of the narratives display a common concern with integration as an underlying principle of social composition. Broadly defined as the incorporation of individual unit into encompassing system, integration implies order and patterns of correlation. Each compositional unit functions within the contextual system and is defined by a specific position within the aggregate design. For nineteenth-century Germany, the concept is applicable to an analysis of the development of the middle classes and to a consideration of the position of the individual within society. As a matter of narrative content in literature, social integration pertains to the composition and function of the social system and to the assimilation of the individual character as presented by the fictional text.

Establishing an analogous pattern in historical context and narrative content is not sufficient to account for the complex relationship of fiction and historical reality. Nor would such an enterprise do justice to the literary work itself, which requires analysis of the mode of presentation as well as of the material presented, of form as well as content. Even establishing structural parallels abstracted from specific content considerations, such as Lucien Goldmann's "homologies," is not adequate to deal with the connection of literary work and historical context.[1] Such an approach, which emphasizes the socio-economic conditions of the genesis of a text, offers ultimately a static model of correspondences. Similar to investigations restricted to content, it relies on concepts of mimesis, the reflection of contemporaneous social conditions or the reproduction of their structures, to delineate the "realism" of nineteenth-century literature.

When examined according to categories of mimesis, especially if restricted to content, German Realism is customarily faulted for deficient breadth, for a failure to achieve what Erich Auerbach's well-known formulation designates as the "European form of realism ... a serious representation of contemporary everyday social reality against the background of a constant historical movement."[2] With the fragmented political and historical situation often given as the reason, the portrayal of social forces in German narrative is designated as limited, static or provincial.[3] The German novel does not offer the encompassing model of society found in Dickens or Balzac, and the mechanisms of social reality are not as critically exposed. German narratives do not carry subtitles such as "les mœurs de province," "chronique du 19e siècle" or "a novel without a hero." Instead, the problematic integration of self and world becomes a peculiarly German theme. The German image is not of the novelist as a "secretary" writing the forgotten history of social customs as Balzac conceived of himself in the preface to *La Comédie Humaine.* Even Gutzkow, whose *Ritter vom Geiste* represented an attempt at a panoramic novel of the total expanse of social reality, retains a Romantic view in his preface of the novelist as occupying the perspective of an eagle soaring in the air. German Realism is rather concerned with the transformation or "poeticization" of reality, and its specific character is not captured with concepts of mimesis, literary reflection of social reality, or structural homologies.[4]

In recognition of the particular caliber of nineteenth-century German Realism, scholarship has turned to questions of form. Otto Ludwig's term "poetischer Realismus" has been appropriated, and consideration of the "Kunstcharakter" of individual works and authors has taken precedence.[5] At the theoretical level, questions of form are often discussed under the rubric of the interrelation of subject and object, terms themselves central to German idealist aesthetics. Richard Brinkmann's *Wirklichkeit und Illusion* (1957) represented the initial innovative effort to concentrate on the structure of the works chosen. Other studies, particularly those of Preisendanz and Ohl, have adapted Hegelian terminology to an analysis of the poetic character of the German novel of the nineteenth century.[6] A concentration on the form and the "poetic" realism of German narrative is definitely a desirable extension of the parameters of research, yet it is often accompanied by a severing of the link between literary work and historical context. If scholarship based on content analysis and the establishment of correspondences between fictional text and social reality denies the specific mode of existence of a work of literature, excessively formal criticism disregards the interrelationship of literature and reality. Such an omission seems hardly tenable when considering a corpus of literature designated as realistic. Gerhard Kaiser offers a succinct formulation of the dilemma in his review essay of Ohl's *Bild und Wirklichkeit:* "so sicher ist es notwendig, den Blick auf die Realität selbst in die Interpretation der Dichtung einzubeziehen, mit anderen Worten: die Frage nach dem Realismus dieses Realismus zu stellen."[7]

The inadequacies of an over-concentration on the formal, poetic aspects of German Realism or on the subject-object dichotomy and its reconciliation become further apparent when the choice of texts is considered. Keller, Fontane, Raabe, and Stifter appear to have been gradually canonized as the primary German realist writers of the nineteenth century. A survey of the century's own discussion of realism reveals, however, rather different emphases. The main texts in the 1850s were not *Der grüne Heinrich* (first version 1854/5), *Die Chronik der Sperlingsgasse* (1857) or *Nachsommer* (1857). Debate in the literary and cultural journals of the time centered on *Die Ritter vom Geiste* (1850/1), *Soll und Haben* (1855) and Alexis' novels. Gustav Freytag, Julian Schmidt, Robert Prutz and Hermann Marggraff were some of the more influential figures, and Berthold Auerbach's *Schwarzwälder Dorfgeschichten* (1843ff) attracted a broader readership than the first installment of Keller's *Leute von Seldwyla* (1856).[8] Studies since 1970 by Helmuth Widhammer, Hermann Kinder, and Hartmut Steinecke as well as the collectively edited *Realismus und Gründerzeit* have readjusted the focus of realism scholarship to include a consideration of the influential texts, journals and debates of the century itself.[9]

An intriguing question arises from the juxtaposition of the forum of discussion in the mid-nineteenth century with realism scholarship in the twentieth. It concerns the historicity of the texts themselves, the discrepancy between the appreciation of certain works for their "realism" at the time and the assessment of the works a century later. The most obvious example is Gustav Freytag's novel *Soll und Haben*. In his 1855 review of the novel, Theodor Fontane designated it as "die erste Blüte des modernen Realismus" and praised it as surpassing the English tradition of Dickens and Thackeray or the American Cooper in its artistic interpenetration of *Idee* and *Form*. Complimenting the tightly-knit composition and convincing motivation in a strict architectonic form, he added of the content of the book, "es ist auch ebenso wahr, wie es schön ist."[10] A good hundred years later, the novel is relegated to the realm of popular literature, the negative stereotyping of Jews is criticized, the narrative structure is characterized as mediocre and predictable, especially in contrast to Keller's *Grüner Heinrich,* and an underlying "mendacity" of the work is suggested.[11]

It is, of course, possible to resolve the apparent divergence in evaluations through recourse to ideological analysis of the content of the work. A novel now viewed as a "Liberal-National Manifesto" (Carter) or "Das Hohelied des bürgerlichen Kaufmannstandes" (Löwenthal) and whose author is characterized as an "Exponent des selbstbewußten, vorwiegend wirtschaftlich orientierten Bürgertums" (Worthmann) would understandably be read as "realistic" by the economically ascendant bourgeoisie of the 1850s. And the varying evaluation of narrative form could be ascribed to increasingly sophisticated expectations for poetic structure in the twentieth century which valorize the complexity of a Keller or a Raabe novel.

Yet both professed explanations for the historicity of this particular text have shifted the plane of discussion perceptibly. The decisive factor is neither the content nor the form of the literary work but the interaction of both with the context of reception, the expectations and attitudes within which the text is read. The answer to the intriguing discrepancies engendered by the juxtaposition of the forum of discussion in the mid-nineteenth century with realism scholarship in the twentieth must be sought in an amended concept of realism which relies neither solely on content analysis of reflected social reality nor mainly on the appraisal of an autonomous poetic structure. The reception of a work, the fact and manner of its being read and its status as communication, is a central category of analysis. The reader, or rather the intersection of reader and literary text, becomes the locus of "realism." Since a "reader" never exists outside of a contextual historical reality, the link between literary work and external reality is retained yet is flexible enough to allow for historical variation. Helmut Kreuzer has described the recognition by the reader of a familiar reality in the text as the criterion of realism, which he views as a "relational" or historically variable property of a work.[12] In a century concerned with integration as a principle of social composition, the function of literature within the pattern and processes of social history is closely connected to its effect upon the reading public, its support or modification of existing reality paradigms. The effect and concomitant function are traceable in the reception of the literary works.

The historical variations in the reception and status of a text as well as the disparate character of German nineteenth-century Realism as a whole may be analyzed in terms of literature as communication rather than representation. The difference between Freytag's *Soll und Haben* and Raabe's Braunschweig novels of the 1890s, for example, is a case of the dialectic reversal within German Realism as postulated by Helmuth Widhammer: "jener dialektische Umschlag ... von der apologetischen und selbstbestätigenden Verklärung zur unbestechlichen und oft melancholischen Selbstkritik."[13] What is implied in the reversal is a shift in the integrative function of the literary works themselves from affirmation to criticism, a shift best analyzed as restructured communication for the reading public.

The reorientation toward the role of the reader in a consideration of literary realism is not a totally unresearched area, but much concrete work remains to be accomplished. In his extensive report on the current state of scholarship in the fourth edition of the volume *Deutsche Literatur im bürgerlichen Realismus 1848-98* (1981), Fritz Martini links empirical investigations of the reading public to studies of popular literature of the nineteenth century.[14] He is more sceptical of the possibility of such investigations in connection with what he terms the "künstlerisch anspruchsvollere Erzählliteratur." For authors such as Raabe, Fontane, Stifter, and Ludwig he sets the task of reconstruction of the "implied" reader through analysis of the strategies and mechanisms of the text itself. Following Martini,

Klaus-Detlev Müller correctly designates a 1972 essay by Horst Steinmetz as opening the discussion regarding German Realism to productive impulses from Wolfgang Iser and Hans-Robert Jauß on reception aesthetics, the role of the reader in literary history and the delineation of the "implied reader" in literary works.[15] A later essay by Steinmetz applies these categories to Ludwig's concept of poetic realism, and Leo Lensing's 1977 study is one of the best examples of an interpretive application, outlining the role of the narrative structure in guiding the reader of Raabe's *Im alten Eisen.*[16]

Hugo Aust's Metzler volume devotes sections to realism as a question of communication and to the reading public in the nineteenth century. He warns against an exaggerated insistence on the primacy of the act of reading, leading to the neglect of the text itself and underscores Martini's call for an analysis of the "Strategie-Elemente" within the literary text.[17] In regarding Martini's, Aust's and Müller's surveys of the possible contributions of reception aesthetics to the study of German Realism and Steinmetz's earlier essay, "Der vergessene Leser," two conclusions may be drawn. One involves a basic reorientation in the definition of a literary work, and the second concerns a tripartite division in tasks facing literary scholars within the framework of a discussion focusing on the intersection of reader and text as the locus of realism.

Including the recipient as an integral part of a literary work and reception as part of the definition of literature entails an understanding of the contextual production of meaning, a sense of the partiality of the text and a concept of literature as a communicative process. In *Theories of Literature in the Twentieth Century,* D.W. Fokkema and Elrud Kunne-Ibsch define the object of literary scholarship as no longer a document, as it was for positivistic research, nor as the monument respected by intrinsic criticism but as a "sign" or "appeal structure" requiring reader cooperation.[18] Wolfgang Iser has offered a phenomenological analysis of the processes of reader realization and supplementation of textual directives, an analysis utilized by Lensing in his book on Raabe.[19] Hans Robert Jauß has dealt more specifically with questions of literary history and has adapted elements of Prague structuralism and Gadamer's hermeneutics to account for the continued vitality and varying evaluations of literary texts. It was Jauß's inaugural lecture at the University of Constance in 1967, later published as "Literaturgeschichte als Provokation der Literaturwissenschaft," which can be credited with the initial impetus to incorporate the reception process as an essential part of literary scholarship.[20] The 1970s witnessed a plethora of contributions, mostly theoretical, to the realm of critical discourse in Germany: Gunter Grimm's introduction and *Forschungsbericht* of 1975 took up the first 73 pages and 371 footnotes of the volume *Literatur und Leser* in an attempted survey of relevant research up to that point.[21]

One of the roots of the work begun in Constance reaches back to Prague in the 1930s, specifically to the theories of the aesthetic function of a work of art as a semiological fact in a specific historical context. The distinction made by Jan Mukařovský between the text as an artefact with a potential only realized in the interaction with the multiplicity of aesthetic and social norms of the context of reception and the aesthetic object which is the final, historically variable product of the process is a basic principle of the redefinition of a literary work.[22] It is a distinction which does not always retain the same terminology; categories of potential text structure and actualized concretization can be traced to Roman Ingarden and have been used by Felix Vodička and Jauß, and a similar duality is evident, for example, in the text-theoretical distinction of Götz Wienold between "Ausgangstext" as the basis and "Resultattext" as the product of "Textverarbeitungsprozesse" by the recipient.[23] The emphasis in any viable variation on the theme is on the partial, potential character of the text and the necessary interaction with the context of reception in a process of constitutive communication.[24]

Such a re-orientation in the definition of a literary work, the denial of its autonomous status or connection solely to the conditions of its genesis, is evident as well in the diffuse domain of scholarship variously termed pragmatics, pragmalinguistics, or text-theory. It is interesting to note that the developments in this direction within linguistics were chronologically parallel to the rise of interest in reception aesthetics in Germany. The basic category of pragmatics goes back further and is founded in Charles Morris' distinction between syntax, semantics, and pragmatics, the last being the relationship between sign and interpreter.[25] And linguistics had considered units beyond the sentence (texts) earlier, but mostly as part of a generative model. It is not until the late 1960s and early 1970s, however, that attempts were made to consider the text in a communicative model stressing the role of the recipient in constituting the message.[26] The proliferation of models and terminologies within this realm of critical discourse defies systematization; two of the most coherent and informative attempts at an overview are Heinrich Plett's *Textwissenschaft und Textanalyse* and Elisabeth Gülich/Wolfgang Raible, *Linguistische Textmodelle*.[27]

The linguistic construct of the text includes the subcategory of literary texts but is not restricted to them; not all categories of analysis are therefore directly applicable to fictional narratives.[28] The reductionism inherent in several models, the tendency to work from paraphrases and schemata, cannot suffice to deal with the complexity of a novel-length narrative, where the "surface manifestations" as well as the "deep-structure" are essential to the production of meaning by a recipient.[29] An ahistorical, idealized concept of the recipient/reader, a *homo linguisticus* parallel to the competent speaker in Chomsky's transformational grammar, is a further deficiency of linguistic text models for literary analysis.[30] Siegfried J. Schmidt, one of the most prolific scholars in the field of text-theory, has drawn a useful distinction between text-linguistics and text-theory. The former, expecially as text-grammar, deals with the systematic representation of the linguistic aspect of communicative acts, and the latter is to be concerned with the relation of text and context.

Schmidt prefers the complex term "kommunikatives Handlungsspiel" to designate the communicative process by which the semantic potential of a literary text is realized as semiotic meaning within a given context of reception.[31] Although the terminology at times seems abstruse, he is contouring areas essential for the analysis of realism in literature. In amending Wittgenstein's term "Sprachspiel," Schmidt emphasizes further the incorporation of non-linguistic elements and the function of texts as socially-determined behavior. The referential relationship of text to contextual reality in his model takes place between the reality paradigm constituted in the reading process and the functional social reality model of the reader's environment. The reading process and the field of reference or reality paradigm constituted in reading are delimited by the structure and content of the text itself. The distinction of semantic potential retains the text as an entity which can be analyzed while maintaining its propensity to assume various semiotic meanings in specific contexts. Schmidt describes the partiality of a text as its regulative character (*Regelcharakter*) for the reader and, in an awkward yet descriptive phrase, designates texts as "teilsinterpretierte Instruktionsmengen." A text enables certain types of reading experiences without permitting totally arbitrary interpretation, an essential observation for nineteenth-century works, which are more determinate than many of the modern works which seem to form the corpus chosen for exemplification in text-theoretical studies. The field of reference of a literary work is constituted according to textual directives and is then placed in reference to the reader's everyday realm of experience.

Realism would therefore be a congruence, at least partial, between the field of reference actualized in reading a work and the reader's contextual, historical field of reference. The integrative function of a narrative would consist in the degree and manner of congruence. Schmidt uses the terms "Situationsabstraktheit" and "Polyvalenz" to indicate the potentiality of a text to be read in a variety of contexts.[32] A text with a highly integrative affirmative character would, however, require a greater congruence of the reader's frame of ordinary experience and that constituted in the reading of the text. Such a work would possess diminished polyvalence as a realistic text. Its realism would be more short-lived historically than a text which relativized or partially opposed a specific reality paradigm. Widhammer's "dialektischer Umschlag," or a discrepancy between *Soll und Haben* and Raabe's Braunschweig trilogy, is describable in such terms. The description is dependent upon the re-orientation in the definition of a literary work central to both reception aesthetics and text-theory: the contextual production of meaning, the partiality of the text, and an understanding of literature as communication.

Placing German Realism within the framework of discussion engendered by reception theory and text-theory generates three tasks for research. Henry J. Schmidt has drawn a careful distinction between reception history, "a reader- or subject-oriented, socio-historical discipline," and reception aesthetics, "a text- or object-oriented phenomenological discipline."[33] The former is an empirical, interdisciplinary analysis of actual readings or concretizations of a text, gleaned from reviews, diaries, literary histories, literary reworkings, etc. Jochen Schulte-Sasse has termed such a task the tracing of the wanderings of a text through its various contexts.[34] In the case of *Soll und Haben*, for example, it would be necessary to refer to contemporaneous reviews such as those of Fontane and Gutzkow, attestations to the book's commercial success in the Wilhelmine period and the debate in 1977 concerning a film version for West German television.

The second category, reception aesthetics, involves analysis of the text and its structure as communication. With regard to readers, necessarily derived from the text itself, the category may be subdivided into two specific tasks. One involves an examination of the reader projected by the author. In a triad of reader types, Gunter Grimm uses the term "imagined" or "intended" reader, as distinguished from the real, historical reader. Lensing works with Raabe's intended reader in his study of *Im alten Eisen*. A distinct, although related, analysis concentrates on the pattern of reader experience established by the text. Iser's "implied" reader is to be understood partially in this sense, especially in his analysis of nineteenth- and twentieth-century novels, where there is not as often an explicit reader addressed in the text. Grimm distinguishes such a reader as the implicit, conceptional or fictive role internal to the work itself. His term "Lektüreanweisungsmuster" is an apt designation.[35]

The difficulty in analyzing the possible pattern of reader experience of a text lies partially, as Henry J. Schmidt has pointed out, in the lack of empirical validation. The reader remains a theoretical construct derived from the critic's or scholar's analysis of a text. However, it does not necessarily follow that such analysis reverts to production aesthetics. A re-examination of specific segments of German Realism with the intent of establishing narrative patterns enabling certain reader experiences is a defensible contribution to an investigation of realism as a category of literary communication rather than representation. The basic suggestion in such a re-examination, that realism involves a degree of congruence between the reality paradigm constituted in the reading process and the functional social reality model of the reader's environment, presents certain difficulties with nineteenth-century texts and twentieth-century readers. The explanation given for the shift in status of *Soll und Haben* remains valid; the congruence for a modern reader is absent and the realism of the text other than as a document is questioned. A novel by Fontane presents a more complex case. Dubslav von Stechlin's estate, the Barby residence in Berlin, or the amusingly awkward dinner parties at Kloster Wutz also lack a congruence with the historical and social reality almost a century later, yet the sense of realism remains.

The subtle yet vital difference lies in the constitution of the reality paradigm of the fictional text. It is not sufficient to regard solely the plot, social and historical elements of the setting or the character types to determine the parameters of the "reality" constituted in the reading of a narrative. The *Junkertum* of the previous century or the etiquette of a *dîner* or a country outing are just as removed from the sphere of everyday experience of most modern readers as the financial ensnarement of the von Rothsattels or the dance lessons Anton Wohlfart attends in Freytag's novel. The latter, however, tenders its field of reference as a "given" entity, and it is experienced as such by the characters in the narrative and by the reader, while the novels of Fontane incorporate the processes of composition of the dominant reality paradigms. The distinction relativizes the weight of a single paradigm and enables a degree of potentially shareable experience in Fontane between the field of reference of the text as communication and that of the reader which is not possible in Freytag. In order to account for the continued realism of narratives, the ability of successive generations of readers to encounter a sense of familiarity and shareable experience, it is necessary to examine the mechanisms of production and legitimation of the social reality composing the field of reference of the text.

For narratives of the second half of the nineteenth century, such analyses entail a focus on the degree and processes of social integration as a matter of narrative content. The novels of the period are concerned with the composition and function of the social system and the assimilation of the individual in much the same manner as is traceable within the context of external social history. An adequate comprehension of the possible reader experience of the works, of the potential realism, relies partially upon an investigation at the level of narrative content of the pattern of social integration. The background pattern of social history is essential for a perception of the original context of reception and of the framework for specific thematic orientations of the texts.

If the possible pattern of reader experience, the "Lektüreanweisungsmuster," is determined partially by the content of a narrative, the concomitant narrative form is equally important. The structure of a text, the elements and pattern of its presentation of content, enables the reader experience. The narrative pattern of specific segments of German Realism includes the manner of integration of the reality paradigm constituted in the text and the structure and strategies of the text itself. The analysis of individual segments must work at both levels, and the ultimate assessment of the integrative function of the literary works rests upon a coordination of the two levels of analysis. The examination of three segments of nineteenth-century literature in the present study is an attempt to describe three patterns of realist narrative in terms of possible reader experience.

The reality paradigms in the works at mid-century by Berthold Auerbach and Gustav Freytag chosen for an initial pattern are characterized by a socially cohesive structure and the unquestioningly approbated integration of the individual. They exhibit a parallel degree of authoritative facticity in the narrative structure itself. A congruence with the reader's context of reception would rest on a narrow basis of shareable experience. A pattern characterized by revelation of the constituent processes of social integration and their constricting influence on the individual is found in Fontane's novels, which allow a broader degree of reader cooperation in Schmidt's sense of polyvalence. A third segment, novels by Wilhelm Raabe, attains a degree of structural complexity appropriate to a pattern of reader experience which enables the perception of the disintegration of the reality paradigm valorized at one level of the text. A closer examination of the constituted realities and the textual strategies according to the precepts set forth in the following two sections will approximate a delineation of the "realism" of the works, its limitations and possible ideological function.

Modes of Integration

It is useful to regard briefly the historical background of the nineteenth century in Germany before turning to a specific consideration of the concerns and content of the narrative texts. Integration, defined as the incorporation of individual unit into encompassing system, is a basic principle in both realms. The primary features of a general definition of integration are the interrelation of individual unit and contextual system, the functional and compositional character of the elements and the necessary assimilation into a comprehensive entity. German social history of the nineteenth century may be read as the attempted realization of a pattern of pragmatic integration. The broad definition of integration is applicable to the specifics of the development of the German middle classes and to the position of the individual within a society increasingly characterized by a drive for national unity and a concern for internal stability. Despite the seeming expediency of specifying dates and political events as the primary factors in the historical movement of the century, it is rather the underlying pattern of economic development and social forces which composes the import of the period.

The first half of the century witnessed the increasing tension between traditional institutions of political, social and economic organization and the need to incorporate new structures. The shift from particularism, agrarian manorialism and small, atomistic producers to the complex consolidation of large industry, commerce and finance in a unified Empire marked a century of adjustment and modernization, of false starts and reversals. Even as the Restoration attempted to maintain the stability of the old order, its inadequacy became apparent.[36] The artisans' and tradesmen's guilds were on the decline, ending the determination of the individual by traditional social divisions. A certain increase in social mobility accompanied the surge in influence of the middle classes as wealth, rather than social estate, became a determining factor.[37] Karl-Erich Born specifies an interim period at mid-century of economic liberalism and pressures for individual self-determination which he labels the "middle-class individualistic era."[38]

It is neither necessary nor possible to detail the variegated and ultimately abortive development of liberalism in Germany within the scope of the present study. Fritz Stern has well captured the post-1878 situation with the designation of "illiberal."[39] Other analyses point out the inherent ambivalencies in the German liberal tradition from its beginning and the early and continued tensions in the position and self-understanding of the middle classes. The optimistic expansion of the 1850s, which Ernest K. Bramstedt characterizes as the aspiring collective consciousness of the middle classes, was short lived.[40] At least three factors enervated the force of the liberal bourgeoisie.

The interrelation of liberal reform and bureaucratic organization, already present in the efforts of Stein and Hardenberg, fostered a social rigidity and reinforced an unwieldy and unresponsive political structure.[41] A second obstacle was the retention of influence by the aristocracy. By 1900 the industrial upper middle class (*Großbürgertum*) had itself adopted aristocratic modes and become "feudalized."[42] A final decisive factor, concomitant to the deliberate blows dealt the liberal cause in the years after Königgrätz, was the volatile economic situation. The economic crises after 1873 underscored the need for stability, and the issues of national unity and economic consolidation took primacy. In a traditional historian's account of the period, Hajo Holborn appropriately entitles the section on the failure of the German liberals "Unification Used to Defeat Liberalism."[43]

The overall pattern of the century leaves the middle classes shaped by social and economic institutions which they do not ultimately determine. There was a brief attempt at mid-century to function as the element establishing the pattern of integration. By the end of the century the German bourgeoisie was an alloy, a social stratum integrated by external necessity. The German situation is fundamentally different from the Second Empire in France or the Victorian period in England, where the middle classes are more firmly established.[44]

The position of the individual in German society corresponds to the pattern of integration of the middle classes in the nineteenth century.[45] At mid-century individual needs and the requirements of the social system seemed to coincide. The conditions for personal fulfillment were apparently reconcilable with the constitution of the aggregate, in this case the emergent middle class. Even granting the setbacks in the political arena after 1848, an optimism obtained. The economic situation of the 1850s allowed the perception of a coextension of personal and social-institutional role. The definition of the individual by the community was not a restricting but a positive factor for both individual and society. Traditional social divisions and institutions had indeed been weakened, but the problem of integrating the self and reconciling change and continuity had not yet become insoluble.

By the 1890s the situation had changed radically. The sense of individual self-determination had given way to a pessimism regarding the compatibility of personal needs and social dictates.[46] Determination by external factors replaced any co-determination of individuals and social institutions. The bureaucratic hierarchy further underscored the regulation of the individual by social institutions.[47] The re-emergence of aristocratic tendencies among the agricultural and industrial proprietors and in the upper echelons of the bureaucracy and military effectively counteracted the "aspiring collective consciousness" of the middle classes at mid-century. Economic conditions necessitated centralization and increasing rationalization. Arnold Hauser describes the situation for France as the increasing subsumption of the individual under economic logic, and similar conditions prevailed in the German Empire. A prime example would be the curtailment of economic individualism and free trade evident in the system of protective tariffs instituted in the years following the crash of 1873.[48] Parallel to the situation of the middle classes, the position of the individual in society moves from the economic mobility of the 1850s to increasing external determination at the century's end.

The pattern of integration traceable within the context of social history is evident as a matter of narrative content in the prose fiction of the period as well. The initial segment of Realism which I shall analyze, Berthold Auerbach's village tales and Gustav Freytag's *Soll und Haben,* is characteristic of the mid-century optimism. Middle-class values are presented as strong integrative forces, and the narratives portray a felicitous coincidence of individual development and societal dictates. The novels by Theodor Fontane considered in the second segment are less affirmative and more analytical. The narrative content is the process of social ritual and its constraint upon the individual, and a tension replaces the earlier optimism. The final section, two novels by Wilhelm Raabe, corresponds to a pessimism regarding the compatibility of personal needs and social dictates. The works scrutinize both the fragility of bourgeois reality and the precarious enterprise of the justification of one's own individual existence. The disjunction of individual and society undercuts the latter and leaves the private sphere, not as a determinant compositional unit, but as a defensive sphere of escape, determined and threatened by the external system. The stories in all three segments are concerned with patterns of social integration, with the composition and function of the social system and the necessary assimilation of the individual.

It is necessary to circumscribe in greater detail the "social system" or "reality paradigm" referred to as composing the field of reference of a text. Realist narrative of the nineteenth century is narrative of everyday existence. The affinity between the novel and quotidian reality is definitely a European phenomenon; the English distinction between romance and novel, for example, emphasizes the proximity to common experience, the recurrent probability of the latter. Walter Scott, an influential figure for German discussions of realism and literature in the nineteenth century, distinguishes the novel as "a fictitious narrative, differing from the Romance, because the events are accomodated to the ordinary train of human events, and the modern state of society."[49] The realism in Germany in the 1850s exhibits similar principles in its stringent criticism of the novels of the first half of the century, in the rejection of the inwardness and fantastic elements of Romanticism and also of the discursive, tendentious character of the Young German novel. The brand of realism propagated by the *Grenzboten,* the prime public forum of the educated middle classes in the 1850s, calls for a representation, albeit selective and optimistically "poeticized," of prosaic reality. The motto for *Soll und Haben,* the sole novel to receive unreserved acclaim in the *Grenzboten,* is an exhortation to ground narrative in quotidian existence: "Der Roman soll das deutsche Volk da suchen, wo es in seiner Tüchtigkeit zu finden ist, nämlich bei seiner Arbeit."[50]

The concept of "work" is meant to encompass an ethical component as well as the daily routine, and the implicit presence of norms and values serves to underscore the manner of "reality" considered to be appropriate narrative material. It is not merely attention to superficial detail and external environment which forms the everyday milieu of realist fiction in the nineteenth century, but a preoccupation with human interaction with the external world. Stifter's passages of nature description are permeated with the effect of human effort on nature and the parallels between the natural and social realms.[51] The minutely detailed description of the location of house and garden in the opening pages of Ludwig's *Zwischen Himmel und Erde* is of import because it determines the routine of Herr Nettenmair's daily existence. In Fontane's novels the field of reference comprises the domain of everyday life as formed by social convention and routine. When Peter Demetz points out the absence of a workday existence and the concentration on social ritual in Fontane, the contradiction to the *Grenzboten* dictum is only apparent.[52] The common basis is the realm of human activity bounded by social conventions, values and norms and the force of the socially defined environment upon the individual. The "reality" of nineteenth-century narrative is not a world external to human activity but one which exists as the result of human endeavor and as such is not immutable. Both E.M. Forster and Ian Watt, in classic studies of the European novel, have emphasized the element of time as a crucial dimension of the novel. For Forster the novel has a double allegiance: "the life in time and the life by values." Watt underlines "the way characters are felt by the reader to be rooted in the temporal dimension." Writing of the early realism of Defoe, he postulates for the reader's perspective on fictional characters: "a sense of personal identity subsisting through duration and yet being changed by the flow of existence."[53]

Continuity and temporality, the interrelation of individual and social world, the force of convention and the transmission of values: such are the basic elements of the reality paradigms constituted in realist narrative of the nineteenth century. Put somewhat differently, it is the pragmatic stock of knowledge regarding everyday social existence which composes the field of reference of the texts. It is not the arcane knowledge of truth valorized in Novalis's *Die Lehrlinge zu Sais,* to take a Romantic counter-example, which shapes the daily lives of the characters in novels by Freytag, Raabe or Fontane, but the knowledge of the proper modes of social behavior. In this sense, Anton Wohlfart's integration into the world bounded by middle-class values of diligence and honor, Innstetten's submission to the dictates of society and Karl Krumhardt's attempts to preserve the authority of the enclave of bourgeois values which define his life are all manifestations of the variety of quotidian reality which is at stake. It is the fabric of social meanings and the commonsense, intersubjective knowledge underlying the everyday routine which constitutes the reality paradigms of the texts.

Siegfried J. Schmidt's model of the referential connection of text to contextual reality would place the paradigm of everyday knowledge available in the text in relationship to what he terms the functional social reality model of the reader's environment. The latter may also be described as the fabric of social meanings and intersubjective knowledge marking the coordinates of the everyday life of a historical reader. The stories of nineteenth-century novels rarely appeal to the reader's stock of theoretical knowledge but most often to the sense of ordinary reality. As was pointed out in the case of Fontane, however, it is not merely the content of the everyday existence in the narrative which is of importance, but the processes of production of that level of reality within the text.

It is necessary to investigate the rather hapless terms "everyday knowledge" and "ordinary reality" to comprehend fully the character of realistic narrative and its concern with social integration. Everyday knowledge is the stock of definitions and meanings shared in a society which outlines the normal, self-evident routines of quotidian existence. Such knowledge is generally taken for granted, and the social routines are actually experienced as self-evident reality. Institutionalized patterns of social behavior, although originally products of human activity, are endowed with an objective facticity through processes of habitualization and transmission to succeeding generations and are internalized as subjective meanings by individuals within a given society. The best analysis of the manner in which socially-produced systems of meaning come to be regarded as the objectively "given" reality of everyday experience is found in a standard treatise in the sociology of knowledge by Peter L. Berger and Thomas Luckmann.[54] Their conclusions have been appropriated in a few instances for the study of literature and are especially fruitful for a consideration of the patterns of realistic narrative in the present study.

In Berger and Luckmann's terms, the stock of commonsense knowledge shared within a society forms the paramount reality, which integrates the values and behavior patterns and provides a stable background and the predefinitions for daily life. The roles assumed by an individual are established by the dominant reality structure and adopted through processes of primary and secondary socialization. The transmission of the institutions of society and of the sustaining processes of legitimation ensures the continuity of the system of meanings and roles composing "ordinary reality" and "everyday knowledge." Language itself, as a prime example of the objectification of originally conventional, socially-produced meanings, is a basic factor in the distribution of knowledge and the reinforcement of the paramount reality. Ranging from basic vocabulary, proverbs and other modes of codified wisdom to explicit bodies of theory and "symbolic universes" which encompass even "deviant" sectors such as dreams and aesthetic production, language is the primary agent for distributing and legitimating knowledge. Even the expression of individual experience in what is termed a "finite province of meaning," an anomalous enclave within the paramount reality, must be phrased in language grounded in the dominant reality. Neither language nor the fundamental institutions of a given social system betray their historical, conventional origin readily.

A social system tends toward stability and toward the integration of all component units into a coherent aggregate which is experienced by participants in the society as a "naturally-given" reality.

The sphere of everyday existence, Scott's "ordinary train of human events, and the modern state of society," can be effectively analyzed for the three segments of German Realism under consideration in terms of the system of meanings and roles composing the field of reference of the texts. The manner and degree of social integration, the pattern of order and the assimilation of the individual character, takes a distinct shape in each section. For Freytag and Auerbach, reality is monolithic, an integrated entity in which the existence of finite provinces of meaning only serves to substantiate the validity of the paramount reality. The narrative concern is with the mechanism of continuity and transmission, and character and social role are co-extensive. Narrative dis-equilibrium is always recuperated, and the reader can only accept or reject the system of social values. At mid-century the texts served to reinforce contemporaneous readers' apperception of their own reality; a century later the texts are quaint or remote, no longer congruent with everyday knowledge.

In Fontane's novels a tension exists between individual and social role. The social mechanisms behind the reality paradigm are the focus of the stories; language and the conventionality of social systems form the fabric of the narrative. Individual characters still perceive the socially-determined "symbolic universe" as an external, objective force, but the reader apprehends the disjunction and the contingency. The novels are concerned with the processes of the social construction of reality, processes still functional beyond the original context of reception. In Raabe's Braunschweig trilogy, the integration of the dominant reality structure which is assumed in Freytag and Auerbach and analyzed in Fontane is revealed as increasingly fragile and conventional. Language itself and the possibility of a valid perception of society and social roles form a major focus of the stories. The process of the novels is a scrutiny and partial betrayal of the quotidian, routinized reality, as the narrator's struggle to retain equilibrium is countered by the disintegrative force of his narrative. The unsuccessfully socialized individuals (Berger and Luckmann would term them carriers of deviant reality definitions) effectively hinder the attempted legitimation of the existing social-institutional order.

Each of the three segments involves narratives of everyday existence and may be analyzed according to the composition and force of the pattern of social integration carried by the content of the works. The structure of the novels as communication and the vitality of the realism are connected to the position of the reader regarding the field of reference actualized in reading the text. The works by Freytag and Auerbach assume the reader's acceptance of the reality presented as self-evident by the text; a congruence of the reader's field of reference with that of the text is presupposed. The works of Fontane and Raabe do not integrate the reader as totally into the system of values which forms the field of reference of the text; partial congruence implies a critical distance. The narrative structure of the works, the pattern of order and strategies of communication, forms the complementary level of analysis which must be considered in delineating the reader experience and the "realism" of each segment.

The Narrative System

In considering the text as a partially determined set of instructions for a reader, as a "Lektüreanweisungsmuster" in Grimm's terms, it is necessary to isolate and analyze the predominant features of the text and their pattern of selection, combination, and variation. The field of reference constituted in reading a work is dependent upon the interaction of the text with the context of reception, and the comprehensive structure and specific strategies of a narrative delimit the available reality paradigm. In making a distinction between the semiotic meaning of a text in a specific historical context and the semantic potential as a constant entity which can be descriptively analyzed, I designated the latter as the object of concern in establishing three separate patterns of reader experience within Realist narrative of the nineteenth century. The manner of integration of the social universe and the degree of stability vary from one pattern to the next and the matters of content are presented in each segment within an appropriate narrative system.

In an introductory study to the adaption of linguistic methods of analysis to prose fiction, Roger Fowler begins with the indisputable statement that all content in a work of literature is represented content, and that the reader's experience of literary content is through the representation as it is controlled by techniques of language.[55] Fowler further characterizes the representation in narrative as a strongly conventionalized process and defines a text of prose fiction as an object whose nature can be specified in terms of elements and their relationships.[56] Following Fowler's specifications, the task of analysis would then be to isolate the central elements and to describe their interrelationships, to examine the conventions behind each distinctive process of narration. The narrative system of a text consists of the internal structures which establish patterns of organization guiding the reader and the compositional elements which elicit reader response. Structure is a popular and perhaps over-used term, and it is necessary to define the sense in which I shall apply it. Rather than mediating among the various specific usages, a broad definition by Robert Weimann is adequate for the present study. He has defined structure in a literary work as the most convenient and comprehensive concept to denote the verbal and conceptual mode of organization of a work of art, and his statement is an appropriate one.[57] The emphasis is on the internal organization rather than on individual elements in their relationship to the author or to external reality.

The importance of integration in narrative prose of the latter half of the nineteenth century is not limited to questions of social integration and the assimilation of the individual at the level of content but is implied in the concept of narrative system as well. The broad definition of integration established at the beginning of the chapter implies order and patterns of correlation, and it is also applicable to questions of narrative structure. Each pattern of realist narrative considered exhibits a specific degree and manner of integration of compositional narrative elements, and the reader experience and the ultimate ideological function of each section within a specific historical context is partially determined by the force of the narrative system.

The centrality of quotidian reality and shared routines of existence for German Realist prose is accompanied by a trait of the narrative system common to all three patterns under consideration: an iterative structure.[58] The realistic dimension of a text, defined as the degree of congruence between the field of reference actualized in the reading process and the reader's contextual, historical field of reference, works with paradigms of ordinary experience, which is characterized by routinization and habitualization. Conveying such a paradigm requires a degree of routinization within the textual structure, and recurrent elements and patterns of repetition are common to all the texts I have chosen. Iterative narrative structures imply a certain degree of stability as well, and all of the stories by Auerbach, Freytag, Fontane, and Raabe exhibit a narrative movement comprising stages of equilibrium, disequilibrium, and a reestablished stability which may be more or less static than the initial condition. It is such a comprehensive pattern, along with distinct narrative strategies guiding and delimiting reader experience, which is to be isolated and described for each segment of realist narrative.

A universal model of narrative is not the project at hand, nor is it a feasible undertaking. A main criticism made of text-theory and text-linguistics is the proliferation of theoretical models of increasing complexity and the resultant neglect or foreshortening of actual literary texts.[59] The specific analyses are meant to originate in and lead back to the texts themselves, and it is neither practical nor desirable to attempt to establish generative models. Descriptive models can be generalized for the reading experience within each pattern of narrative without denying the individual character of the separate texts. It is, for example, not practical to reduce Auerbach's various contributions to the literature of the *Dorfgeschichte* and Freytag's *Soll und Haben* to a single narrative model. The stories do not have an identical structure, but the similarities in the narrative systems as well as in the social system and the manner of integration of individual and society warrant the subsumption of individual works by two separate authors under a single rubric: "reading as reaffirmation." In parallel fashion, *Stopfkuchen* and *Die Akten des Vogelsangs* are each a unique novel, but the tension between narrator and narrated material common to both and the resultant disorientation for narrator and reader connect the two texts by Raabe in a single pattern of reader experience.

The degree of authority exerted by the narrative system of a text is determined to a great extent by the manner of integration of the narrative, and the vitality of the "realism" of novels and stories of the nineteenth century, the potentially shareable experience between the field of reference of the text as communication and that of the reader, depends upon the directed character of the text. The authoritative narrative system common to Auerbach and Freytag presupposes and reinforces reader acceptance of the values and definitions of reality available in the text. The linear, ultracoherent plot and the opposition of clearly defined positive and negative elements leave the reader no option for critical distance within the parameters of the textual structure. Congruent with the perceptions and expectations of the middle-class reading public at mid-century, the narratives afford little experience of familiarity for a modern reader. The more complex tensions of Fontane's novels result in a diffuse narrative system and increased reader participation in constituting the reality paradigm of the work. There is no single perspective which is consistently valorized by the text, but a density of reading and multiple interpretation which emphasizes the contingency and variability of established meanings and reductive readings. The forward motion of the narrative, the linearity of plot, is opposed by compositional elements which call into question the logic of the action advancing the plot. The integration of the social and narrative systems is countered internally, and the resultant position of the reader is one of distanced insight.

In the narrative pattern characteristic of Raabe's late novels, the distance turns increasingly to disorientation. The first-person narrators attempt to order their accounts and integrate them into their own lives and value systems, and a reader "reads," not only the narrator's tale, but also the struggle to maintain order and authority. The tensions are centrifugal, and the final task of constituting a coherent field of reference is left for the reader. All possible perspectives are relativized, and ambiguity and conflict are the primary modes of relationship within the narrative pattern common to *Stopfkuchen* and *Die Akten des Vogelsangs*. In moving from the cohesive structure of *Soll und Haben* and the *Dorfgeschichte* to the constitutive tensions in Fontane and Raabe, the progression is away from an integrated narrative system. In the final patterns of narration, the reader is no longer presented with a fixed system but is led to trace varying perspectives. The patterns of order and the strategies of communication effect a critical distance to the reality paradigm constituted in the reading process, and the polyvalence of the realistic dimension of the works is a function of such a distance. In the following analyses of each pattern of narrative, the reader experience and the resultant "realism" will be carefully defined in terms of both the social system forming the field of reference of the texts chosen and the structure and strategies of the respective narrative system.

II. COHESION AND INTEGRATION: READING AS REAFFIRMATION

Soll und Haben and Auerbach's Dorfgeschichte:
A Parallel Pattern

Gustav Freytag's novel and Berthold Auerbach's village tales share a similar history of reception. Widely acclaimed at the time of their appearance and heralded as appropriate literary phenomena for their era, the *Schwarzwälder Dorfgeschichten* and *Soll und Haben* continued to be popular reading material long after the initial praise had subsided. In retrospect, the more critical among the contemporary assessments of the works have prevailed, and the eventual neglect of Freytag and Auerbach in literary scholarship has only been remedied by a revival of interest since about 1970.[1] The first two volumes of the *Schwarzwälder Dorfgeschichten* were published in 1843, containing stories which had appeared the previous year in various journals. Although Auerbach continued to write village tales in the latter half of the century, and the definitive eight-volume edition was published in 1871, it was the stories of the 1840s and 1850s which figured prominently in the discussions concerning literary realism and which will be of concern in my present chapter. A brief survey reveals a striking parallel in the evaluations accorded the initial volumes of Auerbach's village tales and Freytag's novel, which was published twelve years later. A more careful consideration establishes a parallel ideological function for the narratives, disparate as they might seem in their respective content and in regard to the historical context of their genesis. It is the integrative force of the works, carried by a correspondingly similar communicative structure, which allows the designation of Auerbach's earlier *Dorfgeschichte* and Freytag's novel as a single aspect of realist narrative.

In order to avert the reproach of ahistorical analysis, it is necessary to emphasize at the outset the important distinctions between Berthold Auerbach and Gustav Freytag, the difference in the content of their writings (villagers vs. middle class), and the location of the specific works under consideration on opposite sides of the significant historical year of 1848. Without attempting to offer biographical sketches of the two authors, it is nevertheless possible to summarize the basic divergencies in their positions at mid-century and on into the Empire. Berthold Auerbach remained in many ways an author of the *Vormärz;* despite his initial enthusiasm at the unification of Germany and his eventual disillusionment, it is the liberal humanism of the 1840s which characterizes his political stance and is evident throughout his writings.[2] As a member of the student fraternity "Germania" in the 1830s, he was persecuted for his political activity. In the spring of 1848 he was a candidate for a mandate to the convention in St. Paul's Church but withdrew his application before the local election. The assessments of his politics in the second half of the century vary, partially depending upon the orientation of the biographer or scholar appraising them. Anton Bettelheim's monograph of 1907 emphasizes Auerbach's jubilation over the German unification and only mentions a critical attitude toward Bismarck in another context.[3] Hermann Kinder, in the section on Auerbach in *Poesie als Synthese* (1973), designates Auerbach's stance after 1871 regarding Bismarck as relatively critical.[4] Peter Mettenleitner (1974) entitles a biographical section on Auerbach's political stance "Vom Burschenschaftler zum Chauvinisten" and emphasizes Auerbach's inadequate comprehension of the socio-economic and political factors later in the nineteenth century.[5]

A new, comprehensive monograph on Auerbach has yet to be written; it would almost certainly reveal his important position in the cultural sphere in the nineteenth century and the representative character of his biography for a certain number of Jewish intellectuals. The scholars quoted above, among others, concur in one aspect of Auerbach's life: his final disillusionment over the growing anti-Semitism in the Empire. Zwick quotes a letter from Auerbach after the petition against the Jews and the Jewish debate in the Imperial Diet (1880): "Das war der Sturz von meinem Idealturm, ich bin zerschmettert."[6] A letter gives Auerbach's reaction as a spectator to the Diet: "Vergebens gelebt und gearbeitet."[7] Auerbach's increasing discomfort must be located as well in the widening discrepancy between his liberal humanist ideals, vestiges of the *Vormärz,* and the social historical situation in Germany toward the end of the century.[8]

Gustav Freytag was a personal friend of Berthold Auerbach. He was the witness at Auerbach's wedding in Breslau in 1847, and Bettelheim credits Freytag's review of Auerbach's *Neues Leben* (1852) with convincing the author to return to the genre of village tales.[9] Freytag's biographer Hans Lindau underscores the thematic similarities between *Soll und Haben* and *Diethelm von Buchenberg* (1852), the first of a new series of village tales composed by Auerbach after *Neues Leben.*[10] However, it is necessary to counter Lindau by observing that the ruin of the main character in Auerbach's story, a former farmhand turned estate owner who embarks on financial speculations eventually involving arson and murder, is the result of personal failings and the abandonment of the community values of the village. The fall of Baron von Rothsattel in Freytag's novel is the outcome of a rigidity and inadequacy inherent to the aristocracy as opposed to the solid industriousness of the middle classes. A comparison of the two works serves to illustrate the differences as well as the similarities between the two friends.

A biographical parallel drawn between Freytag and Auerbach in the military campaign of 1870-71 provides a similar illustration. Both authors were called upon to join in supporting the war effort against France. The Crown Prince of Prussia invited Freytag to join his main camp, and the Grand Duke of Baden extended a similar invitation to Auerbach. Auerbach lasted only three weeks, producing fourteen letters as a correspondent for the *Augsburger Allgemeine Zeitung.* Freytag accompanied the Crown Prince through the battle of Sedan, and by the end of the war he had written twenty essays for the *Grenzboten* and the new journal *Im Neuen Reich.*[11] The comparison is not meant to suggest a militarism or a totally uncritical nationalism in Freytag; even a cursory survey of portions of his journal contributions reveals an ambivalence toward Bismarck and moderation in his support of military action.[12] But the contrast accentuates the deeper affinity between Gustav Freytag and the developments in the latter half of the century. In 1848 he had favored a moderate constitutionalism and Prussian hegemony, and his allegiance to the National-

Liberal party and his position in the North German Parliament after 1867 indicate that his nationalism was stronger than his support of parliamentary reforms.[13]

The yoking of two such distinct personalities as Berthold Auerbach and Gustav Freytag is perhaps not as disquieting as the deliberate connection of literary works across the watershed year of 1848 within a single pattern of realist narrative. The two village tales selected for detailed analysis, *Die Kriegspfeife* and *Befehlerles,* are from the initial volume of *Schwarzwälder Dorfgeschichten* (1843), and it would seem that the reality and the "realism" could hardly be commensurable with Freytag's novel of 1855. Secondary scholarship has generally apportioned separate chapters to the two authors, most often connecting Freytag with Julian Schmidt. There is a tendency to treat the literary works of both authors as documents, representative of a stage of the German cultural forum in the *Vormärz* for Auerbach and of the literary and cultural precepts propagated by the influential journal *Die Grenzboten* in the German realism discussion of the 1850s in the case of Freytag. The content of the works is usually summarized and scrutinized in order to circumscribe the position of the texts and their authors in the inauspicious development of liberalism in Germany in the nineteenth century and in the various literary debates at mid-century.

In the case of Auerbach, the main themes of his village tales can be catalogued and placed within the context of structural changes in the agrarian sector in the course of the century.[14] Beyond such obvious thematic connections, the social-historical framework is that of the insistent expectations of the liberal bourgeoisie in the 1840s for political and social reform. It is the middle classes which provide the readers, critics, authors and main concerns of the *Schwarzwälder Dorfgeschichten.*[15] The basic form of social organization in the stories, the village community (*Dorfgemeinde*), exemplifies the liberal ideals of the *Vormärz*: a self-governing body with an equitable and legitimate authority structure, the compatibility of individual and social role and a strongly cohesive social ethos. Auerbach's concept of *Volk,* which is best gleaned from *Schrift und Volk,* his programmatic treatise of 1846, corresponds to the same nexus of ideals. "Das Volk" is not strictly a sociological or a class distinction, but a force carrying historical weight, capable of establishing and maintaining itself against encroachment by tyrannical and arbitrary authority structures in much the same manner as was advocated by the liberal causes in the 1840s.[16]

Gustav Freytag's novel of commerce and character development with its strong emphasis on solid middle-class values and Prussian nationalism belongs to the retrenchment of the bourgeoisie in the 1850s. The political setbacks of 1848 were partially balanced by an economic ascendancy in the following decade, and the portrayal of "Das Volk bei der Arbeit" as solicited by Julian Schmidt and exemplified by *Soll und Haben* reveals the import of the compensatory realignment. The editors of the *Grenzboten* used the term "Volk" in a distinctly class-specific sense, referring to the "Besitz- und Bildungsbürgertum" which was establishing itself as dominant in the 1850s. The valorized form of social organization in Freytag's novel is the hierarchically structured firm of T.O. Schröter, and a distinct work ethos advocates the production efforts of the middle-class figures as opposed to the self-seeking speculation of the aristocracy or the frenzied activity of the Jewish financial manipulators.

Despite the obvious differences, biographical and thematic, between the two authors and their works, there is a distinct parallel in the evaluations accorded Auerbach's *Schwarzwälder Dorfgeschichten* and Freytag's *Soll und Haben*. It is the realism of the stories and their relevancy to the current age which is repeatedly emphasized, especially as a welcome contrast to the excesses of Young German prose, regarded by many as a variation of the extreme subjectivity of Romanticism. A comparison of reviews of the village tales and Freytag's novel reveals similarities in judgment and terminology. Fontane's review of *Soll und Haben* has already been mentioned; in it the adoption and refinement of the English novel for German circumstances is praised, and Freytag is commended for surpassing Dickens and Thackeray in "die ideelle Durchdringung," the artistic interpenetration of *Idee* and *Form*. Fontane characterizes the basic ideational conception of the novel (*Idee*) as "eine Verherrlichung des *Bürgertums* und insonderheit des *deutschen* Bürgertums."[17] Robert Giseke's review cites the "Darstellung der Gesundheit und Idealität" in Freytag's novel and contrasts it to Gutzkow's *Ritter*

vom Geiste, which he finds to be lacking in the representation of positive aspects of contemporary reality.[18] Berthold Auerbach's own review stresses the realism of the work, the portrayal of "das unmittelbare Leben, wie es sich täglich vor unseren Augen bewegt." The book demonstrates for Auerbach "wie gesund das Mark des Nationallebens im ehrenfesten Bürgertum sich hält."[19] Felix Dahn summarizes the import of the novel approvingly: "daß das arbeitstreue, glanzlose aber kraftvolle Bürgerthum mit seinem Fleiß und seiner sittlichen Gediegenheit die höchste und edelste Macht unserer heutigen Culturwelt ist."[20]

The reviews of the initial volumes of the *Schwarzwälder Dorfgeschichten* provide similar characterizations for the contribution of Auerbach's stories: their salubrious effect, the immediacy and realism of the prose, and the appropriate underlying conception. In 1849, Freytag is enthusiastic about the village tales: "Die Stoffe werden vaterländischer, die Darstellung des Details wird genauer und objektiver, die Sprache wird charakterisierende Prosa. Alles dies ist ein Fortschritt."[21] Another reviewer likens Auerbach to Eugène Sue, whose *Mystères de Paris* appeared in 1844. The ground for the comparison is the basic orientation of the works, the common attempt to acquaint the reader with the lower classes. In the case of France, the result is a portrayal of "die untersten Classen in der verdorbenen Hauptstadt." Auerbach's village tales, by way of contrast, follow a different intent: "das Publikum wieder auf das Volk, auf die Bauernschaft aufmerksam zu machen und namentlich auf den guten Kern, der in demselben noch liegt." Auerbach "hebt den gesunden Sinn des Volkes ... hervor." The German variant of a literary portrayal of the lower classes is of political importance: "denn nur auf einer breiten Grundlage vermag das Prinzip unseres Jahrhunderts sein Ziel zu erreichen: und diese breite Grundlage bildet unser gemeinsames Volk."[22] Similar sentiments and an emphasis on the realism of Auerbach's tales are expressed by Freiligrath in verse:

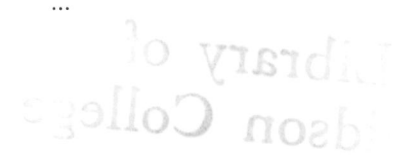

> Das alles aber ist dir nur gelungen
> Weil du dein Werk am Leben ließest reifen;
> Was aus dem Leben frisch hervorgesprungen
> Wird wie das Leben selber auch ergreifen,
> ...

> O, das erhebt! Wer mag ihn unterdrücken,
> Den Kern im Volk, den ewig tücht'gen, derben?
> So laß uns frisch denn auf und vorwärts blicken:
> Ein Keim wie der wird nimmermehr verderben!
> Der fängt erst an, in Pracht sich zu entfalten –
> Mag Gott die Hände segnend drüber halten![23]

Allowing for the altered emphasis in assessments, the specific orientation toward *Bürgertum* in Freytag and *Volk* in Auerbach, the positive reception of their works is based on analogous criteria. It is the selective and optimistic representation of prosaic reality which is singled out for praise, and in both cases the accent is on a positive quintessence of the contemporary historical context: "das Mark des Nationallebens," "die höchste und edelste Macht unserer heutigen Culturwelt," "der gute Kern," "die breite Grundlage." Yet it was just such principles of selectivity and idealization which elicited the more critical reception of the works, and a similarity between *Soll und Haben* and the *Schwarzwälder Dorfgeschichten* obtains here as well. It is necessary to distinguish between the earlier village tales of Auerbach, which are under consideration in the present study, and *Barfüßele* (1856), an extremely popular, sentimental tale which was widely criticized for its saccarine optimism. The more fundamental criticism in the 1840s and 1850s touched upon the limited scope of the stories and the exclusion of the negative aspects of the peasant milieu.

Ferdinand Kürnberger, a well-known Austrian critic, acknowledges a dissatisfied reaction to Auerbach's village tales: "die Empfindung eines Fragmentarischen ... sie [die Geschichten] sind unvollendet und unfertig im Verhältnis zur großen Weltsumme überhaupt, davon sie nur Bruchtheile geben."[24] Hermann Marggraff, in *Die Entwicklung des deutschen Romans* (1844), disapproves of the partiality of content. The village tales remain "zu sehr in der Beschränkung eines gewissen Standes und provinzieller Besonderheit."[25] Auerbach's more radical companion Moses Hess criticizes the tendency, "das arme, enterbte, entmenschte Volk zu *idealisieren.*" Hess suggests that Auerbach could have chosen a more viable form of expression: "Du wärest mit mir in die Hütten der Unglücklichen eingedrungen und hättest die furchtbaren Geheimnisse der depravierten Menschheit entdeckt und vielleicht besser als Sue, der französische

Bourgeois, sie dargestellt und so mitgearbeitet an der Erlösung der Menschheit."[26]

Similar criticism of the one-sided, overly positive character was applied to *Soll und Haben* as well. Giseke qualifies his initial praise of the novel in pointing out that Freytag evaded some of the very problems and tensions of contemporary society: "es [das Buch] bietet uns eine bereits wiederhergestellte Gesellschaft, oder vielmehr jene Gesellschaft, die noch nicht in Frage gestellt, von dem socialen Drange der Gegenwart noch nicht berührt ist."[27] Robert Prutz criticizes the narrow scope of Freytag as the author of a comfortable, self-satisfied bourgeoisie who favors his subject with "rosafarbenes Licht" and a "poetische Glorie."[28] Hermann Marggraff echoes the critique and the rhetoric in his review of the novel: "der Verfasser beabsichtigt, wie es scheint, das Contorleben mit einer poetischen Aureole zu verklären, er schreibt eine Kaufmanns- oder vielmehr eine Commisidylle."[29] An extremely perceptive anonymous review places the idealizing tendencies of Freytag's novel, which is characterized as "nichts weiter als eine Apotheose des innerlich cruden Materialismus," in a broader historical perspective:

> Seit die Professoren der Paulskirche in ihrem Problem – die Wohlfahrt der deutschen Nation herzustellen, Bankrott gemacht und das Publicum um ein zwar unklares und nebelhaftes Ideal gebracht haben, ist eine merkwürdige Compensation auf dem Wege. [...] Die Erzähler haben gleichsam das Amt des Frankfurter Parlaments geerbt und suchen nun ihre Wohlfahrts-Tendenzen auf ihre Weise plausibel zu machen. Zwar könnte man über die Art des Optimismus, der dabei eingerissen, sehr bedenklich werden und keinen großen Werth auf diese Constructionen des 'glücklichen Lebens' legen, wenn deren Helden mit rosenfarbenen Brillen die Gewitterwolken betrachten, an Abgründen tanzen, allen Gefahren ohne große Mühe entgehen und schließlich in einen Glückshafen einlaufen [...] Glücklicherweise rufen dergleichen naturalistische Apotheosen des 'Wohllebens' schlechthin ihre Gegengewichte idealistischer Romane von selber hervor.[30]

The passage is enlightening because it actually faults the work for the lack of a concrete ideal. Such a contrast to Fontane's commendation of the fundamental *Idee* of Freytag's novel is evident in Gutzkow's trenchant criticism as well. One of Gutzkow's main objections in his 1855 review is the shallowness of the book: "die endlose Nüchternheit ... die trostloseste Leere des Gemüts," "wenn man im Interesse seines horriblen Verstandes, seiner nüchternen realistischen Doktrin und seiner admirablen Illusionslosigkeit à tout prix einen Roman *ohne idealen Hintergrund* schreiben zu können glaubt."[31] The celebration of the German middle classes, for Fontane the *Idee* of the novel, is not sufficient for Gutzkow. A relentless opponent of the principles of literary realism propounded by the *Grenzboten* editors Schmidt and Freytag in the 1850s, Gutzkow insisted that literature should extend beyond a mere "Spiegel des Nationallebens." He envisioned:

> eine Wahrheit der Dichtung ... die in den uns umgebenden Konstitutionen nichts entspricht, eine ideelle Opposition, ein dichterisches Gegenteil unsrer Zeit, das einen zweifachen Kampf wird zu bestehen haben, einmal gegen die Wirklichkeit selbst als konstituierte Macht mit physischer Autorität, sodann einen gegen die Poesie der Wirklichkeit, welche so viel Dichter und so viel Kritiker für sich hat.[32]

Gutzkow's criticism reaches the core of the realism of the *Dorfgeschichte* of the 1840s and Freytag's novel of the following decade, and yet a slight refinement of his evaluation is necessary for an adequate comprehension of the exact position and function of such "Poesie der Wirklichkeit." The apparent contradiction between the praise of an underlying ideational conception and the denial of such a dimension can only be resolved satisfactorily by examining the manner in which Auerbach's *Dorfgeschichte* of the *Vormärz* and the variety of literary realism represented by *Soll und Haben* in the 1850s presupposed a dual perspective with regard to external, historical reality. Despite the insufficiencies of existing conditions, the potential direction of historical development was viewed optimistically, and it was the positive foundation which was to be reinforced by the literature hailed as realistic. The rhetoric of the positive reviews quoted above illustrates the pervasive aspect of such a perspective, which is consistent with the period at mid-century characterized in the previous chapter as evincing an optimistic self-assurance of the middle classes, a conviction that they were the historical force establishing the pattern of integration.[33]

At the abstract level, it is such a two-tiered conception of an ultimate resolution to contemporary dissonances which forms the functional social reality model or reality paradigm behind the original, favorable reception of Auerbach's tales and Freytag's novel. There is an undeniable shift in the content of the conceived resolution; the political optimism is replaced by expectations of economic prosperity after the losses of 1848. Yet the disparity is not as great as it might seem. Auerbach's portrayal of *Volk* and *Dorfgemeinde* was oppositional within the context of the *Vormärz* but by no means radical. The idealization in Auerbach's works could also be termed compensatory, in contrast to his friend Hess or to the more democratic literature of the *Vormärz*. The fundamental model of the ultimate success of a potential already extant in present reality outweighs any true opposition in the sense of Gutzkow's stipulation.

The literary and the historical models are conjoined; it is the optimistic historical perspective in the literary precepts of the *Grenzboten* and in Auerbach which underlies the selectivity, the *Verklärung* and the *Idee*, which receive criticism as well as praise. When Hess chides Auerbach for neglecting to portray "die furchtbaren Geheimnisse der depravierten Menschheit" and when Gutzkow counters Freytag's novel with the rebuke: "Gab es Menschen, die 1848 nur allein an Wolle und Talg dachten, es sollte sich ein Dichter schämen, sie als verehrungswürdig hinzustellen,"[34] they are both in fundamental disagreement with the main principle of the variety of realism under consideration. It is not the contradictions and social conflicts which are deemed suitable literary material, but rather the continuity of a positive stratum characterized as "das Wesen der Dinge" or "das Wahre." Julian Schmidt requires of authors: "daß man Sinn für Realität hat, für den wahren Inhalt der Dinge."[35] He specifies "ein idealer Dichter, der auch in den Verirrungen der Menschen das Allgemeine, Positive und Nothwendige herauskennt."[36] In a *Grenzboten* article on Schiller from 1858, Schmidt characterizes the idealistic basis of such realism:

> Wenn man nun das, was wir als wahren Realismus bezeichnet haben, Idealismus nennen will, so ist auch nichts dagegen einzuwenden, denn die Idee der Dinge ist auch ihre Realität. Wenn der wahre Idealist mit seiner Idee das Wesen der Dinge trifft, so bildet sich der falsche Idealist eine Idee, die der Wirklichkeit nicht entspricht, weil sie überhaupt keinen Inhalt hat.[37]

Portions of Fontane's essay of 1853, entitled "Unsere lyrische und epische Poesie seit 1848," are very close to the position of Schmidt and Freytag in the 1850s. The images he utilizes of the artist as a sculptor awakening prestructured forms in a marble quarry are indicative of the double perspective.[38] Freytag strikes a similar note in the dedication to *Soll und Haben,* claiming for his novel: "daß er wahr nach den Gesetzen des Lebens und der Dichtkunst erfunden und doch niemals zufälligen Ereignissen der Wirklichkeit nachgeschrieben ist."[39] Auerbach establishes the same process for literature in *Schrift und Volk:* "Die Poesie wiederspiegelt die Welt, zunächst ohne andere Tendenz als die, der Wahrheit, das heißt der ewigen, wie sie in den mannigfachen Gestaltungen sich kund giebt, die Ehre zu geben."[40]

Given the common confidence in historical processes and in the positive elements of the contemporary context, the task of literature for Auerbach and for the *Grenzboten* brand of realism was the reinforcement of the progressive tendencies. The rejection of a naturalistic portrayal of existing inequities and the prerequisite *Verklärung* are related to the function of literature. Auerbach's *Schrift und Volk* stresses the pedagogical value of the *Volksschrift,* based on a law of historical necessity: "Mit dem Streben, aus dem Volke heraus sein innerstes Wesen erkennen zu lassen, geht nothwendig auch das hervor, auf dieses Wesen einzuwirken, denn nicht das schlechthin Wirkliche ist Gesetz, sondern das Höhere, in der ewigen Natur gegründete."[41] He compares the task of literature to preventative medicine, which establishes and maintains a condition of health while avoiding crises.[42] Hermann Kinder has effectively outlined the manner in which Auerbach's pedagogical intent designated literature as *Vorschein,* as the prescient representation of historical progress. For Auerbach, the harmonious existence depicted in literature represented not only eternal human values but also an attainable future state of affairs.[43]

The programmatic realism of the 1850s was also characterized by a didactic intent, and Kinder emphasizes the anticipatory function of literature after 1848 as well. He describes the intent of programmatic realism as the accomplishment of the remaining historical synthesis between an anticipated future state and present reality.[44] Helmuth

Widhammer expressly disagrees with Kinder on the issue and designates the main concern of Freytag and Schmidt as the reaffirmation of existing conditions rather than the anticipation of future progress.[45] Widhammer calls for a re-analysis of the reception aesthetics of programmatic realism and the connection to an inherent idealism.[46] The disagreement between Kinder and Widhammer is only apparent; the anticipatory function of literature as based on a reinforcement of positive tendencies within contemporary reality is necessarily also affirmative for both Auerbach and Freytag. In neither case does the ideational conception behind their works, the reality as projected, represent fundamental opposition to the reality as given. The reinforcement of the former involves a basic reaffirmation of the latter.

The parallel between Auerbach's village tales and Freytag's novel extends beyond a coincidentally similar history of reception. Within the dual perspective which formed the reality paradigm for the genesis and original favorable reception of the works, they exerted a common ideological function. Berger and Luckmann have defined ideology as the attachment of a particular definition of reality to a specific vested interest within a historical period. They emphasize the fact that the same external world may be interpreted simultaneously in varied ways by different groups, although a shared "core universe" is most often taken for granted.[47] The abbreviated survey of the contemporaneous reception of Auerbach's early village tales and *Soll und Haben* suggests a common definition of reality behind the approbation, one shared by the authors. The narratives supported the functional reality model and exercised an affirmative function within the contextual ideology, which is attached to the liberal bourgeoisie in its moderate form in the *Vormärz* and in the 1850s.

Were it the purpose at hand to trace convincingly the roots and extent of the ideology in reference, the selected excerpts would hardly suffice. It is problematical to predicate the ideological foundation of a portion of the reception history of literary texts solely on reviews and the stated positions of authors. Nor is it sufficient to concentrate on the contemporaneous discussion carried out in essays and neglect the literature itself. The literary work then often becomes a document, especially in the consideration of the programmatic realism of Freytag and Schmidt.[48] Studies by Dieter Kafitz and Michael Schneider have proved productive in their focus on the formal aspects of *Soll und Haben* as well as on its exemplary position in literary discussions at mid-century.[49] I extend such an analysis to examine a similar structure and function for Freytag's novel and Auerbach's early stories.

The parallel reception pattern for the village tales of the 1840s and *Soll und Haben* and the common ideological function of the works within the original context of reception attest to the manner in which the texts may be said to compose a single aspect of realist narrative. The integrative force of the works, the affirmative ideological function, requires a considerable degree of congruence between the field of reference actualized in the reading process and a reader's contextual, historical field of reference. In order to read the works as "realistic," it is necessary to accept the reality paradigm delimited by the content and structure of the texts. The narratives of Auerbach and Freytag possess diminished polyvalence as realistic works because of the strongly directed character of the social system which forms the content and also of the narrative system which co-determines the reader experience. The communicative structure is cohesive, not only in the sense of a logical coherence of narrative elements, but in the composition and functioning of a unified, dominant social system which is monolithic, an integrated entity within which aberrations and challenges serve only to substantiate the validity of the paramount reality. Character and social role are coextensive, and the narrative concern is with mechanisms of continuity and transmission, with the assimilation of the individual character into the unquestioningly approbated pattern of social order. The reality paradigm exhibits objective facticity, appearing as a quasi-natural force, and the reader's acceptance of the field of reference is presupposed. The narrative structure itself engenders an authoritative facticity, and the narrative strategies effect experience and reaffirmation of the fictive field of reference as given. An analysis of both aspects of *Soll und Haben* and representative *Dorfge-*

schichten, the social system and the narrative structure, shall substantiate the connection between Auerbach's tales and Freytag's novel as a single segment of realist narrative.

The Cohesive Social Universe and the Integration of the Individual

The possible pattern of reader experience established by literary texts, designated by Gunter Grimm as "Lektüreanweisungsmuster," is circumscribed by the reality paradigm constituted in the reading process and partially determined by the narrative content. For the aspect of realist narrative under consideration in my present chapter, it is not solely the details of the plot, setting, and character types which determine parameters of the field of reference of the works but rather the common emphasis on the social universe as a comprehensive entity which encompasses and defines the individuals inhabiting it. The system of meanings and roles providing the fabric for the quotidian reality of the narratives is an unquestioned basis. In Berger and Luckmann's terms, the paramount reality is all-pervasive; there is no incorporation of the historical processes of production of the dominant reality structure which appears as a natural, objective order, and there is no valid challenge to the overarching "symbolic universe" which provides the final frame of reference legitimating the paramount reality. The emphasis is on processes of "universe maintenance" and on the successful assimilation of the individual.

Berger and Luckmann define the symbolic universe as "the matrix of *all* socially objectivated and subjectively real meanings."[50] It fulfills a "nomic, or ordering" function and incorporates even deviant or marginal enclaves of experience. The symbolic universe provides a canopy spanning the routines and behavior patterns of the institutional order and the progression of individual biography. In terms taken from *The Social Construction of Reality:*

> this nomic function of the symbolic universe for individual experience may be described quite simply by saying that it 'puts everything in its right place.' What is more, whenever one strays from the consciousness of the

order (that is, when one finds oneself in the marginal situations of experience), the symbolic universe allows one to 'return to reality' — namely to the reality of everyday life. Since this is, of course, the sphere to which all forms of institutional conduct and roles belong, the symbolic universe provides the ultimate legitimation of the institutional order by bestowing upon it the primacy in the hierarchy of human experience.[51]

The symbolic universe and the underlying social order must be asserted and maintained against internal and external threats. The narrative pattern comprising Auerbach's village tales of the 1840s and *Soll und Haben* incorporates assaults upon the dominant social system, but the cohesive matrix of meanings and values is never seriously questioned. The advancement of plot requires conflict and the perturbation of a stable system, but equilibrum is always restored. The origins of the paramount reality and of the pervasive scheme of explanations and behavior patterns are never an issue, as the narrative concern is with mechanisms of continuity and transmission, with the reinforcement of the accepted order and the assimilation of the individual character. Rhöse has pointed out parallels to a principle of divine *ordo* evident beneath the prevailing conception of the middle-class citizen as securely rooted in a fixed, universal order of existence, and his thesis restates in different terms the manner in which the aggregate order is the "natural" given, embedded in the past and characterized by continued, unrefuted validity.[52]

The sanctioned *ordo* is presented as a monolithic entity, and the individual inhabitants of the pervasive social order and its symbolic universe are in a position of mutual definition with the contextual system. Defined by their position within the aggregate design, they contribute to the continuing existence and reinforcement of the paramount reality through their acceptance of the ordered matrix of meanings and their total integration. There is no disjunction between individual, personal needs and societal dictates, no residual, subjective requisite beyond the realm of activity bounded by social conventions, values, and norms. The ultimate coextension of personal and social-institutional roles allows the definition of the individual by the community and the approbated social order to be regarded as positive factors both for social stability and for personal development. The social systems constituting the reality paradigms of the pattern of realist narrative exemplified by *Soll und Haben* and the early village tales of Auerbach are centripetal, stabilizing and integrating all component units into a cohesive aggregate experienced as a "naturally-given" order of reality.

The penchant for "naturalization" of historical phenomena has been designated as a characteristic trait of bourgeois ideology, and the literature hailed as "realistic" in Germany at mid-century provides an appropriate illustration. Rhöse's category of an unchanging *ordo,* Berger and Luckmann's analysis of the functioning of the symbolic universe as a continual legitimation of everyday roles and knowledge *"sub specie universi"*[53] and Roland Barthes's delineation of the mode of operation of myth and the presuppositions of realist literature in his early essays are all applicable to the communicative structure common to the *Dorfgeschichte* and Freytag's novel. Barthes's description of myth as "depoliticized speech," as the self-presentation of a state of affairs purged of the complex relations behind it and his specification of the traditional "readerly" text as "a circle of *solidarities,"* in which "everything holds together" are pertinent to the pattern of narrative in which a single reality paradigm prevails as the natural order integrating all characters and events.[54] At mid-century the narratives of Auerbach and Freytag reaffirmed the reader's perception of reality as ordered and progressive and were accordingly praised as the realistic literature appropriate for the contemporary age.

Yet the same facet of the texts, the insistently monolithic character of the reality paradigm composing the field of reference, is largely responsible for the diminished polyvalence of their realism. Without incorporation of the historically relative character of a specific reality paradigm, without admission of the conventionality of the paramount reality and its force upon the individual, the works cannot be read as even partially congruent with a reader's frame of ordinary experience beyond a narrow context of reception. The communicative structure common to Auerbach's early *Dorfgeschichten* and *Soll und Haben* evinces a comprehensive social order which is never questioned or revealed as itself a historical product of social interaction. External threats are repelled, and internal enclaves of deviant experience form finite provinces of meaning which are nevertheless integrated into the overarching matrix of knowledge and values designated by Berger and Luckmann as a symbolic universe. The narrative concern is with the maintenance of a stable order, the continual re-establishment of equilibrum, and with the successful assimilation of individual characters such that no figure granted a positive role is defined either against or outside the dominant symbolic universe.

The substantiation of the cohesive social order composing the field of reference of the works by Auerbach and Freytag depends upon detailed examination of the texts. In order to facilitate an illustrative analysis in the case of Auerbach, it seems expedient to concentrate upon two village tales from the initial volume of *Schwarzwälder Dorfgeschichten* published in 1843. It would be neither possible nor desirable to assert that the texts can be reduced to an identical narrative structure, one which would prevail for all the village tales and be conveniently applicable to *Soll und Haben* as well. Yet the individual analyses will demonstrate the manner in which the type and force of the pervasive social order and the position of the individual figures form a common basis for the village tales and Freytag's novel. The shorter *Dorfgeschichten* are an advisable prelude to the more complex narrative of *Soll und Haben. Die Kriegspfeife* and *Befehlerles* are two of the earliest Auerbach stories; both appeared in 1842 in the *Zeitung für die elegante Welt*.[55] The tales have been contrasted as representing the idyllic (*Die Kriegspfeife*) and the overtly political (*Befehlerles*) as two polar possibilities of peasant or village literature.[56] A similar social system composes the substance of both works, however, and they are representative for the prevalence of what I have termed a monolithic reality paradigm in Auerbach's village tales at mid-century.

Paraphrases of the two works are a useful preliminary step, as Auerbach's stories are not as well-known as Freytag's novel, and a summary also indicates already the fundamental characteristics of the everyday reality of the village circumscribed by the tales. *Die Kriegspfeife* is the story of Hansjörg, the narrator's neighbor, who shoots off his trigger finger to avoid military duty in 1796, a year of French forays into Black Forest territory. He is nursed back to health by Kätherle, whom he eventually marries. His final and total reintegration into the community (*Dorfgemeinde*) requires one further symbolic step — he has to give up smoking his pipe out of consideration for Kätherle, which he does, and the pipe is hung over their marital canopy bed. Even a three-sentence summary reveals the issues of prime importance: the reestablished equilibrium of the village order against the external threat of the French invaders, who eventually retreat, as well as against the internal insubordination of Hansjörg's *Selbstverstümmelung,* and the successful reintegration of the individual.

The same concerns obtain in the second story, and a comparison at the schematic level of paraphrase emphasizes the common narrative movement toward re-establishment and maintenance of an originally accepted order with collective values given priority over singular, individual action. An amplified analysis of each story may then buttress the broader parallels. The second story, *Befehlerles,* is divided into two sections. In the first segment, Mathes puts up a May tree in front of his sweetheart Aivle's house in violation of a new ordinance forbidding the practice because it is ostensibly depleting the forests. Mathes is arrested, Aivle is interrogated, and he has to pay a fine. The authorities are rather rude, but their ordinance is not totally unjust, for ecological reasons. The tree symbolically grows new roots "als ewiges Liebeszeichen an dem Hause der Glücklichen."[57] The second segment of the tale mirrors the first with important variations. The tradition which is forbidden is the right of village men to carry a hand-ax. Again the reason is "zuviel Waldfrevel," but this time it is unjustified. Buchmaier, a relative of Mathes, leads a collective protest. The ordinance is rescinded, the responsible "Beamter" is removed, and the traditional order is reaffirmed.

Although *Befehlerles* is longer and outwardly more complex, it is actually the more transparent of the two tales. The reader is explicitly directed to modify and abstract the basic principles of the first story of Mathes and Aivle in considering the second section, which begins: "Mit dieser Geschichte [the foregoing section concerning the May tree] hängt aber noch eine andere von allgemeiner Bedeutung zusammen" (170). It is the composite of the two segments, the variations on a common theme, which constitutes the unified field of reference of the work.[58] The basic model is the external interference with a long-established mode of social behavior, protest against the interference and the resultant sanctions, and a final re-established stability. In the initial section it is the action of a single figure, and the conclusion involves the altered position of the individual within the community. The succeeding section, "von allgemeiner Bedeutung," entails collective action and results in restoration of the prevalent everyday routine: "Nach wie vor tragen die Mannen ihre Axt am linken Arme" (183).

The opening of *Befehlerles* locates the action within the accepted tradition of May Day festivities: "Nach alter Sitte" (154). Shared knowledge and respect of the customs is assumed, as evidenced by the "Mayman" in his attack on the constable after the latter has arrested Mathes: "Der Bub verließ sich wol darauf, daß er als Mai eine geheiligte Person und unverletzlich sei" (156). But the constable has allied himself with the authorities who are interfering with the community of May festival tradition. The nickname scornfully applied to him by the village children underscores his exteriority. "Soges" is a reminder of his attempts to ingratiate himself with the previous Austrian administration by adopting their dialect ("i sog es"). Language is a marker of allegiance in *Befehlerles,* and "Soges" is associated with superimposed authority ("der österreichischen Herrschaft"). The constellation of external threat to the natural order embodied by choice and use of language may appear somewhat forced in the positioning of Soges, but it is a constellation which is repeated and reinforced in both sections of the short tale. Aivle is intimidated by the language of the civil authorities and scarcely recognizes her own statements when they are translated into standard, coherent German for the court protocol. What is lost is the immediacy and the human sentiment; the reader is given a sympathetic portrayal of Aivle's fear and dismay during the questioning, but the official record disregards such elements: "von all dem Weinen und den Qualen des Mädchens stand kein Wort darin" (168). The language of authority is a transgression of the sphere of village custom and common dialect.[59]

The connection of external interference to artificial language is more explicit in the second section of the story. The opening paragraphs juxtapose the official, written ordinance of Oberamtmann Rellings with the dissatisfied murmurings of the village inhabitants. Buchmaier's impassioned speech against "so ein verzwängtes Schreiberle," "ein Schreiberschultheiß nach dem anderen," "Beamtenstuben," and "Schreiberordnung" leaves no doubt as to the character of the interlopers (178). In the story of Buchmaier versus Rellings, both of whom appear in other village tales as well, there is more at stake than violation of established social ceremony. The carrying of a hand-ax is also firmly anchored in immemorial custom: "Seit alten Zeiten," "wie die Sage geht" (170-1). However, the habit has definite political overtones, as it is not only a custom but a justified privilege and a sign of an individual's stature within the community. Only married men, "die Mannen," were granted the right to carry the implement. As Hahl has pointed out, a vaguely surmised connection to practices of general conscription ("allgemeine Wehrhaftigkeit") links the custom to liberal demands of the *Vormärz*.[60] Especially Buchmaier's words convey the variety of liberal social community (*Dorfgemeinde*) typical of Auerbach's narratives.

The interference with the traditional order in the second half of *Befehlerles*, therefore, carries overtly political emphases beyond the structural level of attempted disturbance of the established social universe. Yet what Buchmaier is advocating within the framework of the story is the preservation of the existing system, which is embedded in the past and which establishes roles and definitions for its inhabitants. Relling's attempted circumvention of the valid train of ordinary events must be opposed, and Buchmaier states the opposition in strong terms as he shatters the posted ordinance with his ax: "Wir sind Bürger und Gemeinderäthe; ohne Amtsversammlung, ohne Beistimmung von allen Gemeinderäthen kann man keine solche Verordnung erlassen" (173). His final speech reverses the attempted intervention and specifically incorporates the pretentious "Herrle" into the established order:

> Was sag' ich da? Herren! Unsere Diener seid ihr, und wir sind die Herren. Ihr meinet immer, wir sind euretwegen da, damit ihr was zu befehlen habt; wir bezahlen euch, damit Ordnung im Lande ist, und nicht, um uns cujoniren zu lassen. Staatsdiener seid ihr, und der Staat, das sind wir, die Bürger (180).

The effectively defended stability of a cohesive, self-determining community in *Befehlerles* manages to integrate even the external threat.

The re-established equilibrium at the end of the first section of the tale, marked by the re-rooted May tree, is of a slightly different character, and the difference is relevant for the integration of individual and community within the reality paradigm common to Auerbach and Freytag. The ordinance prohibiting the custom of presenting a May tree to one's sweetheart does indeed have some basis, and Mathes' musings in prison concerning the beauty of a fir twig lend substance to the case against him. He explicitly envisions the twig as the tree he cut down and set in front of Aivle's house, and the next itself specifies the twig as "das Sinnbild seiner Anklage" (159). In a certain sense it is a recognition for Mathes: "Er sah jetzt zum erstenmal, wie schön so ein Reis ist" (160).[61] But the fir twig is connected to a broader theme and ultimately to the distinction between Mathes' action in section one and Buchmaier's conduct in the following portion of the story. Following his release from confinement, Mathes meets Aivle at the exact spot where he had broken off the twig, and he ignores her. Aivle brings about a reconciliation which leads to the happy end in the house with the revitalized fir tree. Mathes had been the only one to transgress the ordinance and fell a tree for the May Day custom, and his solitary deed is not entirely condoned within the framework of the narrative. However, the issue extends beyond the possible harm to the forests, as the charge of "Waldfrevel" is mitigated by the choice of a tree due for felling anyway. The fir twig designated as a symbol of the accusation is also labelled "das sichtbare Sinnbild seines Schweigens über den Maibaum" (159), and the difference between Matthes' protest and that of Buchmaier is the personal, solitary character of the former. Mathes is justified in disputing the necessity of his incarceration; the narrative voice appends the adverbial phrase "mit Recht" to his insistence that he certainly won't run away before a court hearing (157), and in the second section Buchmaier and the other village men successfully refuse similar treatment (175).[62] But Mathes' silence regarding the May tree is tantamount to a lie, as contrasted to Buchmaier's open and verbal defense. In addition, Buchmaier speaks with the force of the community behind him, as he refuses to comply with Relling's intent to question the villagers singly, stating to his companions: "Kommet 'rein, ihr Mannen, wir haben gemeinschaftliche Sach', ich red' nicht für mich allein" (177). The contrast between the two sections, one of subtle variation on a common theme, emphasizes the necessary congruence of individual action with the stable social order. The first segment reintegrates the individual into the community, and the second maintains the identity of the established aggregate system of values.

Such a detailed analysis of an outwardly straightforward story exceeds the reflective processes of most readers, and yet it is the ordered coherence of the field of reference of such simple texts which shapes the assessments accorded the works and which ultimately functions through the manner and composition of the everyday order of reality suggested. *Die Kriegspfeife* provides a similar illustration, sanctioning even more strongly the assimilation of the individual into a cohesive network of social conventions, values, and norms. The existence of a symbolic universe which integrates all spheres of meaning and behavior forms the presupposed basis of Auerbach's "idyllic" tale. The more earnest disturbance in *Die Kriegspfeife* is internal — the action of Hansjörg in maiming himself to avoid military duty. Hahl's estimation of the deed as a "berechtigte, doch nur 'negative' Tat" and his conclusion of a political tinge to the story insofar, "als sie die Gesellschaft gegen den Obrigkeitsstaat ausspielt" tend to foreshorten the text to conform to his thesis of the prevalent themes of *Vormärz* liberalism in Auerbach.[63] The introduction to the tale does indeed imply that the peasant was often the pawn of kings and emperors, but the external threat to the village order in the story itself is the presence of the marauding French troops and not the military draft system of superimposed authority. Hansjörg's act is marked "als Sünde gegen das Vaterland" (54), and his imitators are unsuccessful in their attempts to avoid military service (57).

The comprehensive matrix of values and norms which define the community in *Die Kriegspfeife* is a particularly dense one, and it is necessary to examine closely the compositional elements in order to determine the manner in which the reality paradigm of Auerbach's text is tendered as a cohesive entity, a "circle of solidarities" in Barthes's terms. The narrative progression is from a violation of accepted, permissible behavior to an atonement for that violation and the reacceptance of the transgressor into the prevailing order. Hansjörg's successful attempt to circumvent military conscription is clearly branded as a negative act, and the path of expiation is implied from the beginning. Couched in religious terms as a sin, his deed is a transgression of divine order, and it is further presented as an obstacle to his possible social position and a danger to his very existence. Joking with Kätherle on the topic of marriage, by which he is referring to their own future wedding, Hansjörg admits the intent behind the loss of his finger. Kätherle's agonized outcry combines the condemnation of his action from three standpoints: divine order, social position and individual existence:

> O, du lieber Heiland, was hast du für eine Sünd' gethan, Hansjörg! Du hättest dich ja auch todt schießen können; nein, du bist ein wilder Mensch, mit dir möcht' ich nicht hausen, ich hab' Angst vor dir (51).

Sin is connected to death and yoked with exclusion from the social institution of marriage. The same intermingling of systems of values is evident at the ceremonial burial of the finger. Hansjörg is struck by thoughts of his own death, he admits to Kätherle that he has sinned and must attend confession, and her reconciliatory kiss is designated as "die seligste Absolution" (54).

The implication of marriage as an encompassing value in the story is relatively transparent. The shot is fired the day before a village wedding, the admission to Kätherle results in her refusal to be a bride, and the final wedding scene re-establishes equilibrium and provides a happy end. Kätherle's eventual acceptance of Hansjörg's marriage proposal is connected to the motif of the pipe, as she acquiesces in order to deter him from the dangerous pursuit of the French soldiers who stole it. The passing of her earlier outburst of horror had also been joined to the pipe, through her conciliatory lighting of it, a difficult task for Hansjörg's maimed hand. The pipe, labelled by the narrator as "ein Hauptstück in unserer Geschichte" (49), is Hansjörg's most valued possession, and his final renunciation of the habit of smoking it, even after Kätherle had restored to him both the pipe and the right to resume smoking, marks the final recognition of the primacy of community values over individual identity.

In a feverish dream during Hansjörg's recuperation, pipe and finger are equated even before the specific pipe is introduced into the story (48-9). It is "die schönste Pfeife im ganzen Dorfe" (49), and the narrator compares the sentiments of its owner to the attachment of a hero of antiquity to his shield.[64] When the pipe is stolen from Hansjörg, it almost appears as a justified punishment for his stubborn refusal to part with it when a wounded French soldier with only four fingers pleads for a smoke. The Jewish merchant who restores the pipe to Kätherle advises her: "Er hat sie [die Pfeife] so gern gehabt, wie er dich hat, und wenn es gegangen wär', ich glaub', er hätt' sie geheirathet" (63). Hansjörg, overhearing the conversation but missing the referent for the personal pronoun "sie," assumes his future bride is being informed of rumors concerning his former love interests, and his semi-guilty conscience forces an open discussion of the issue. It is an amusing misunderstanding, yet the narrative function of the pipe parallels the role accorded it in the story as a whole. The absence of the object, here the ambivalent grammatical substitution, effects a realignment of the principal characters. The final stage reincorporates the object and clarifies all remaining issues and misunderstandings. When the pipe reappears at the wedding, Hansjörg admits to having eavesdropped and drawn a false conclusion. Similarly, the absence of the pipe in the broader frame of the story leads to the marriage. Its reappearance is accompanied by Kätherle's offer to allow Hansjörg to resume smoking, and the latter's refusal is the final reconciliatory step. The pipe, connected throughout the narrative with Hansjörg's deviant behavior and stubborn individuality, is restored and renounced. The re-established equilibrium is transmitted to the succeeding generations; none of the children nor grandchildren up to the narrator's present point of writing have ever taken up smoking.

The cohesive social order and the definition of the individual by established social roles is readily analyzable in the abbreviated narrative form of the *Dorfgeschichte*. The expanded narrative of *Soll und Haben* would seem to render more difficult a similar extraction and tracing of compacted themes contouring the field of reference of the text. Indeed, the objection could be raised that the reality paradigm constituted in reading Freytag's novel is not monolithic, that it is not possible to speak of a comprehensive social universe as it is in the case of Auerbach's *Dorfgemeinde*. In addition to the "exterior" realm of the Poles, there are three distinct spheres in the novel: the German middle class, the aristocracy, and the cast of Jewish financial manipulators. Fontane writes of three dramas composing the work: the "bürgerliches Schauspiel" of Anton Wohlfahrt and the tragedies of Baron von Rothsattel and Veitel Itzig.[65] Lindau acknowledges the structural function of the three spheres: "Die Verschiebung und Durchdringung der drei Kreise bildet gleichsam den auf eine Formel gebrachten Inhalt des Romans."[66] Dieter Kafitz, in an excellent analysis of *Soll und Haben*, examines three basic constellations of characters and social forces: the middle-class and Jewish merchants, who carry the themes of family and work; the opposition of nobility and bourgeoisie; and the contrast of nationalities between the Poles and the Germans.[67]

The German middle-class is the one term common to all of Kafitz's juxtapositions, as even the contrast of Germans and Poles, outwardly the defense of an aristocratic estate, actually illustrates the efficacy of middle-class industriousness and valor. The complexity of Freytag's novel must not be allowed to obscure the predominance of a single social order as the final frame of reference for the work.[68] The unifying, pervasive aspect of the values of diligence, honest endeavor, prosaic achievement earned through persistent assiduity rather than by privilege of birth, and respect for order and community is reflected in the accepted designation of the novel as an integral element of the ideology of the German bourgeoisie in the 1850s.[69] Despite its intricacy of plot, *Soll und Haben* is permeated by a cohesive system of values and emphasizes a specific segment of society as the determinant unit establishing and maintaining the present and future social order.

The firm of T.O. Schröter embodies the cohesive matrix of meanings, values, and roles central to Freytag's novel. Not only does it present a model of social organization contrasting with the other spheres, but it is the fixed point to which the narrative returns in a continual re-establishment of equilibrium. Within the novel, Schröter's firm possesses unquestioned validity, and its stability is never seriously threatened. The reader is informed early in the first book that Schröter's business is "ein Warengeschäft, wie sie jetzt immer seltener werden," and there is doubtless significance in the anachronism.[70] As the narrative progresses, however, a disjunction between the time of action and the moment of narration is not maintained, and the firm displays a timeless endurance, a quality eliciting "feste Gesinnung und ein sicheres Selbstgefühl bei seinen Teilhabern" (56). Schröter's firm does not go unscathed, but the losses incurred due to the unrest in the provinces are recuperable. The narrator acquaints the reader with the seriousness of the situation after Anton's return from the first sojourn in Poland:

> Vieles war verloren und nicht weniges noch gefährdet. Erst in der Ferne war Anton mit dem ganzen Umfange der Gefahr bekannt geworden, welche das Geschäft bedroht hatte. Und er erkannte, daß die Tätigkeit vieler Jahre nötig sei, um die Verluste wieder auszugleichen und an Stelle der abgerissenen Fäden neue anzuknüpfen (421).

The "danger," reassuringly phrased in the pluperfect tense, is hardly more than a passing tremor in comparison to the cataclysmic changes for the von Rothsattel estate.

On only two other occasions is there any indication of a deeper disturbance in the routine and orderly existence of T.O. Schröter's firm. On the first, the reassuring resolution is clear to the reader and other characters, even if not immediately to Schröter and Sabine. Pix's departure and the unsettling news of Fink's disappearance bring forth a moment of despondent reflection for Schröter. He confesses to his sister and aunt, "Ich werde alt und es wird leer bei uns" (577). His hopes for continuity in the firm through Sabine's marriage and future offspring seem unfulfilled. It is not an immediate threat to stability which concerns him but the question of perpetuation of a stable order. Again, the problem is not insoluble. Even though the aunt's mention of Anton Wohlfart is rebuffed by both brother and sister, it is firmly implanted in the reader's mind and reinforced by the successive narrative action, as the irrepressible aunt consults with Baumann, who writes a letter to Anton. Anton's return to the capital after a year in Poland is the other occasion for mention of disruption for the firm. Schröter is described as having aged (758), and the following passage indicates fluctuations in the firm's fortunes:

> Durch viele Jahre war hier alles fest gewesen, jetzt war das Geschäft in unruhiger, schwankender Bewegung. Viele von den alten Verbindungen des Hauses waren abgeschnitten, mehrere neue waren angeknüpft. Er fand neue Agenten, neue Kunden, mehrere neue Artikel und neue Arbeiter (796).

Yet the passage itself balances the possible losses with new connections, customers, and wares. Baumann and Specht plan to leave shortly, but the gain of Anton as a partner more than compensates, and the happy end to the novel ensures the continuity.

The stability of Schröter's firm as a model of social order is further emphasized by the severed continuation in both of the other spheres of action. Eugen von Rothsattel, a focal point of all his father's endeavors and sense of family pride, is killed, and any continuity implied in the future of Lenore von Rothsattel and Fritz von Fink involves a radical break with the order of aristocratic existence exemplified by the Baron. Von Rothsattel's loss of his son is paralleled in the deaths of Bernhard Ehrenthal and Veitel Itzig, Bernhard, hardly a suitable heir to the financial affairs of his father but nevertheless a source of pride and motivation to the latter, is an aberrant figure in the circle of Jewish characters.[71] His frailty and death terminate Hirsch Ehrenthal's hopes and future plans and contribute to the speculator's final state of mental imbalance. It is actually Itzig who is groomed as the successor to Ehrenthal, and his betrayal and death mark the discontinuity in the sphere of financial speculation. Itzig is also the heir to Hippus, to whom he is a pupil and in addition the object of such affection as the derelict lawyer can display (118-120). Itzig's reciprocal sentiments cease abruptly the night his mentor demands five percent of his first successful venture, and he becomes acquainted with "den Fluch der Argen, daß sie elend gemacht werden nicht nur durch ihre Missetaten sondern auch durch ihre bessern Neigungen" (280). The treachery inherent to Freytag's portrayal of the realm of parasitical existence of Hippus and the Jewish characters precludes stability and continuity.

The plot strand of *Soll und Haben* which traces the biography of Veitel Itzig reveals to the reader the process by which Itzig literally assembles his own sphere of everyday existence. The stages may be traced from his original statement of intent to Anton on the way to the capital that he is seeking the "Rezept, durch das man kann zwingen einen jeden, von dem man etwas will, auch wenn er nicht will" (25) through his apprenticeship to Hippus and gradual ingratiating ascent with Ehrenthal to a position of power over both his mentor and former employer. Just before the final turn of events precipitated by Anton's return from the provinces and Itzig's murder of Hippus, both the coveted von Rothsattel estate and a union with Rosalie Ehrenthal are within his grasp. And his downfall is partially effected with the same methods he had used to engineer von Rothsattel's ruin. The extended passage at the end of Book V, Chapter 5 (788-91) depicting Itzig's frame of mind and his tortured existence after the murder of Hippus and the Dickensian description of his panicked flight from the bridal party to eventual death (816-20) illustrate the efficacy of the advice Hippus gave Itzig regarding Ehrenthal's attempts to ensnare von Rothsattel: "Sorgen muß er ihm machen ... Sorgen durch Arbeit, große Arbeit, immerwährende Unruhe, tägliche Sorgen, die nicht aufhören ... Es gibt wenige, die den Kopf nicht verlieren, wenn eine große Sorge das ganze Jahr in ihrem Schädel herumbohrt" (226). Veitel Itzig becomes the victim of psychological mechanisms he once manipulated to secure the collapse of others.

The gradual assembly of requisites for Veitel Itzig's ascendant career and resultant fall finds a narrative parallel in the equally transparent disintegration of the accepted order of existence for the von Rothsattels. The narrative block of exposition in Book I, Chapter 3 characterizes the Baron as "das Musterbild eines adligen Rittergutsbesitzers" (29), whose main concern is the preservation of the modest family fortune for future generations of von Rothsattels. Ehrenthal's visit in the same chapter portends the ensuing events. The

Baron's answer to Ehrenthal's suggested financial investment is unambiguous, but so is the accompanying narrative clause: " 'Ich mache keine Geldgeschäfte,' antwortete der Freiherr stolz, aber in seiner Brust klang die Saite fort, welche der Händler angeschlagen hatte" (34). The careful reader can plot the trajectory of von Rothsattel's fall, from the initial mortgage for 45,000 Taler through the assumption of a mortgage on the Zaminsky estate, the erection of a factory on his own property, the fradulent double disposition of a mortgage for 20,000 Taler and the forced exile in Poland following the thwarted suicide attempt.

The variable fortunes of von Rothsattel, Hippus, Itzig, and Ehrenthal, as well as of the other Jewish figures and the lack of ordered continuity in their respective spheres of action are contrasted to the stability of Schröter's firm. Freytag's novel renders the specifics of Ehrenthal's and Itzig's manipulations and a detailed account of the disintegration of von Rothsattel's order of existence, but the solidity of the firm of T.O. Schröter is a constant, an unchanging principle of *ordo* within the narrative. Contrary to the network of consequences growing more complex with each additional mortgage or promissory note, the business of Schröter's company displays no real fluctuation and the reader learns very few of the details. The most extensive sections of description of actual business dealings are devoted to interchanges with Schmeie Tinkeles (esp. 57-60) and to salvaging the firm's interests in the provinces (Book III, Chapters 1-3). The former are described in great detail but are of little consequence, and the latter activity is depicted in terms of general characterization, as Anton's association with Eugene von Rothsattel and his military comrades is of more import for the story than his duties as a representative of the company. The actual processes and practices of Schröter's firm are not told. External threats do not generate severe upheavals, and internal disturbances are limited to inconsequential squabblings among the employees which leave the substance of the firm untouched.

The organization of Schröter's firm has been well characterized as "das Bild einer patriarchalischen Großfamilie."[72] It is the routinized aspect of the established order which exercises the nomic function described by Berger and Luckmann as "putting everything in its right place." Schröter's company may be regarded as a fixed system of definitions and roles which orders the quotidian existence of the participants. The mechanism and contingent variables are never exposed; the block of exposition in Book I, Chapter 5 initiates the hero Anton Wohlfart and the reader into a comprehensive and cohesive order. Already presented as a singular entity in the initial chapter of the novel, it requires no justification and undergoes no real alteration. There are changes in personnel, but the roles remain essentially invariable. A smaller version of Father Sturm eventually heads the *Auflader,* Jordan is replaced by Baumann, and Pix is succeeded by Balbus, who proves to be just as recalcitrant in the ongoing "war" with Schröter's aunt over the use of the attic (793). Fink's location within the hierarchy is an exception, since he begins as a *Volontär.* His aberrant position is signaled by such breaches of custom as the repeated damage done to Sabine's fine damask napkins (94-96) and his thoughtless killing of the sparrow on the anniversary outing (266-7). Yet Anton's intercession soothes ruffled spirits on the latter occasion and reveals how Fink has gradually taken over a regular post in the firm (270). When Fink leaves for America, Anton takes over one of his rooms and his dinner-table assignment and is designated as Fink's heir (318-19). Anton manages to combine both the unique aspects of Fink's position and the ordinary routines of the firm, adopting and integrating his predecessor's role.

The solid base of T.O. Schröter's firm is a fixed point of orientation within the novel to which the centripetal pattern of narrative movement repeatedly returns. The bond established in the opening chapter between the Wohlfart family and Schröter's company is a determinant one: "und doch wurde es für Anton ein Leitseil, wodurch sein ganzes Leben Richtung erhielt" (14). Each of the first three books ends with a redefinition of Anton in the company's terms: Book I marks the transition from apprentice to colleague, Book II the assimilation of Fink's position, and Book III the offer and refusal of Jordan's position as *Stellvertreter* and subsequent departure. Books IV and V form a unit surrounding Anton's efforts in Poland. The one chapter devoted to the firm (IV:5) documents the effects of Anton's absence — Schröter's despondent reflections on the future of the company. Baumann's letter to Anton leaves the latter equally troubled, and he is alienated from his immediate environment in Poland and inaccessible to Lenore (583-4). The final book brings the elevation of Anton to partner and husband, ensuring the continuity and stability of the firm.

The underlying narrative movement of *Soll und Haben* is similar to that of the *Dorfgeschichte,* the re-establishment and maintenance of an originally accepted stable order with collective values stressed over singular individual action. The length of the novel expands the pattern into a recurrent structure, traceable along the path of Anton Wohlfart's biography. Anton's earliest self-definition is in congruence with the presence of Schröter's firm in his life. He wants to become a "Kaufmann" (14). The final scene of the novel is the attainment of that goal, representing a felicitous coincidence of personal identity and social role. The position and integration of the individual within the encompassing social system is a major factor in the composition of the reality paradigm characteristic of Auerbach and Freytag, and the recurrent pattern of Freytag's novel embeds the hero ever more securely into the stable social order represented by Schröter's firm until the final stage of total congruence and equilibrium is reached. The unquestioned system of meanings and roles which forms the frame of reference for Anton's biography and Freytag's novel increasingly manages to encompass even the deviant enclaves of experience. The continually renewed interaction of Anton with Schröter's firm is the "return to reality" characteristic of the pervasive influence of a single, cohesive symbolic universe, and the manner in which Anton comes to repudiate his fascination with the aristocratic mode of existence represents the incorporation of a "finite province of meaning" within the dominant reality structure.[73]

The designation of Schröter's firm as a system of meanings indicates a stock of shared knowledge, a body of definitions and norms which provides a stable background and the predefinitions for daily behavior patterns. *Soll und Haben* contours Anton Wohlfart's acquisition of such a stock of knowledge, his internalization of the objective order embodied in Schröter's firm. Berger and Luckmann define socialization as "the comprehensive and consistent induction of an individual into the objective world of a society or a sector of it."[74] Anton's socialization process includes the "primary socialization" of appropriating his father's attitudes and the extensive "secondary socialization" process which is the "acquisition of role-specific knowledge" and the internalization of a specific system of values.[75] Anton's socialization process can be traced through the increasing primacy of the values connected with Schröter and their ultimate delimitation of his perception of the sphere of experience centered around the von Rothsattels.

Anton's concrete introduction to the routines and roles of Schröter's firm (Book I:5) is preceded by the significant encounter with Lenore on the von Rothsattel estate (Book I:2). His initial reaction to the estate is one of humble admiration, an attitude as ingrained as his desire to become a *Kaufmann*: "Der Respekt vor allem, was stattlich, sicher und mit Selbstgefühl in der Welt auftritt, war ihm, dem armen Sohn des Kalkulators, angeboren" (19). He dons a pair of gloves "von gelbem Zwirn" in an attempt to adapt to his surroundings, and the incident leaves a lasting impression. One of his first activities in his new environment is to sketch the von Rothsattel mansion and hang it over his sofa (55). His next extended contact with aristocratic society and Lenore is the dance sessions he attends at Fink's instigation, this time properly attired with "Glacéhandschuhen." Anton's participation in aristocratic circles alienates him from the firm's sphere of everyday existence. His colleagues are critical and withdrawn, and Anton and Fink are set apart "als aristokratische Coterie" and expressly excluded from Pix's birthday celebration (190-93). Yet Anton has not forsaken the underlying system of values. He is attracted by the behavior patterns ("Ton und Benehmen") of the circle around Frau von Baldereck, but his own popularity grows due to "die bürgerlichsten aller Tugenden, durch Ordnung und Pflichttreue" (170-1). When Fink's web of half-truths is revealed as the enabling factor in Anton's acceptance in the dance sessions, his farewell speech attests to a basic adherence to Schröter's values: honesty and a rejection of unearned privilege (198-200). It is the basic consistency in Anton's character which caused T.E. Carter to assess the hero of Freytag's novel as an essentially static figure: "Anton dancing or in the office remains true to himself."[76]

Throughout the work there is a consonance between the hero and the social environment into which he is finally integrated. Yet despite the consistency of Anton's motivations and actions, the connection to Lenore and the von Rothsattels remains a disturbing element, a detached province of meaning only absorbed into the prevalent symbolic universe after Anton's extended stay in Poland. The innate respect and the fantasy elements which formed his initial impression on the aristocrat's estate remain with him until the basis for the respect is revealed as hollow and fantasy is nourished within his own reality. The final condition of the once proud family on their paltry Polish estate no longer deserves the epithets "stattlich" and "sicher." The mutation implied in the marriage of Lenore and Fink is the final demise of the finite province of existence and privilege which von Rothsattel sought to retain. The new pair is apotheosized as the beginning of "ein neues deutsches Geschlecht, dauerhaft an Leib und Seele ... ein Geschlecht von Kolonisten und Eroberern" (830).

The position and function of fantasy in *Soll und Haben* is a carefully woven thematic complex, and the final fusion of fantasy with the predominant order of everyday reality marks the closure of the symbolic universe of Freytag's work, the integration of all spheres of personal experience under the pervasive reality definition.[77] There are two distinct strands of dream and fantasy motifs in the novel, the "Poesie des Geschäfts" (326) and the "träumerisches Entzücken" (19) linked to Anton's "Sehnsucht nach dem freien, stattlichen, schmuckvollen Leben der Vornehmen" (147). The former first appears as the smell of coffee, "ein poetischer Duft," which accompanies the Christmas package from Schröter's firm and helps influence Anton's decision to become a merchant. The second motif surfaces with the idyllic preliminary encounter with Lenore, and the dual threads of the imaginative elements of the daily routine connected with Schröter's company and Anton's attraction to the world of Lenore are carefully drawn through the novel.[78] The introduction to the company becomes for Anton "die Quelle einer eigentümlichen Poesie" (64), a quality he later earnestly defends to Bernhard Ehrenthal (239-241) and senses most strongly in the face of the threat to the firm in Poland (326). The counter-sphere resurfaces as "undeutliches Traumgesicht" at the Balderecks (170), and the opening idyll finds a correspondence in Anton's sleigh ride with Lenore, "das Schlittenmärchen," in Book IV (543-46). Yet the extended exposure to the von Rothsattels' habits, attitudes, and everyday routine brings the final disillusionment, the repudiation of the finite province of meaning. H. Kaiser has termed the final stage of Anton's biography "die Überwindung der trügerischen, blendenden Poesie ... durch das Leben selbst."[79] Anton returns from his year with the von Rothsattels "frei von dem Zauber" (752), and it is quite graphically a "return to reality" from a "marginal situation of experience" in Berger and Luckmann's descriptive terms. The final union with Sabine and the partnership in the firm are a reaffirmation of the predominant system of values and definitions within the novel and a conclusive reestablishment of equilibrium. In the final pages of the text, Sabine is expressly connected to Anton's father and the initial chapter of the novel. It was she who interceded for Anton's initial employment with the firm, and her brother had always referred to him as "her" apprentice (833). Her actions in putting the "Samtkäppchen" on the elder Wohlfart's head during his visit, an incident related in the final chapter, parallels Anton's childhood game with his father (833, 11). The reckoning of accounts implicit in the title of Freytag's work reaches its final, orderly state of balance. The congruence of individual and social order is total, and the final paragraph emphasizes the fulfilling integration of the realm of personal experience:

> Die poetischen Träume, welche der Knabe Anton in seinem Vaterhause unter den Segenswünschen guter Eltern gehegt hat, sind ehrliche Träume gewesen. Ihnen wurde Erfüllung, und ihr Zauber wird fortan sein Leben weihen (836).

As in Auerbach's *Dorfgeschichte,* a single reality paradigm retains ultimate validity and integrative force over personal, individual biography and experience. The field of reference constituted in reading Freytag's lengthy work is as cohesive and monolithic as the more readily transparent *ordo* of the shorter tales. The issues established in Chapter I of the present study as the main concerns of nineteenth-century German realist narrative, questions of the interrelation of individual and social world, the force of convention and transmission of values, stability and continuity, are resolved in Freytag and Auerbach in a narrative pattern of distinct univocality. A single social order prevails, possessing unquestioned validity and imposing itself upon the reader. The communicative structure common to *Soll und Haben* and Auerbach's early village tales presupposes acceptance of the dominant system of values and operates to reaffirm the univocality of the fictive field of reference.

The Authority of the Narrative System

One aspect of the communicative structure of Auerbach's village tales and Freytag's novel is the content of the texts, analyzed in the previous section in terms of social systems and the integration of the individual figure. The univocality of the works, the predominance and unquestioned approbation of a single, stable social order, has a correspondence in the composition and force of the narrative structure itself. *Soll und Haben* and Auerbach's village tales are highly directed texts which allow little latitude for reader concretizations. The vitality of the "realism" of the works, of a congruence between the field of reference actualized in the reading process and the reader's contextual, historical field of reference, is limited. The overdetermination of the narrative presupposes and reinforces acceptance of the cohesive system of meanings and values which forms the axis of each work. The narrative system itself is a model of *ordo* and imposes its authority upon the reader.

The authoritative stance of the texts by Freytag and Auerbach extends beyond the linear, rational mode of narration and the contrastive technique of characterization which clearly juxtaposes Buchmaier and Rellings, Anton and Itzig. There have been several analyses of Freytag's novel in connection with the aesthetic principles advocated in the author's *Technik des Dramas* (1863) and as an exemplary work for the literary precepts of the *Grenzboten*.[80] The compositional aspects of Auerbach's tales have received most attention in comparison with other authors.[81] The purpose of the present analysis is to isolate additional comprehensive patterns and distinct strategies within the texts at hand which guide and delimit reader experience. A pattern of narrative described as overdetermined must yield the tactics of its strongly directed character to close examination. It is not possible to exhaust all the nuances of any text, but specific narrative patterns and strategies common to *Soll und Haben* and the village tales can be ascertained and analyzed as to their mode of operation and resultant function.

The comprehensive pattern of narrative movement from a stable state to a re-established equilibrium has already been indicated in the previous section. Jonathan Culler's designation of plot as "the temporal projection of thematic structures" is pertinent for the works of Auerbach and Freytag.[82] *Die Kriegspfeife* accomplished the basic pattern in a single movement, and the parallel stories in *Befehlerles* duplicate the scheme with the plot variations which emphasize the underlying themes. *Soll und Haben* is a complex but unambiguous narrative, and the recurrent structure of disequilibrium and recuperation, the repeated return to the order implicit in Schröter's firm until the attainment of a final, reestablished stability, forms the plot and contours the import of the novel. The progression of action in all three texts is marked by an inevitability, and the individual stages are readily evident to the reader. There is a necessity and inner logic of action; all mysteries are eventually explained, from the misunderstanding concerning the pronoun "sie" in *Die Kriegspfeife* to Fink's America adventure and the fate of the purloined documents in *Soll und Haben.* The narrative logic is similar to the character of Anton Wohlfart, comprehensible and reliable.

A strict temporal and causal progression obtains in all three works. When simultaneous levels of action are narrated in Freytag's novel, care is taken to clarify the fact, and the synchronization often serves to underscore a significant contrast between the main spheres of action. The adverbial phrases "unterdes," "zu derselben Stunde," "zu derselben Zeit" signal the shift in the realm of action. The most striking use of the technique for contrastive purposes occurs in Book I, Chapter V, where the respective arrivals of Anton and Itzig in the firm of T.O. Schröter and the house of Hirsch

Ehrenthal are paralleled (40-55). The stages of their receptions are analogous, from the presentation of a letter of introduction to their dreams and their first activities the following day. The content of the initial welcome already indicates the difference in milieu; the "freundliches Licht" in Schröter's eye and his measured consideration (42) are opposed to Ehrenthal, whose manner is characterized with the verbs "anschnarren" and "entgegenschleudern" (47-8).

The continuous chronology of plot and the recurrence of an established point of reference guide the reader through the text. There is a causal and temporal connection between events in the narrative progression, as no action is unmotivated and there is never a reversal of an accepted state of affairs. The disintegration of the von Rothsattel family fortunes is a measured, inevitable process. The "reversal" of the ordinance regarding the handax in *Befehlerles* is actually the logical result of the narrated action and the restoration of an accepted order. The texts exemplify what Roland Barthes has termed the "readerly": "controlled by the principle of non-contradiction but by multiplying solidarities, by stressing at every opportunity the *compatible* nature of circumstances, by attaching narrated events together with a kind of logical 'paste.' "83

The lack of contradiction within the narrative pattern common to Freytag and Auerbach does not imply the absence of tension. *Befehlerles* and *Soll und Haben* contain elements of suspense which sustain reader interest. The Polish adventures and the financial intrigues in the latter and the actions of Buchmaier in the Auerbach text set up constellations of opposing forces and give rise to conflict. Yet it is a tension with an ultimate resolution, and the opposing positions do not define themselves in the telling of the story nor are they subject to modulation within the narrative progression. Hansjörg's "Selbstverstümmelung" in *Die Kriegspfeife* is censured from the outset, and the positive sphere of order and stability associated with Schröter's firm is established early in Freytag's novel and the values are never questioned within the narrative. The use of contrast, the juxtaposition of static, predefined positions, extends beyond a schematic method of composition and is indicative of a strategic binarism central to the works of both authors.

Binarism or a system of binary oppositions are terms originally borrowed from linguistics, and they have been variously applied to the study of narrative prose.[84] The use of the terms in the present context is meant to describe a series of oppositions and equivalencies with the ultimate valorization and totalization of one set of terms. In decoding the oppositions the reader realizes the values suggested by the positive terms. The function of such a textual strategy is to reinforce the dominant system of values composing the field of reference of the text, and the extensive use of the technique contributes greatly to the strongly directed character of the narratives under consideration. *Die Kriegspfeife* is rather strictly constructed on such a basis, and its brevity allows a thorough examination of how the strategy can function at a very elementary level.

Several pairs of opposites should have become evident in the paraphrase and initial analysis offered in the preceding section. In a text as short as *Die Kriegspfeife,* terms may include verbal concepts as well as figures and objects significant for the action of the story. A clear opening opposition is "Vaterland" : "Franzos'." Others evident from the plot paraphrase include "Gemeinde" : "Sebstverstümmelung," and "Ehe" : "Pfeife" (individuation). A brief, compacted section of the story allows the extraction of several other pairs. It is the passage referred to earlier in which Hansjörg has just buried his finger, which Kätherle has refused to accept as a present.

> Hansjörg stand sinnend dabei, als das Kätherle das Loch wieder zuschaufelte. Die Sünde gegen das Vaterland, die er durch seine Selbstverstümmelung begangen hatte, kam ihm nicht in den Sinn; dagegen erwachte in ihm der Gedanke, daß hier ein Theil der ihm von Gott verliehenen Lebenskraft eingescharrt wurde, für die er Rechenschaft ablegen müsse. Er stand so zu sagen lebendigen Leibes bei seinem eigenen Begräbniß, und der Vorsatz stieg in ihm auf, alle ihm noch gebliebenen Kräfte nach Pflicht und Gewissen treulich zu üben und anzuwenden. Ein Todesgedanke überschauerte ihn, und mit Wehmuth und Freude schaute er auf, sah sich lebend und neben sich sein geliebtes Mädchen (54).

Even though the transgression against the homeland is explicitly presented as *not* occuring to Hansjörg, the sentence of course brings it unavoidably into the reader's mind. Further elements are readily evident, and a partial listing for the tale yields the following series:

"Vaterland"	"Vaterland"	Kätherle	"Pflicht/Gewissen"
"Franzos"	"Selbstverstümmelung"	"Finger"	"Sünde"
"Religion"	Kätherle	"Ehe"	"Ehe"
"Selbstverlust/Tod"	"Pfeife"	"Selbstverstümmelung"	"Pfeife"

The terms are not necessarily uniform nor all explicitly mentioned in the text. "Religion" is perhaps a debatable choice, but the story does suggest the term through the verbal echoes of "Sünde" and "von Gott verliehen." Kätherle's kiss is designated as "die seligste Absolution," and Hansjörg attends confession following the burial scene. Further additions would be conceivable, as binarism is understood as a recurrent textual strategy and not as an exhaustive structural pattern. An explicit substantiation of the equivalencies established by the bottom line is the statement by Kätherle: "Laß die Pfeif' beim Franzos und beim Teufel" (62). The effect of a consistent binarism is the univocality of the work. All terms and values are positionally defined, and a reader can only accept the validity of the "top line" or dismiss the story. It is not a strict homological patterning of oppositions which is decisive but the process by which already defined terms are juxtaposed and carried into new oppositions, retaining the positive or negative marking. The result is an ostensibly self-evident division of values. Even in as short a tale as *Die Kriegspfeife* the process is an intricate one. Ultimately the field of reference of the text associates and affirms religion, patriotism, marriage and the primacy of communal concerns over individuation, which is presented as actual loss of self. It is a monolithic paradigm in which all terms composing the "top line" are compatible. The line of demarcation is consistently upheld, as the valorized terms never appear in a negative position in another opposition.

Binarism in *Soll und Haben* is readily evident in the schematic parallel of the biographies of Anton Wohlfart and Veitel Itzig, in the contrast of Germans and Poles and in the thematic opposition of "Poesie des Geschäfts" and unchecked fantasy. The strategy in Freytag's novel extends to plot segments as well as isolatable elements, and the decoding process is more complex. The function for the reader is, however, the same, and binarism remains an authoritative textual strategy which effects acceptance of the fictive field of reference and reaffirmation of the "top line" of values established by the text. One example of the juxtaposition of plot segments has already been mentioned: the introduction of Anton and Itzig into their respective spheres. The opposition of the two characters in Book I, Chapter 4 reinforces a previously established contrast and opens a further pair of terms with Schröter's firm: Ehrenthal's family. The decoding process involved in the system of binary oppositions in *Soll und Haben* can be exemplified in the first book of the novel. In a more complex variant of the "reading" of oppositions than in *Die Kriegspfeife*, it is necessary to go beyond the simple juxtapositions to extract the values asserted by the text.

Anton and Itzig are first juxtaposed in Book I, Chapter 2. The school-days' anecdotes with which Itzig is introduced establish him as weak, dishonest and scheming. The ancillary exposition of Anton's character reinforces the childhood characterization of Chapter I. The same marking is evident in the opposition of Schröter's firm : Hirsch Ehrenthal in Chapter 4 as Anton and Itzig enter the capital. Anton is welcomed into an existing order, and Itzig and Ehrenthal gauge each other's character and maneuver for position. The negative marking of scheming and manipulative speculation is shared by Itzig and Hirsch Ehrenthal in the oppositions Anton : Itzig as schoolboys, Anton : Itzig in the paralleled segments of Chapter 4, and Schröter : Ehrenthal. Schröter receives the positive marking of order and routine. Chapter 5 and 7 underscore the firm of T.O. Schröter as the locus of stability and recurrent, predictable order, and Chapters 6 and 8 provide the negative contrast, opposing Itzig and Rothsattel to the values of order and stability.

Chapter 5 first introduces Anton to the predictable regularity of his new environs. As Schröter informs him: "es ist eine strenge Regelmäßigkeit in unserem Hause" (62), and Chapter 7 characterizes the unchanging routine of *Comptoir* and *Vorderhaus* as congruent with the systematic aspects of a comprehensive polity and with the order of nature itself. Anton becomes a "kleiner Vasall eines großen Staatskörpers" (78), and his new colleagues are designated as "Minister," "Würdenträger," and "Generalstatthalter seiner kaiserlichen Firma" (78-9). Even the sun, despite Liebold's mistrust, adheres to the "altertümlichen Gesetzen des Universums" and respectfully spares the balance sheets of the firm. Drawn with humor and Dickensian overtones, the world of Schröter's firm nevertheless retains the character of the language used to describe it.

Chapter 8 is the negative pole to Anton's systematic environment. Itzig's variegated existence includes days spent on the streets and nights passed in the acquisition of an arcane knowledge which sometimes seems to him "als ob man durch die Benutzung dereselben in Gefahr gerate, sich dem Satan zu verschreiben" (113). Hippus, a vagabond former lawyer given to drink, initiates him into "Schlupfwinkel" and "Schleichwege" (116). The contrast to Anton's ordered life is reinforced in details: Itzig's meagre meals and single glass of beer in his first year (196) are the counterpart to Anton's dinner routine at Schröter's: "am Sonntage ein Gericht mehr und ein Glas Wein vor jedem Couvert" (63). The opposition Anton : Itzig in their new environments can be decoded as orderly routine : lack of a stable order/speculation.

Chapter 6 establishes the sphere of growing financial disorder surrounding von Rothsattel, and it is a clear contrast to Schröter's business. There is no work being done, no goods being examined and exchanged, and no bustle of customers. Instead there are the mortgage documents, the repeated intrusion of Ehrenthal and the questionable *Holzhandel.* Rothsattel is marked as the negative term by increasing instability, speculation and poor judgment. The opposition Schröter : Rothsattel is again that of order and routine : instability/speculation. The values opposed in the first book are carried throughout Freytag's novel, and the positive terms of order, routine, stability, and honest work are continually reinforced. The reader is easily oriented by the consistent binarism, and even the "anomalous" figures such as Bernhard Ehrenthal or the Polish aristocrat who aids Schröter and Anton are congruent with the prevailing system. Bernhard is an aberration within a schematic opposition of Jews and Germans but acts to reinforce the positive terms of the novel's underlying value system as he opposes Itzig and his own father.

The system of binary oppositions established in Book I is never radically altered. The expansion of the scene of action to Poland only provides new variations on established themes. The opening paragraph of Book III, beginning with "Ein böses Jahr kam über das Land," describes the atmosphere in such terms of disaster and chaos that when "Das Schreckenswort 'Revolution in Polen' " finally appears as explanation in paragraph two, the reader associates with it all the dire disruption of order conceivable. Even the landscape in Poland is bleak and desolate, and the new estate is unfit for human habitation. Karl's exclamation upon encountering the well-kept cottage of the *Vogt* in Book IV emphasizes the positive terms of opposition: "Hier ist eine Hausfrau, hier ist Vaterland, hier sind Deutsche" (513). The positive values associated with Schröter's firm are extended to encompass the outpost of German culture and middle-class order in Poland. The Rothsattels' socializing with the Polish aristocracy and refusing to attend church services with non-aristocratic German settlers (540) position them on the negative side and continue the claim to privilege rooted in Book I in the Baron's concern to retain the family estate and heritage for his son. The retention of unearned privilege had been most strongly opposed by Schröter in his later justification to Anton of his refusal to aid the Rothsattels: "Jeden, der auf Kosten der freien Bewegung anderer für sich und seine Nachkommen ein ewiges Privilegium sucht, betrachte ich als einen Gegner der gesunden Entwicklung unseres Staates" (480-1).

The only real exception to the schematic arrangement of binary opposition within *Soll und Haben* is the figure of Fritz von Fink. His mobility and alienation from his own class plus his incompatibility with the sphere of Schröter's firm preclude his being relegated to a fixed category. He manipulates the Baldereck social circle and reveals his scorn for the social conventions of his class of origin, stating to Anton: " 'Was meinen deutschen Adel betrifft, so viel darauf!' — hier schnalzte er mit den Fingern, — 'er hat für mich ungefähr denselben Wert, wie ein Paar gute Glanzstiefel und neue Glacéhandschuhe' " (98). In the course of Schröter's anniversary outing he thoughtlessly kills Sabine's favorite sparrow and praises the American mode of life above that of his homeland (266-8). Due to his irresponsibility in considering the limitations of his companions, Anton almost drowns (Book I:9) and Lenore spends the night alone in the woods with a twisted ankle (Book V:3). Yet it is also Fink who offers the toast at the firm's outing "in tiefem Ernst: 'Trinken Sie mit mir auf das Wohl eines deutschen Geschäfts, wo die Arbeit eine Freude ist, wo die Ehre eine Heimat hat; hoch unser Comptoir und unser Prinzipal!' " (274). And it is Fink's energy and capital which will revitalize the Rothsattel estate and establish the bulwark of German culture in Poland. Fritz von Fink defies the binary system of Freytag's novel, and his figure is almost in competition with the narrative voice and also with the character of Anton as the locus of proffered reader identification.

The reliable point of orientation for the reader in Freytag's novel and a means by which the reader is led to reaffirm the positive terms in the binary system of values is the character of Anton Wohlfart. He is clearly the "hero" of *Soll und Haben,* and the suggested identification with his figure is relatively transparent. The novel begins with background of the Wohlfarts and of Anton's childhood. The reader's curiosity about the figure of Anton is stilled by the narrative use of descriptive detail to convey the fullest possible picture. Such details as his early predilection for using the handle instead of the bowl of his spoon for eating purposes (11) are calculated to engage the reader's sympathy. The first chapter of Book I, hardly essential to the action of the narrative except to establish the link between Anton and Schröter's firm, fulfills the communicative function of establishing Anton as the character on whose side the reader's loyalties are to lie. The opening descriptive paragraph of Chapter 2 could well be the beginning of the novel. It is an objective landscape description similar to the opening chapter of the first version of Keller's *Grüner Heinrich.* The important difference is that "der Wanderer" in *Soll und Haben,* who is named in the second paragraph, is already familiar to the reader, while the initial reaction to the designation "ein junger Mensch" and the name "Heinrich Lee" in Keller's novel is neutral anticipation. By the time Freytag's novel actually begins, the reader has already entered the fictive world of the hero and now enters the novel at his side.

The function of Anton as the reliable guide for reader involvement in the action of the novel and in the strongly directed system of values forming the field of reference of the work is well illustrated by his connection to Schröter and by the position and structure of his role in the two Poland adventures. Anton's initiation into the stable order of T.O. Schröter's firm in Chapters 5 and 7 of Book I is also the exposition for the reader, who becomes acquainted with the colleagues, the figure of Fritz von Fink and the everyday routine as Anton's initial weeks are related. Similarly, in both Poland episodes Anton is drawn into a situation which he did not create and in which he is initially not the central figure. In the first episode (Book III), he goes to protect Schröter and help him regain his property. In the second adventure (Books IV-V), he goes to aid the von Rothsattels and manage their property. In both cases he is drawn into the conflict and then becomes the central protagonist. Correspondingly, the reader enters the realm of adventure and gradually becomes involved along with the hero. The parallelization of Anton and the reader is necessary in order to establish the standpoint dictated for the reader by the narrative. The strongest statements of the underlying values of the work are actually voiced by Schröter, usually in conversation with Anton.[85] The proffered identification with Anton places the reader in a parallel role of recipient of Schröter's statements and implicitly creates ties between Anton's position (that of general agreement with Schröter) and the attitudes to be taken by the reader. A good example of such a narrative strategy based on reader identification is to be found in Schröter's remarks in the first Poland adventure. In their conversations Anton makes statements of fact, and Schröter draws the tendentious conclusions for Anton and the reader:

"Es ist besser, wir beschränken uns auf die Waffen, die wir zu gebrauchen gewöhnt sind," bemerkte er [Schröter] gutmütig, indem er Anton die Pistolen zurückgab, "wir sind Männer des Friedens und wollen nur unser Eigentum zurückhaben ...
Dort drüben erheben die Privilegierten den Anspruch, das Volk darzustellen. Als wenn Edelleute und leibeigene Bauern einen Staat bilden könnten! ..."
"Sie haben keinen Bürgerstand," sagte Anton eifrig beistimmend. "Das heißt, sie haben keine Kultur," fuhr der Kaufmann fort (330-1).

A further example of the parallel positions of Anton and the reader of *Soll und Haben* is found in the description of the party at the Tarowskis (546-50). The passage consists largely of narrative description, and any dialogue involves comments and questions directed at Anton. The reader only has access to Anton's thoughts and reactions in the section, and they are quoted directly and also rendered in indirect discourse and in the mixture of narrative voice and individual character stance termed free indirect discourse. The result is the alignment of reader, narrator and character on the outskirts of an activity which is positioned negatively within the text. Anton's censure of the entire episode is clear, and the reader perceives the Rothsattels and the Polish aristocrats through his eyes and with the further support of the narrative perspective. Anton's increased distance from the Rothsattels in Poland is meant to elicit a similar attitude on the part of the reader, placing both in the position of reaffirmation of the positive values associated with Schröter and the final scenes of the novel.

If Anton is evidently the "hero," Fink is just as clearly the more interesting figure. Especially upon a rereading of the novel it is Fink who retains the reader's interest, as Anton is not only reliable and predictable but totally programmed. Fink eludes the binary system of Freytag's text and occasionally usurps the function of the narrator. He is the only major figure to offer his own character exposition (101-3), and it is his language in general which sets him apart from the other characters and undercuts the narrative voice. On two occasions he demonstrates the power of words to create reality, and he also is the only character consistently capable of metaphorical speech. In the preparatory efforts for Anton's introduction to the Balderecks he neatly evades the question of Anton's family and points to the conventionality of language in his answer:

"Ist denn das Gut groß, welches Sie abgetreten haben?" fragte Herr von Tönnchen. "Ein Gut?" fragte Fink und sah nach dem Himmel, "es ist gar kein Gut. Es ist eine Bodenfläche, Berg und Tal, Wasser und Wald, ein kleiner Teil von Amerika. Und ob dieser Besitz groß ist? Was nennen Sie groß? Was heißt groß auf dieser Erde? In Amerika mißt man die Größe des Landbesitzes nach einem anderen Maß, als in diesem Winkel von Deutschland. Ich für meinen Teil werde schwerlich je wieder eine solche Besitzung mein Eigentum nennen" (50).

In the following conversation with Frau von Baldereck he demonstrates the gap between language and communication, as she "understands" a number of things Fink never says at all (151-4). He plays a similar role on the evening with the Ehrenthals, where his well-chosen words to mother and daughter have the effect, "daß beide bezaubert wurden" (249). Anton's censure in both cases is swift; he leaves the dance lessons when the ruse is revealed and forces Fink to discontinue his affair with Rosalie Ehrenthal. Yet Fink retains linguistic control of Anton as well and rivals the narrator in finding formulaic descriptions for the hero. He chides him affectionately for believing "ehrlich handeln sei eine so einfache Geschichte, wie ein Butterbrot streichen" (426) and titles him a "spitzfindiger Hamlet in Transtiefeln" in Poland (649).

The conclusion that Fritz von Fink "seems to elude the author's control,"[86] or at least the narrator's, is appropriate. It is the ironical tone in Fink's speech and attitudes which is generally absent from the narrative voice in *Soll und Haben* as well as in Auerbach's *Dorfgeschichte*. There is little of the distance between narrator and story which is essential for irony. The few times that the narrative voice assumes an ironical tone in Freytag's novel, it is for a brief characterization and can be regarded as a rhetorical embellishment. An early example is the explanation of Itzig's having to wait outside Ehrenthal's door because "der Geschäftsmann erst das Familienglück des Abendessens genießen wollte, bevor er dem künftigen Millionär Audienz gab" (46). At Anton's first encounter with Eugene, the narrator assumes the hero's perspective with a touch of irony and describes the resemblance of Eugene to Lenore as "so ähnlich wie bei einem jungen Reiteroffizier in Beziehung auf das allerschönste irdische Fräulein nur möglich ist" (333).

Such passages hardly constitute an ironical level to the text, and the general posture of the narrator in *Soll und Haben* is that of sympathetic mediation between reader and story. The strongly directed character of the novel, the univocality of its field of reference, is reinforced by the narrative voice, which shares the constitutive values carried by other strategies within the text. On several occasions the narrator addresses individual figures in the story, and his attitudes are clearly those to be assumed by the reader as well. At the end of the Book V the following passage addresses von Rothsattel:

> Wo seid ihr, lustige Pläne des blinden Mannes, der gebaut, gesündigt, gelitten hat, um euch lebendig zu machen? Horche, du armer Vater, mit verhaltenem Atem; es ist still geworden im Schloß und auf den Gipfeln der Bäume, und doch vermagst du nicht mehr zu hören den einen Ton, an den du immer gedacht hast bei deinen Luftschlössern, unter deinen Pergamenten, den Herzschlag deines einzigen Sohnes, des ersten Majoratsherrn der Rothsattel (723).

Any sympathy with the Baron implied in the phrase "du armer Vater" is cancelled by the references to the suicide attempt, unrealistic dreams, the mortgages and the original intent to retain and transmit a position of privilege, all terms with a negative marking within the text. The reader's reaction to Eugene's death as a human loss for Rothsattel is channelled in accordance with the priorities of the narrative system. A parallel function of the narrative voice is the extended passage addressed to Rosalie Ehrenthal after Itzig's death (817-9). It begins "Lege deinen Brautschmuck ab, schöne Rosalie ..." and continues to strip her of her finery and then to prophesy a future suitor desirous of her inheritance and a final unhappy marriage reminiscent of that of her mother with which the reader is acquainted. The final sentence reveals how close the narrative stance is to the consistently valorized position of Schröter:

> Das Geld aber, welches der alte Ehrenthal durch Wucher und Schlauheit mit tausend Sorgen für seine Kinder zusammengebracht hat, das wird wieder rollen aus einer Hand in die andere, es wird dienen den Guten und den Bösen, und wird dahinfließen in den mächtigen Strom der Kapitalien, dessen Bewegung das Menschenleben erhält und verschönert, das Volk und den Staat groß macht und den einzelnen stark oder elend, je nach seinem Tun (818).

There are definite verbal echoes of Schröter's earlier explanation to Anton of the necessary fall of Rothsattel:

> Wo die Kraft aufhört in der Familie oder im einzelnen, da soll auch das Vermögen aufhören, das Geld soll frei dahinrollen in andere Hände, und die Pflugschar soll übergehn in eine andere Hand, welche sie besser zu führen weiß. Und die Familie, welche im Genusse erschlafft, soll wieder heruntersinken auf den Grund des Volkslebens, um frisch aufsteigender Kraft Raum zu machen (480).

The positive pole is, of course, the final paragraph of the text, which addresses, not a narrated character, but the house of T.O. Schröter itself, stressing the stability and continuity of the central force in the novel, the total integration of the individual and the final equilibrium. It begins "Schmücke dich, du altes Patrizierhaus ..." and ends with the final balance: "Das alte Buch seines [Antons] Lebens ist zu Ende, und in eurem Geheimbuch, ihr guten Geister des Hauses, wird von jetzt ab 'mit Gott' verzeichnet: sein neues Soll und Haben" (836).

The passages of generalized narrative commentary in Auerbach's village tales are similar in structure and function to those in *Soll und Haben*. They are incorporated into the field of reference of the text and often coincide with the perspective of a specific character.[87] The following passage from *Befehlerles* consists of narrative commentary, but it is presented partially as the sentiments of Mathes, refined by the narrator, as the first two sentences actually form the antecedent for the pronoun *das* in the last sentence:

> Wer nie in den Händen des Gerichts war, weiß nicht, welch' ein schreckliches Los es ist, so auf einmal nicht mehr Herr über sich zu sein; es ist, als ob einem der eigene Körper genommen wäre. Von Hand zu Hand geschubt, muß man freiwillig seine Füße aufheben, um doch nur dahin zu gehen, wohin Andere wollen. Das fühlte Mathes, denn er war in seinem ganzen Leben zum erstenmale vor Gericht (159).

In Auerbach's tales the narrator is a more perceptible guide, and the assumed reader identification is with the narrator and not directly with an individual narrated character. Yet the result is similar to the alignment with Anton in *Soll und Haben*. Reading becomes a process of consensus, an acceptance of the field of reference of the text. Auerbach's commentary on the *Schwarzwälder Dorfgeschichten*, "Vorreden spart Nachreden," states the intent of the stories to offer a comprehensive picture of the author's home village: "ein ganzes Dorf gewissermaßen vom ersten bis zum letzten Hause zu schildern."[88] The narrative tone is meant to certify factuality and carry exemplary character: "Ich habe mich fast immer als mündlich erzählend gedacht; die Ereignisse stehen als geschichtliche Thatsachen da. Daher mußte es kommen, daß hin und wieder manche Lebensregel und allgemeine Bemerkung eingestreut wurde."[89] The claim made for the author and consequently for the narrator of the following tales is one of authority. The narrator/author is acquainted with the material being related and asserts its actuality. Within the tales themselves the narrative voice finds a medial position, one of familiarity with the characters, milieu, and story and at the same time a position external to the story at the reader's side. The beginning of *Die Kriegspfeife* informs the reader that it is the story of "meinem Nachbar Hansjörg" and also parallels reader and narrator as spectators from a different era:

> Es war im Jahr 1796. Wir in unserer mäuschenstillen Zeit, wir Kinder des unbefriedigten Friedens, können uns kaum einen Begriff von der damaligen Unruhe machen; es war als ob die Leute gar nirgends mehr fest zu Hause wären, als ob das ganze Menschengeschlecht sich auf die Beine gemacht hätte, um Einer den Andern da und dorthin zu treiben (45).

The sentence is characteristic for the dual function of Auerbach's narrator as an authority who can relate and interpret the events: "es war als ob ... als ob ..." and still share the reader's perspective: "wir."[90]

In *Schrift und Volk,* Auerbach recommends a balanced partiality as the appropriate narrative stance: "Die Theilnahme des Erzählers an seinen Geschichten darf sich aber nicht in salbungsvollen überschwenglichen Ausrufungen, sondern muß sich in der ganzen Haltung kundgeben."[91] As in *Soll und Haben,* there is no ironical distance, and the narrative voice functions to reinforce the univocality of the works. A related narrative strategy characteristic of the strongly directed communicative structures common to Freytag and Auerbach is the persistence of the texts in providing their own commentary. In *Befehlerles,* the narrative itself labels the defiant defacing of the posted ordinance as "sinnbildliche Handlung" (174) and refers to the fir twig Mathes plucks as "das sichtbare Sinnbild seines Schweigens" and "das Sinnbild seiner Anklage" (159). Similar passages can be found throughout Freytag's novel as well. Following an unfavorable description of Ehrenthal's house, the narrator adds the unnecessary commentary: "Es war kein guter Charakter in dem Hause" (46). As Itzig leaves Ehrenthal's house after the initial meeting, the narrator is not content to describe his smile of pleasure and reproduce his thoughts of pride but adds the superfluous interpretation: "offenbar war er mit seinem Handel zufrieden" (51). The use of rhetorical questions follows the same pattern. The narrator in *Die Kriegspfeife* not only informs the reader that the pipe is a central object in the story but reemphasizes the fact after the extended description: "War diese Pfeife nicht schön, und hatte Hansjörg nicht recht, daß er sie liebte, wie ein Held des Altertums seinen Schild?" (49). Freytag's narrator makes sure that the anomalous aspect of Bernhard Ehrenthal is duly noted by the reader: "Wie aber kam der Sohn in diese Familie?" (50). The strongly directed character of such narrative devices leaves little latitude for the reader.

A variant of such a strategy is a recurrent narrative pattern of thesis and illustration or, sometimes in reverse order, *exemplum(a)* and conclusion. The initial sentence of Book I, Chapter 5 states that Anton is confused as he attempts to orient himself in Schröter's firm. The following pages bring a variety of scenes in staccato tempo, illustrating the everyday bustle which confuses him. The beginning of Book III is an example of the reverse order. The illustration, the *exampla,* are the dire pictures of disorder, and the conclusion is "das Schreckenswort, 'Revolution in Polen'." The first Poland episode itself then functions as the thesis for which the extended second Poland adventure offers the confirming illustration. The passages of interpolated generalized commentary function in the same manner and point to the exemplary aspect of the narrated action. The opening sentence of *Die Kriegspfeife* claims the story itself as exemplum: "Das ist eine ganz absonderliche Geschichte, die aber doch mit der neueren Weltgeschichte, oder was fast einerlei ist, mit der Geschichte Napoleons, ganz genau zusammenhängt" (45). The function of such a pattern is to embed the narrative action in a broader context and to offer the reader consistent reinforcement. It is a pattern of authority and is congruent with the other narrative strategies which characterize the communicative structure of *Soll und Haben* and the *Dorfgeschichte.*

The strongly directed character of the narrative system common to Freytag's novel and Auerbach's tales: the persistent narrative voice, the determined position of the reader, the constitutive binarism, and the comprehensive pattern of re-established equilibrium, contributes to the underlying univocality of the works. The reality paradigm constituted in the reading of the texts is monolithic. The approbated social order is an integrated entity which aberrations and challenges only serve to substantiate, and the uniformity is carried by the narrative strategies as well, which effect experience and reaffirmation of the fictive field of reference as given. Although disparate in content and in regard to the historical context of their genesis, Auerbach's *Dorfgeschichte* of the 1840s and Freytag's *Soll und Haben* share a cohesive communicative structure, one which determined the parallel reception pattern of the works and the original ideological function and which delimits the vitality of their "realism." The similar narrative pattern and the analogous composition of the social system within the works permit the designation of village tale and commercial novel as a single aspect of nineteenth-century realist narrative.

III. CONVENTION AND NARRATIVE REFRACTION: READING THE SOCIAL CODE

The novels of Theodor Fontane, written in the last quarter of the previous century, have retained an appeal for twentieth-century readers. The "Fontane renaissance" has become a virtual topos of literary scholarship, and three major editions of Fontane's works have been published since 1959.[1] Although Walter Müller-Seidel's appraisal of the world-wide popularity of Fontane's novels is overly enthusiastic, the continued interest in the works is more extensive and of a different character than the revival of interest in Freytag and Auerbach described in the last chapter.[2] *Soll und Haben* and the *Dorfgeschichte* have become primarily objects of scholarly concern, while Fontane's novels are read and recommended as literature for enjoyment as well as material for analysis from a historical perspective. In 1975, a three-part television version of *Der Stechlin* (1898) was presented by the North German Radio and Television Network (NDR). In 1979, the same work was selected by the West German weekly *Die Zeit* as one of the hundred best works of world literature.[3] There have been four film versions of *Effi Briest* (1895), including Rainer Werner Fassbinder's 1974 rendition. Fassbinder had also proposed a television film of *Soll und Haben* in 1977, and a brief comparison of the mode of adaptation of literature for the screen in each case is enlightening for an understanding of the basic differences in the narratives themselves.

The controversy which ensued upon the announcement of a ten-segment television film based on Freytag's novel resulted in the eventual cancellation of the project in early 1977. The anti-semitic, chauvinistic character of the book was deemed improper material for a series by the West German Radio and Television Network (WDR). In an article published at the time in *Die Zeit,* Fassbinder outlined his intended adaptation and emphasized the manner in which the film perspective would have provided a distance to the ideological identity of the historical text: "Ein Film 'Soll und Haben' wird 'richtig' das als falsch erzählen, was Freytag und mit ihm seine Figuren und seine Leser für 'richtig' hielten."[4] The univocality of Freytag's narrative, the alignment of reader, story and narrative voice within a fixed system of attitudes and values, requires a definite perspective of film presentation to compensate for the lack of critical distance within the text itself. The projected television series was to reveal the historical stance of the text and was not intended as a popularization or recommendation of the novel as it stands.

The filming of Fontane's *Effi Briest* in 1974 was based on other principles. Although the film bears the unmistakeable stamp of Fassbinder's cinematographic technique, it is not a rectification but an extension of the original narrative perspective. Fassbinder has stated that he followed Fontane's attitude towards the story and the society portrayed in his film. He speaks of a "built-in 'distance' " which allows the audience "to discover its own attitude to society."[5] The perspective which Fassbinder extrapolated for his film is inherent to Fontane's texts and is partially responsible for their vitality. The authoritative narrative system characteristic of Freytag's *Soll und Haben* and Auerbach's village tales presupposes and reinforces reader acceptance of the field of reference of the works. The reality paradigm constituted in the reading of the narratives is regarded as a "given entity," without incorporation of the underlying mechanisms of production and legitimation of that reality. Fontane's novels present a distinctly different reader experience. The potential text structure enables a wider range of concretizations and a broader scope for the degree of congruence between the reality paradigm constituted in the reading process and the functional social reality model of a reader's environment. It is this congruence which I have termed the realistic dimension of a text. The increased polyvalence of Fontane's realism can be ascribed to the distinctive composition of the social system composing the field of reference of his works and to the comprehensive patterns and strategies of the concomitant narrative structure. Reading is no longer a process of consensus or reaffirmation, but rather a tracing of variable perspectives within the text.

The narrative system in Fontane's novels refuses to exert the authoritative facticity which I have established for the communicative structure common to Freytag and Auerbach. Victor Lange has suggested that a narrative text provides a model of understanding, and Fontane's texts present a framework of reading and multiple interpretation in which the indeterminacy of meaning is itself a structural element.[6] The narrative progression in Fontane's stories is basically linear, but the temporal movement is not central to the narrative logic. The action of the advancement of plot does not carry meaning as it does in Freytag and Auerbach. As the plot is less important, the reader will find other principles which encode meaning and organize the text. It is the rituals of social interaction which constitute the dominant dimension of Fontane's novels and, as has been duly noted, shape the very rhythm of the texts.[7] A narrated event is embedded in a field of varying interpretations, which are of more import than a resultant plot development. Apperception of character and narrated event is refracted, and all thematic issues are facetted, with disparate weight accorded the variants by the underlying textual pattern.

A similar analytical perspective dominates the social world which composes the field of reference of Fontane's novels. The milieu of Fontane's "Gesellschaftsromane" is the realm of human activity bounded by social conventions, values and norms. Yet such a socially-defined environment and its effective force upon the individual characters inhabiting it are common to all three patterns of German realist narrative which I am considering. The specific quality of Fontane's presentation of the fabric of socially-established meanings and quotidian routines is the degree to which the contingency of the institutionalized patterns of social behavior and their constricting influence upon the individuals who perceive the social world as an objectively "given" entity are perceptible to the reader. Fontane's characters are not rebels against society; the closest they come is a sceptical submission to its dictates, an attitude contributing to the designation of their author's stance as one of "resignation."[8] Yet the disjunction of individual and social role, the incomplete integration of character and encompassing society, exposes the constructed and constraining nature of social reality. In Berger and Luckmann's terms, the analysis of social roles is of particular significance "because it reveals the mediations between the macroscopic universes of meaning objectivated in a society and the ways in which these universes are subjectively real to individuals."[9]

The objectivated universe of meaning, the institutional world which the individual inhabitant experiences as everyday reality, is carried to a great extent by language, which marks the coordinates of commonsense knowledge and social routine. Social institutions, evolving from the transmission of habitualized action, provide the stable background and predefinitions for human interaction within a given social reality. As detailed in *The Social Construction of Reality*:

> The institutions, as historical and objective facticities, confront the individual as undeniable facts. The institutions are *there*, external to him, persistent in their reality, whether he likes it or not ... They have coercive power over him, both in themselves, by the sheer force of their facticity, and through the control mechanisms that are usually attached to the most important of them.[10]

Although the institutional order is itself originally a product of human interaction, it is experienced as a reified, legitimated entity, and language is a specific factor in the distribution of knowledge and in the reinforcement of the paramount reality:

> Language provides the fundamental superimposition of logic on the objectivated social world. The edifice of legitimation is built upon language and uses language as its principal instrumentality. The "logic" thus attributed to the institutional order is part of the socially available stock of knowledge and taken for granted as such.[11]

The idiom of sociological categories seems harsh when applied to the nuanced prose of Fontane's narratives, yet it is not irrelevant. Already the emphasis accorded language is consistent with the well-recognized function of language as conversation and social interaction in Fontane's works.[12] A careful examination of three of the most subtle novels will substantiate the pertinence of the analysis. *Schach von Wuthenow* (1883) is generally regarded as a transitional text in Fontane's *oeuvre,* an amalgamation of historical narrative and "Gesellschaftsroman."[13] *Effi Briest* (1895) and *Der Stechlin* (1898) belong more exclusively to the latter category, and all three have received considerable critical attention. My purpose is not to attempt an additional, exhaustive interpretation of each work, but to outline the common communicative structure, the manner in which the narrative itself enables a degree of distanced insight into the social processes composing the text. The ultracoherence and univocality of the narrative in *Soll und Haben* and the *Dorfgeschichte* and the presence of an approbated social order as the fulcrum of the texts are replaced by a finite plurality. The locus of Fontane's realism is not to be found solely in his critical treatment of the petty bourgeoisie and segments of the gentry nor mainly in such techniques as objective narration, scenic representation, or "Verklärung," but more fundamentally in the unfolding of the constitution of social reality and the relative character of its validity.

Social Event and Individual Perspective: Schach von Wuthenow

The historical moment of the action in *Schach von Wuthenow* was important for Fontane. He inquired carefully concerning the exact date of the actual incident of Major von Schack and Victoire von Crayen and subsequently altered the specific circumstances, shifting the date from 1815 to the period immediately preceding the collapse of the Prussian state. Bülow's letter to Sander, which forms part of the conclusion of the story, is dated exactly one month before the defeat of the Prussian army at Jena, and the subtitle for the work, "Erzählung aus der Zeit des Regiments Gensdarmes," emphasizes the connection of the story to its historical epoch.[14] The book, however, is not exclusively a historical narrative, and it has been suggested that Fontane's selection of the years 1805-1806 illuminates aspects of the composition of the Second Empire as well as of the demise of the Prussian order at the beginning of the century.[15] The historical context of the original reception of the work was the 1880s, which I characterized in my initial chapter as a time of growing pessimism regarding the compatibility of personal needs and social dictates, a period of tensions and increasing rigidity in Germany's socio-economic structure. The semantic potential of Fontane's text comprises an incident set at the beginning of the nineteenth century, while the semiotic meaning for a reader is not completely circumscribed by the Regiment Gensdarmes, Zacharias Werner or the imminent battle of Jena.

It would be equally difficult to read *Schach von Wuthenow* solely as a psychological novel, as the story of a man driven to suicide by an exaggerated sense of superficial status and a distorted conception of honor.[16] The historical setting and the pervasive theme of Prussia's political decline are too insistent to be regarded as incidental. Before the title figure even appears, the tension in the salon of Frau von Carayon concerning political events of the day introduces the counterpart to Schach's personality. Disagreement is immediately apparent between Alvensleben, as the sole representative of the Regiment Gensdarmes present, and Bülow, who is introduced as the leader of the "Frondeurs" currently forming the critical opposition in Berlin. The latter offers a harsh portrayal of the contemporary condition of the legacy of Friedrich the Great, quoting Mirabeau's simile of a piece of fruit rotting before it ever ripens.[17] Schach's entrance with the news of riots heightens the tension, and there is a sharp exchange of words between Bülow and Schach (276-8). Although Frau von Carayon attempts to divert the conversation toward cultural topics, her mention of Zacharias Werner's Luther drama *Die Weihe der Kraft* results in a renewed interchange between Bülow and Schach connecting the Lutheran heritage with the historical phenomenon of Prussian national identity. Bülow's critique again carries the theme of decline, and Schach's objection is equally adamant. It is evident from the outset that Fontane has deliberately chosen actual events and topical items of the period as basic narrative elements, and the story cannot be totally detached from them.

The manner of composition of the narrative material, however, carries *Schach von Wuthenow* beyond historical fiction and marks the continuing realistic level of the work. The factuality of specific incidents and persons referred to in the text is subordinate to their function in constituting the fictional field of reference. The historical and political dimension which is expressly tied to the years 1805-1806 is not primarily a retrospective critique of the epoch for a reader presumably familiar with the details. While an annotated edition certainly clarifies specific elements, the semiotic meaning of the work is not impaired by the lack of such assistance. It is interesting to know the historical identity of Pauline Wiesel or Christian von Massenbach and Karl Ludwig August von Phull, but the uninitiated reader could manage without the specialized knowledge. Pauline's position as the mistress of Prince Louis Ferdinand is indicated by both the narrator and the Prince himself in Chapter 7 (317, 320-1). It is later specifically referred to in a significant conversation between Schach and Victoire in which the illicit nature of the relationship is criticized by both but the sovereign power of society to condone any action is explicitly recognized by Victoire (326). The position of Pauline and her function in the conversation in Chapter 8 and as a foil to the sincerity of Victoire are clear within the narrative completely independent of the question of her actual historical existence. Similarly, Victoire's letter to Lisette introduces Massenbach and Phull (306), linking them to Sander's publishing house and thereby assigning them a position among the "Frondeurs" familiar to the reader from the opening three chapters. Their intended inclusion at the Prince's *dîner* and his designation of them to Schach as invigorating opponents (307) betray the playful side of the Prince which has no correspondence in Schach, who is relieved that they decline the invitation (308). Their function within the narrative system does not rely upon a reader's acquaintance with their historical identities but upon the attitudes with which they are introduced and regarded by other figures in the story.

An early example of the function of a factual person or event within the text is the person and mission of Count Haugwitz. He forms a main topic of conversation in the opening two chapters, and the manner in which his figure contributes to the reader's perception of the situation in the work reveals a basic structuring principle of the narrative system in *Schach von Wuthenow*. It is informative and perhaps expedient for a more rapid orientation if a reader is acquainted with the details leading up to the disputed agreement with Napoleon which resulted from Haugwitz' efforts in 1805-1806, but the knowledge is not essential for constituting the fictional field of reference of Fontane's text. The sentence with which the topic is introduced provides the necessary details, and it is the interpretation of Haugwitz' actions and the resultant exposition of the various positions of the individual characters which is vital to the reading process. The first mention of the issue is Bülow's positive assessment of Haugwitz' diplomatic mission: "die, nach Bülows Ansicht, nicht nur ein wünschenswertes Einvernehmen zwischen Preußen und Frankreich wiederhergestellt, sondern uns auch den Besitz von Hannover noch als 'Morgengabe' mit eingetragen habe" (273-4). Alvensleben, Frau von Carayon, and Victoire are in disagreement with the tenor of Bülow's remarks. Schach enters with news of disturbances in the streets at the Haugwitz residence, and his opening statement distances him from Haugwitz' politics and aligns him with Alvensleben against Bülow: "Ich komme von der Gräfin Haugwitz, bei der ich um so häufiger verweile, je mehr ich mich von dem Grafen und seiner Politik zurückziehe" (276). The alignment of Frau von Carayon's guests had already been indicated in Schach's reserved greeting of Bülow and Sander as opposed to the heartiness of his greeting of Alvensleben, and it is reinforced in the ensuing discussion, as Alvensleben and Schach share the disapproval of Haugwitz' achievements by the Regiment Gensdarmes and Bülow defends the rapprochement with France.

Frau von Carayon's objection is more personal than political. She comments that the additional "dowry" ("Morgengabe") of Hanover is hardly tenable, not for political, tactical reasons, but on general principle: "weil man nicht gut geben oder verschenken könne, was man nicht habe" (274). Both Josephine von Carayon and her daughter tend to interpret external events in personal terms, as the latter's advocacy of the Poles in the face of Bülow's disparaging comments illustrates: "Ich liebe sie [the Poles], weil sie ritterlich und unglücklich sind" (275). Similarly, the cultural event of the day, the production of Werner's *Weihe der Kraft,* elicits personal as well as discursive political reaction and interpretation. Victoire and Alvensleben object to the portrayal of Luther on the stage for reasons of personal reverence, while the theatrical production gives rise to a dispute between Schach and Bülow concerning the social and political repercussions of the Reformation. They again interpret the phenomenon from divergent standpoints: Bülow underscoring the necessarily transient, historical character of the Lutheran and the Prussian "episodes" in German history, and Schach disagreeing (280-2). As in the case of Haugwitz, Werner's play is subject to varying interpretations, and it is the interpretations, or "readings" of an external event which constitute the import of the text. The opening salon of Frau von Carayon establishes the initial constellation of figures, characterized by their interpretations of current events. The narrative "event" of the initial two chapters is the social interaction of conversation and polite disagreement, which establishes variant versions of the meaning of specific political and cultural incidents. The interchange of varying personal and political interpretations evident in the opening section indicates the pervasive pattern of Fontane's *Schach von Wuthenow*: the refraction of a concrete fact or specific event in a network of divergent perspectives.

The production of a textual referent through alternative versions within the narrative has been recognized by Gilbert, von Wiese, Ohl, Demetz, and Mittenzwei, among others, as the predominant means of character exposition of the title figure in the work.[18] The narrative does not totally clarify the person and actions of Schach but leaves the reader to construe the story and its possible significance. The basic pattern of reader experience, the "Lektüreanweisungsmuster" of the brief novel, is determined by such a structure of perspectival narration, which extends from individual narrative strategies to the comprehensive organization of the text. There is a continual interaction of individual event and framework of significance, and the result for a reader is the constitution of the fictional field of reference through the constant modulation and refinement of the varying perspectives. The authority of the narrative discourse is not convincingly located in any single angle of vision, and the reading process effects realization of the conventionality of the social institutions and definitions accepted by the characters in the story. The communicative structure of *Schach von Wuthenow* consists of formative tensions, of equivocal readings of narrated events, and the social system composing the reality paradigm of the work is itself subject to interpretation, stable yet not absolute in its authority as apprehended by the reader. The mechanisms of production and legitimation of the dominant social order and their impelling logic as perceived by individual figures are strikingly evident to the reader of Fontane's "social code."

The initial two chapters of the text present the reader with a narrated event which is a particular instance of an established social ritual, Frau von Carayon's customary *Empfangsabend*. It is followed by a typical Fontane "Nachgespräch," in which Alvensleben, Bülow and Sander are joined by Nostitz.[19] The central topic of conversation is Schach, both in his personal relationship to the von Carayons and in his political identity as a representative of certain aspects of the contemporary Prussian state. The assessments vary from Bülow's unyielding association of Schach with the petty masquerade of Prussian complacency as embodied in the Regiment Gensdarmes to the analysis of Alvensleben and Nostitz of the underlying consistency in Schach's character which distinguishes him from his superficial comrades so scorned by Bülow. The discussion composing the third chapter is an example of the technique of character exposition through the exchange of varying perspectives on a specific figure by others in the text. It also exemplifies the basic structuring principle of *Schach von Wuthenow,* the refraction of a narrated social or public event in the divergent interpretations of individual characters. The import of Fontane's novel encompasses more than the intriguing title figure but provides a model of the constitution and force of the social world through the processes of perception of its inhabitants.

The pattern evident in the alternation of salon and "Nachgespräch" is repeated throughout the text. The reader is presented with an episode or a series of events of a public or social nature followed by one or more "readings" or interpretations which impart meaning and constitute the consequence of the event. The significance of a narrated event lies in the perception of the principal characters, and the resulting refraction of an episode hinders a reader's assumption of the immediate comprehensibility of social phenomena as unquestioned facts. A clear parallel to the sequence of salon and "Nachgespräch" is visible in the excursion to Tempelhof and Victoire's subsequent letter to Lisette which constitute Chapters 4 and 5. Similar to the evening gathering at the von Carayons', the outing is a single narrated episode of an established social practice, one well familiar to Fontane readers.[20] Victoire's letter reveals her personal reading of several implications of the excursions, and her version partially reinforces the preceding narrated account and partially differs from it. Her reluctant interpretation of Schach's change of partners upon reentering the village as a conscious avoidance of being seen at the side of an unattractive woman coincides with the emphasis placed on the incident in the previous chapter. Schach, engaged in conversation with Victoire on the way back from the church, stops at the outskirts of the populated area to wait for Tante Marguerite and Frau von Carayon:

> Als sie heran waren, bot er der Frau von Carayon den Arm und führte *diese* bis an das Gasthaus zurück. Victoire sah ihnen betroffen nach und sann nach über den Tausch, den Schach mit keinem Worte der Entschuldigung begleitet hatte. Was war das? Und sie verfärbte sich, als sie sich, aus einem plötzlichen Argwohn heraus, die selbstgestellte Frage beantwortet hatte (303, emphasis in the original).

The emphasis placed on the gesture by the italics and the suggestion in the neutral narrative voice before the interpolated question that the action warranted an apology lend credence to Victoire's explanation to Lisette: "daß es ihm peinlich gewesen sei, mit *mir* und an meinem Arm unter den Gästen zu erscheinen" (306, original emphasis).

In two related matters Victoire's perception is not as reliable. She persists in hoping for a marriage between Schach and her mother and assures Lisette that she could easily assume the appropriate posture of respect toward a new stepfather (306). Schach's noncommital behavior in conversation with Frau von Carayon on the leisurely walk to the church, as well as the assessments offered in Chapter 3 contradict Victoire's hopes, and her own emotion for Schach is inadequately described as respect. Lisette answers with a different reading of the Tempelhof episode, chiding Victoire for her mistrust and for her self-delusion in designating her sentiments as respect (324). It is Lisette's letter and her version which Victoire is contemplating in Chapter 8 when Schach calls and finds her alone.

The moment of seduction in the eighth chapter combines the effect of Lisette's letter with Schach's retention of the topic and tenor of conversation at a *dîner* at Prince Louis Ferdinand's. Again, it is a character's perception of a narrated social event which is of consequence for the story, and the contingency of that perception is evident to the reader. Chapters 6 and 7 correspond to the von Carayon salon, a narrated example of conventionalized social behavior. The sequence of conversational topics is even equivalent, as is the division of guests. Haugwitz, Protestantism and Prussia, the decline of the latter in the era of Napoleon; such themes once again oppose Bülow and Schach, to the delight of the Prince. The arrival of an additional guest brings a shift of topic to the theatre, Iffland, and Werner's play, which leads back to politics. Yet the general tone of the *dîner* is different from the opening salon and has been well described by Ingrid Mittenzwei as "ein selbstgenügsames Spiel."[21] Beauty is present at the Prince's dinner only as a linguistic concept, as the object of witty formulations and casual consideration. The presence of Josephine and Victoire von Carayon as variant forms of feminine appearance is replaced by the categorization of beauty in borrowed words. Schach retains the language, and the suggestion of the internal charm of "beauté du diable" plays its role in the understated love scene in Chapter 8, as he assures Victoire:

> Der Prinz hatte doch recht, als er enthusiastisch von Ihnen sprach. Armes Gesetz der Form und der Farbe. Was allein gilt, ist das ewig Eine, daß sich die Seele den Körper schafft oder ihn durchleuchtet und verklärt (327).

The final sentence and Schach's admonishment "fassen Sie sich und glauben Sie wieder an Ihr Anrecht auf Leben und Liebe" (328) echo Lisette's letter to Victoire:

> ... sei guten Mutes und halte Dich ein für allemal versichert. *Dir lügt der Spiegel.* Es ist nur *eines,* um dessentwillen wir Frauen leben, wir leben, um uns ein Herz zu gewinnen, aber *wodurch* wir es gewinnen, ist gleichgültig (324, original emphasis).

Schach's sober interpretation of the spirited superficiality of the evening with Prince Louis and the reverberation of Lisette's analysis of the Tempelhof episode work together to effect the inadvertent union. The coincidence and the "misreadings" should be evident to the reader.

The eighth chapter represents a decisive juncture in the novel, and there is a shift within the pattern of reading as well. The narrated events assume a more public nature: the performance of Werner's Romantic play and the ensuing sleigh-ride parody by the Regiment Gensdarmes, the circulation of cruel caricatures of Schach's relationship to the von Carayons, and the intercession of the royal couple to insure the marriage. The communicative structure of the text remains the same, the interaction of event and framework of significance, both personal and political. Werner's drama divides Berlin into two factions: "Alles was mystisch-romantisch war, war *für*, alles, was freisinnig war, *gegen* das Stück" (332). The sleigh parody, a prank in the best tradition of the Regiment Gensdarmes, is to a certain extent also a reading of the play, a scornful judgment of Werner's "Lutherkarikatur" (336). The reader knows of Schach's aloof abhorrence of the mischief of his comrades, but Victoire's perception of the masquerade and her fear that Schach was even peripherally involved lead to her collapse and confession.

Following the confrontation between Schach and Frau von Carayon on the day after the sleigh parody, the narrative becomes increasingly the tracing of Schach's perception of events and of his own future path. Scarcely has he managed to reconcile himself to the finality of the wedding, a year in Italy, and a subsequent married life with Victoire in Wuthenow and himself in Berlin, when the series of mocking cartoons appears. In the isolation of his retreat to Wuthenow (Chapter 14), Schach succumbs to his tunnel-vision perspective on society and on his future plight.[22] Frau von Carayon, unaware of the public ridicule, interprets Schach's retreat in her own fashion and invokes a separate instance of public judgment in the form of a royal intercession. The interviews with the king and queen finalize Schach's decision for suicide. The favor of the queen and her sanction in the form of the desire to be godmother to the child cannot penetrate his already formulated conviction: "Ich bin rettungslos dem Spott und Witz der Kameraden verfallen" (344). Persisting in his perception of an intolerable future, he also establishes a correspondingly appropriate definition of life: "Was ist leben? Eine Frage von Minuten, eine Differenz von heut auf morgen" (373). Acquiescence in the wedding and subsequent suicide form the only conceivable solution.

The framework of reading and interpretation of narrated events which offers the reader variant versions concludes with the dual epistolary optic of Bülow's political and Victoire's personal construing of Schach's suicide. The variegated field of reference of the work, the intersection of the personal and the political and the relative validity of all standpoints, finds no singular concluding perspective. The narrative pattern of *Schach von Wuthenow* requires the reader to effect the final construction of the reality paradigm of the text and its significance. The equivocal nature of Fontane's narrative is already apparent in the opening paragraphs of the text, where the syntactical configuration indicates the pattern of reading culminating in the juxtaposition of the final letters. Müller-Seidel has pointed to the significance of Schach's "presence" as an object of reference while he is still absent, and a similar equivocation is evident at the level of syntax.[23] The initial posture of a text influences the cognitive orientation of the reader, and the beginning of *Schach von Wuthenow* continually qualifies its own statements, effectively undercutting the authority of the narrative discourse.

The opening sentence establishes the customary social ritual of the von Carayon salon but qualifies in a second clause the fact that this evening, however, only a few guests are assembled. Similarly, the following sentence relates the fact that officers of the Regiment Gensdarmes are rarely absent from such evenings, but only one has appeared on this particular evening. The following paragraph elicits a parallel effect through the use of supplementary clauses with "nichtsdestoweniger," "beziehungsweise," "wenigstens." The beginning of the third paragraph affects only partially reliable knowledge of the narrated action: "Das Gespräch, das eben geführt wurde, schien sich um die kurz vorher beendete Haugwitzsche Mission zu drehen" (273). The rest of the sentence, which I quoted earlier, then assumes Bülow's perspective on the Haugwitz mission and blends direct and indirect discourse in the pronoun "uns."* Frau von Carayon's objection to the term "Morgengabe" immediately modifies the weight of Bülow's statement.[24] From the outset, the narrative

---

* "die nach Bülows Ansicht nicht nur ein wünschenswertes Einvernehmen zwischen Preußen und Frankreich wieder hergestellt, sondern uns auch den Besitz von Hannover noch als 'Morgengabe' mit eingetragen habe" (273-4).

elements of Fontane's text are defined through tension, not by the binary opposition of already defined positions so readily apparent in Freytag and Auerbach. There is no immediately sanctioned perspective or figure of proffered identification for the reader.

Bülow is often designated as the dominant voice in Fontane's narrative, and he is indeed a privileged character and an unrelenting analyst.[25] Yet he is not allowed to stand unchallenged, and his reliability as a reader of social environment is undercut at several points in the novel. As Müller-Seidel has pointed out, his susceptibility to the Romantic songs from Werner's play is a contradiction to his self-professed critical stance.[26] The end of Chapter 2 is explicit on the issue:

> Nur Bülow schwieg. Er hatte, wie die meisten mit Staatenuntergang beschäftigten Frondeurs, auch seine schwachen Seiten, und eine davon war durch das Lied getroffen worden ... Wider Wissen und Willen war er ein Kind seiner Zeit und romantisierte (283).

Bülow's perspicacity is undercut with regard to the personal level of the story as well. The fact that Bülow either doesn't notice or pays no heed to Victoire's disfigurement (275) could be understood in his favor, but his insensitivity to the relationship between Schach and the von Carayons casts doubt upon his position as the sole reliable guide in the narrative. Nostitz chides him early in the novel for his lack of discernment: "Was doch die Gelehrten, und wenn es gelehrte Militärs wären, für schlechte Beobachter sind. Ist Ihnen denn das Verhältnis zwischen beiden entgangen?" (287). Nostitz, in turn, is amended by Alvensleben, whose psychological insights recognize the validity of Nostitz' allusions but deny the possibility of a marriage between Schach and Frau von Carayon. In the postscript to Bülow's final interpretive letter on the symptomatic case of Schach the reader is expressly reminded of Bülow's blind spot and the evening at Sala Tarone, a *caveat* against acceptance solely of Bülow's political reading of the issue (385). The mutual corrective is found in the composite of Bülow's and Victoire's perspectives.

The most unreliable "reader" of the social environment is Tante Marguerite, who consistently jumbles characters, settings, and plots of her narratives. Even her language is incongruous, and in one instance her inability to adequately recount an event, the appearance of the caricatures, is of unfortunate consequence for Schach, who is thereby denied a possible modicum of understanding by Frau von Carayon (359). Her wedding toast with the anecdote of Victoire's bouquet on the Tempelhof outing, which was meant for Schach but cast upon a child's grave, is marked by narrative irony. She assures the guests of the significance of the gesture (379), unaware of the telling connection to death and child to come.

If Tante Marguerite's misreadings are comic and ironic, Schach's flawed perception is ultimately tragic. His inability to extend his own narrow perspective, most tellingly portrayed in Chapter 14, leaves him trapped in a situation he perceives as intolerable and unalterable. Yet Schach's dilemma is more than a fatally narrow apprehension of his social environment but reveals the inadequate co-extension of personal and social roles, the incomplete integration of individual and contextual social system characteristic of the reality paradigm of Fontane's narrative. The discrepancy becomes visible when roles shift and the resultant friction exposes both the constraining influence of the social system and the insufficiency of individual self-definitions. For both Schach and Victoire, the prospect of an altered social status is disturbing and of serious consequence. In her earnest conversation with Schach in Chapter 8, Victoire states her assessment of society and her place within it:

> Die Gesellschaft ist souverän. Was sie gelten läßt, gilt, was sie verwirft, ist verwerflich. Außerdem liegt hier alles exceptionell. Der Prinz ist ein Prinz, Frau von Carayon ist eine Witwe, und ich ... bin ich (326, ellipsis in original).

Against Schach's protest at the harshness of her self-definition, Victoire defends the freedom she has gained through her loss of beauty and identifies herself with the similarly disfigured Mirabeau. But Schach's words and Lisette's letter open to her the vista of a different role, no longer severed from love and marriage, and she succumbs to her unconscious hopes and needs: "Ach, das waren die Worte, nach denen ihr Herz gebangt hatte, während es sich in Trotz zu waffnen suchte" (328).

Schach's forced redefinition of his social position and his inability to cope with his perception of the repercussions of a marriage to Victoire not only are indicative of his self-definition in terms of societal categories but also reveal the perils of a mode of thought and perception rooted in absolute, invariable categories. A definitive point of distinction between Schach and Bülow, the issue of perception in unquestioned, fixed terms is fundamental to the constitution of both the social system and the narrative system in Fontane's text. Bülow allows no concept to stand absolute; Victoire's defense of the Poles for their aid in rescuing Vienna meets with his admission of "meine ketzerischen Ansichten über Rettungen" (275). He expresses similar scepticism at the Prince's dinner concerning "unter dem Leibe erschossene Kaiserpferde" (312) and rulers who are designated with the attribute "the Good" (313). Prussia and Lutheranism are "episodes" for him, "hinschwindende Dinge," "künstliche Größen," designations vehemently opposed by Schach (281). Bülow perceives the hollowness of his own historical epoch, evidenced most clearly in his succinct statement to the Prince: "Der Geist ist heraus, alles ist Dressur und Spielerei geworden" (310). His final analysis of the symptomatic aspects of Schach's case rests on the same judgment, the assessment of a fatal adherence to empty concepts of honor (Chapter 20).

Schach's mode of perception and analysis establishes either/or categories and results in the aporia which he can solve only by suicide. Alvensleben and Nostitz characterize him as genuine, as not affecting a pose or posture like so many of his comrades (288-9). In his tortured retreat in Wuthenow, Schach is incapable of envisioning mitigating circumstances or alternatives to his projection of a secluded life with Victoire. The constricting circularity of his thoughts is explicitly underscored in the repeated pattern of his nocturnal pacings in the garden on the estate.* The assimilation of the categories of beauty offered in jest by Prince Louis was a

---

* "Nur ein schmal Stück Wiese lag noch dazwischen, und auf ebendieser Wiese stand eine uralte Eiche, deren Schatten Schach jetzt umschritt, einmal, vielemal, als würde er in ihrem Bann gehalten. Es war ersichtlich, daß ihn der Kreis, in dem er ging, an einen anderen Kreis gemahnte, denn er murmelte vor sich hin: 'Könnt ich heraus.' " (353).

major factor in the seduction in Chapter 8; in Chapter 14, as well as in the final decision for suicide after the interview with the king and queen (373-4), it is Schach's narrow perception, his inability to surmount the categories he regards as absolute, which seal the tragedy.

Victoire also succumbs to either/or modes of analysis in her acceptance of Lisette's reading of the Tempelhof episode*, but it is the ability to transcend such narrowed perception that makes her an accurate reader in her final letter of the side of Schach for which Bülow is blind. At Tempelhof, Schach admits his inner affinity for the Templar order because of the unyielding nature of their vows (302). Victoire teasingly declares him "einen nachgeborenen Templer," and she returns to the theme in all seriousness in her letter from Rome. She describes Schach's inability to switch his self-definition into the categories which marriage to her would have brought and draws a fitting comparison: "Ein Kardinal ... läßt sich eben nicht als Ehemann denken. Und Schach auch nicht" (386). Catholicism is a prevalent theme in the final pages of Fontane's novel, and it stands in only apparent contrast to the emphasis on Luther otherwise evident in the work. The paradox that Victoire, the staunch defender of Luther, should write from the holy city of Rome concerning a "miracle" healing of her child is ironic in the manner of Fontane's narratives, an irony which offers the reader insight beyond a subtly amusing shift of fate. Victoire even incorporates Tante Marguerite's probable "reading" of the "miracle" (387-8), and the suggestion again is of the refraction of an event in the perception of its interpreters. No institution stands unquestioned in Fontane's text, from the army to the church. Even the royal authority is relativized by the humorously clipped language of the king (370-1). The paradox of Araceli is open to interpretation and emphasizes one final time the relative character of the reality paradigm of *Schach von Wuthenow,* the locus of significance in the interplay of varying perspectives, and the fallacy of perceiving reality in invariable terms. The faulty integration of individual and social environment, the constitu-

---

* From Lisette's letter: "Ich finde, je mehr ich den Fall überlege, daß Du ganz einfach vor einer Alternative stehst und entweder Deine gute Meinung über S. oder aber Dein Mißtrauen *gegen* ihn fallen lassen mußt." (324, emphasis in original).

tion of the social system through convention and interaction, and the consistent position of the reader at the intersection of narrated event and variable interpretation span the field of reference and the reader experience of Fontane's text.

The Opacity of the Social System: Effi Briest

Victoire's final letter to Lisette in *Schach von Wuthenow* counters the latter's continued puzzlement regarding Schach's behavior with the statement that final explanations are not possible: "Ein Rest von Dunklem und Unaufgeklärtem bleibt, und in die letzten und geheimsten Triebfedern andrer oder auch nur unsrer eigenen Handlungsweise hineinzublicken, ist uns versagt."[27] The reader of Fontane's novel reaches the same conclusion; the narrative refraction results in only partial validity of each perspective represented. The perception of the characters is, in every case, limited, and final explanations are not attainable. Each angle of vision contributes to the reader's understanding of a narrated character or event, and the variants encourage an awareness of the partiality of all attempted solutions. Roy Pascal has pointed out that it is the lack of empathetic identification with any single character which enables a reader to observe what I have designated as the constitution and force of social reality, which he terms "the play of the whole."[28]

Effi Briest (1895) would seem to follow other principles of narrative composition. There is a more definite plot line and a central figure who arouses a reader's sympathy. Yet there remains "ein Rest von Dunklem und Unaufgeklärtem" in the novel which has led several critics to write of an atmosphere of fate prevailing in the work.[29] It is the dual aspect of "fate," inevitability and opaque intangibility, which characterizes both the social system and the narrative system of *Effi Briest*. From the initial scene where Effi is called from the games of childhood to assume the adult role of fiancée and a position of social status as future wife and mother until the final yielding of the rigorous social code to parental affection as she returns to Hohen-Cremmen, it is the logic of social categories which determines the course of action of the text. It is a logic which does not go unchallenged, as the cohesive matrix of meanings and values which orders Effi's existence is questioned by every character with the exception of Johanna, whose rigid judgment surpasses that of her master.[30] Berger and Luckmann locate the logic of social institutions not in the institutions themselves but in the reflection upon them by the inhabitants of a particular social universe, a reflection carried mainly by language.[31] The varying degrees of discomfort with which the characters ponder the necessity of Effi's plight coincides with the extent to which they accept and thereby reinforce the social logic which dictates it.

The novel contains numerous passages of reflection by the characters upon the train of events consisting of Effi's marriage, infidelity, and resultant position outside her inherited social environment, and they exercise an important function in the rhythm of the narrative. The events themselves proceed in a not unexpected manner; no development actually surprises the reader. Even the two central contingencies of the novel, the letters and Innstetten's initial conversation with Wüllersdorf, are not incongruous. It is symptomatic of Effi's very inexperience in social intrigues and extramarital affairs that the letters were not destroyed, as the Geheimrätin Zwicker regretfully emphasizes in outlining the incident to a friend (394). And Innstetten's insistence that he has no alternative, especially after taking Wüllersdorf into his confidence (372-375), is consistent with his character. Mittenzwei astutely observes that the nobleman triumphs over the husband in Innstetten's decision,[32] and it is a priority of social categories over personal consideration for which the reader is well prepared. Already in his refusal to consider seriously his young wife's anxieties during the first separation of their marriage, Innstetten follows similar principles, explaining that he left her alone out of necessity:

> Meine liebe Effi, ich lasse dich ja nicht allein aus Rücksichtslosigkeit oder Laune, sondern weil es so sein muß; ich habe keine Wahl, ich bin ein Mann im Dienst, ich kann zum Fürsten oder auch zur Fürstin nicht sagen: Durchlaucht, ich kann nicht kommen, meine Frau ist so allein, oder meine Frau fürchtet sich. Wenn ich das sagte, würden wir in einem ziemlich komischen Lichte dastehen, ich gewiß, und du auch (234).

His refusal to consider selling the house is based on similar arguments about the resultant ridicule of "die Leute" (235). His insistence upon the duel is an understandable extension of his character, position, and attitudes.

The progression of the plot in *Effi Briest* is causally motivated; the events follow a transparent logic. Yet at intervals the narrative coalesces in reflective conversation or monologue, and such junctures undermine the forward movement and challenge the necessity of the causally-motivated progression of events.[33] The most radical and emotional example is Effi's outburst following Annie's visit (Chapter 33). Her child's rote answers, specifically the refrain "O gewiß, wenn ich darf," shatter her reserve of strength. In a prayer which turns to a curse, she reviles Innstetten as a "Streber" driven by an exaggerated concept of honor. The monologue begins with the "ich" and "du" of religious supplication and switches to "er" as Effi affixes blame for the excessive punishment: "Denn das hier, mit dem Kind, das bist nicht *du, Gott,* der mich strafen will, das ist *er,* bloß er!" (408-9, original emphasis). The monologue culminates in a rejection of "euch" and "eure Tugend," and the pronoun would seem to extend beyond husband and child to indict a state of affairs for which she finds no words.

Innstetten's initial conversation with Wüllersdorf, which has been described as the most magnificent conversational scene in the German novel,[34] is a vital passage of reflective dialogue which controverts the necessity of the narrative action and exposes the "social logic" as convention. Innstetten also finds no exact words for the state of affairs which dictates his actions but resorts to "das Ganze," "ein Etwas," "jenes, wenn Sie wollen, uns tyrannisierende Gesellschafts-Etwas" (373-4). The language of society has no term for the totality of its own reified structures, and Innstetten's attempts to circumscribe the force which outweighs "Liebe," "Verjährung," and Wüllersdorf's promise of "Verschwiegenheit" reveal the limits of language as the vehicle of reflection upon social institutions. Wüllersdorf's final answer is a similar circumlocution:

> Die Welt ist einmal wie sie ist, und die Dinge verlaufen nicht wie *wir* wollen, sondern wie die *andern* wollen. Das mit dem 'Gottesgericht,' wie manche hochtrabend versichern, ist freilich ein Unsinn, nichts davon, umge-

kehrt, unser Ehrenkultus ist ein Götzendienst, aber wir müssen uns ihm unterwerfen, solange der Götze gilt (375, original emphasis).

Wüllersdorf utilizes tautology, unspecified nouns and indefinite pronouns ("die Dinge," "die andern"), and metaphorical language in an attempt to express the inexorable constraint determining their actions. He even rejects the reference to "true" religion for the extended metaphor with "false" idolatry, itself of limited duration.

Innstetten's monologue following the duel and his final conversation with Wüllersdorf exercise a similar function of counteracting the narrative action. In the former, he opposes his conviction of the necessity of his deed with the suspicion that a statute of limitations must exist which renders his course of action questionable:

> [Innstetten] wiederholte sich's, daß es gekommen sei, wie's habe kommen müssen. Aber im selben Augenblicke, wo dies für ihn feststand, warf er's auch wieder um. "Es *muß* eine Verjährung geben, Verjährung ist das einzig Vernünftige; ..." (380, original emphasis).

The obligatory character of the action ("müssen") confronts the equally strong imperative nature of its contingency (*"muß"*). The aggregate system of values blurs, and absolute definitions become elusive. In the final conversation after reading Roswitha's letter requesting Rollo, Innstetten and Wüllersdorf agree on the ambiguity of their entire endeavor. Again they have no words for the totality of the social system. Innstetten, who has just been named "Ministerialdirektor," senses "daß dies alles nichts ist" (419). He speaks of "dieser ganze Krimskrams" and of "bloßen Vorstellungen" (420). Wüllersdorf expresses the questionable aspects of "alles andere" (419) and once again resorts to metaphorical language, modestly suggesting that the best one can do is to develop "Hilfskonstruktionen" (421). Their analytical conversation is as shattering and revelatory for a reader as is Effi's impassioned outburst.

Another major complex of conversations which reveal the force of social convention underlying the causality of the narrative progression are those directly touching Effi. As in *Schach von Wuthenow*, it is often a shift in Effi's role which exposes the incomplete integration of individual and contextual social system and gives rise to reflective conversation. There are two fundamental types of dialogue involved, one in which Effi is the topic and another in which she acts out her role in exchanges with Innstetten. In the latter, it is the manner of speaking which is important, and it is often that which is left unsaid which is telling. The friction is already evident in their correspondence before the wedding. Effi's infrequent letters to Innstetten are "voll reizend nichtigen und ihn jedesmal entzückenden Inhalts" (184). Her future husband settles all important matters with Frau von Briest, and his thoughtful, well-formulated letters to Effi arouse the latter's uneasiness. A letter reproduced for the reader at the end of Chapter 4 causes Effi to emphasize unwittingly in an exchange with her mother the discrepancy between the role she is about to assume and her own personal needs and desires. Instetten promises her jewelry on their Italian honeymoon, and the gift has little meaning for Effi, who explains to her mother:

> Ich klettre lieber und schaukle mich lieber, und am liebsten in der Furcht, daß es irgendwo reißen oder brechen und ich niederstürzen könnte. Den Kopf wird es ja nicht gleich kosten (194-5).[35]

She continues to insist that Innstetten is the correct choice for a husband, as he has the proper qualities to attain important social status, but she fears his stiff integrity of character, a trait she finds lacking in her own self (195).[36] The language and the sentiments summarize the opening chapters of the novel and indicate the vital disjuncture between Effi Briest and the role of Baronin von Innstetten which awaits her.

The first scenes of the novel are characterized by a perceptible tension between Effi's knowledge of the definitions and categories of the world she inhabits and her individual nature. Contrary to the opening of *Soll und Haben,* where Anton Wohlfart's intention to become a "Kaufmann" is not in contradiction to his character as presented in narrated action, Effi's generalized statements to her playmates are in conflict with her unbridled behavior, which is "wild," "stürmisch," and "leidenschaftlich" (172), as well as with her uninhibited tone, which causes Hulda Niemeyer to comment: "Du sprichst wirklich wie ein Midshipman" (178). Hulda's consistency in manner, attitude, and speech is missing in Effi, and the discrepancy highlights the conventionality of the socially-determined meanings to which Effi unthinkingly adheres. She parrots the predefinitions of her social environment, using emphatic pronouns and adverbs, unaware of the lack of integration of language and speaker so evident to a reader:

> "Eine Geschichte mit Entsagung ist nie schlimm" (174).
> "Nun, es kam, wie's kommen mußte, wie's immer kommt" (175).
> "Jeder ist der Richtige. Natürlich muß er von Adel sein und eine Stellung haben und gut aussehen" (182).
> "Wenn man zwei Stunden verlobt ist, ist man immer ganz glücklich" (182).[37]

Effi's introduction to Kessin takes the form of a conversation with her husband during the ride from the train station to her new home (202-207). Innstetten summarizes the people and character of Kessin, and his manner and tone project an air of intriguing instability. Effi's reaction captures the ambiguity of staid society and implied enigma: "Es klingt erst spießbürgerlich und ist doch hinterher ganz apart" (206). Innstetten's reassurance is only partial, and he reminds her of "die Geschichte von dem Chinesen," although he has not yet related it (207). The dialogue opens up a new dimension in the narrative, a shifting ground underlying Effi's future social role. Her household is a mixture of fixed routines and inexplicable detail, and the conversations with Innstetten maintain the ambiguity. The first morning in Kessin he evades the issue of the nocturnal rustling (216). Later, his conciliatory suggestion of a sleigh ride after their first marital quarrel over Effi's fright during his absence includes a route passing the Chinaman's grave, which results in disclosure of the unsolved incident (239-241). A man of disciplined daily behavior, Innstetten neglects the thoughtful attention which Effi needs: "Er hatte das Gefühl, Effi zu lieben, und das gute Gewissen, daß es so sei, ließ ihn von besonderen Anstrengungen absehen" (255). Upon completion of the obligatory round of social calls he is at a loss for a proper gesture of celebration; Effi reproachfully remarks that an expression of affection for her never occurs to him (224). His idea of entertainment is a series of evenings reviewing and studying their Italian journey, a project contrasting sharply with Crampas' lively plan for a community production of the drama "Ein Schritt vom Wege" (291-292).[38]

As Effi grows accustomed to her social role, the conversations with Innstetten increasingly emphasize the artificiality of their marriage and the distance between them. After Annie's birth and Effi's visit in Hohen-Cremmen, Innstetten comments that she has changed, that her tone and manner are seductive and no longer childlike (273). Effi laughingly quotes Niemeyer on the necessarily seductive character of the feminine role (273-274). Significantly, it is at that moment that Crampas drops by for a visit. The day remains in Effi's memory as the beginning of the affair, and she returns to it and to the question of the feminine character in her monologue concerning guilt and remorse, which she finds lacking in herself:

> Aber Scham über meine Schuld, die hab ich *nicht* oder doch nicht so recht oder doch nicht genug, und das bringt mich um, daß ich sie nicht habe. Wenn alle Weiber so sind, dann ist es schrecklich, und wenn sie nicht so sind, wie ich hoffe, dann steht es schlecht um mich, dann ist etwas nicht in Ordnung in meiner Seele, dann fehlt mir das richtige Gefühl (359).

Effi's reflection on the description which she is forced to maintain indicates the discrepancy between her character and the role she must assume: "Immer war es mein Stolz, daß ich nicht lügen könne und auch nicht zu lügen brauche, lügen ist so gemein, und nun habe ich doch lügen müssen" (359). The inevitability of the deceit and the social origin of its necessity are evident to the reader, who perceives the incompatibility of personal needs and social dictates. The artifice to which Effi must resort ranges from seductiveness to pretense and dishonesty.

The other central series of dialogues directly concerned with Effi's integration into established social patterns are the conversations between Frau von Briest and her husband about their daughter. If what is left unsaid is important for the level of conversational situations involving Effi and Innstetten, it is what is left unsettled in the exchanges between Effi's parents which provokes a reader to further thought. The conversations emphasize specific aspects of the narrated action and offer interpretation without presenting a final answer to the questions raised. In Chapter 5, the ambition and intolerance for boredom which Effi had demonstrated in assembling her trousseau and in conversation with her mother are underlined by

Frau von Briest, and the possible pitfalls of "Vergnügungssucht und Ehrgeiz" are suggested (199-200). Innstetten's pedagogical bent, later well analyzed by Crampas in connection with the Chinaman motif (282-283), is already apparent in the tenor of the honeymoon as reflected in Effi's postcards to Hohen-Cremmen, which cause her father to draw the categorial conclusion: "Das ist eben das, was man sich verheiraten nennt" (202). His final comment in the chapter, his refrain throughout the novel, leaves open the issue of whether marriage must be so: "Das ist wirklich ein zu weites Feld" (202).

The last three chapters of the novel contain several conversations between Briest and his wife, and the questions left unanswered effectively challenge the entire course of the narrative action. Frau von Briest's ineffectual objections as to the regulatory force of society are brushed aside by her husband's insistence that Effi return to Hohen-Cremmen: "Eins geht vor ... Liebe der Eltern zu ihren Kindern" (411). And the conciliatory ending of Effi's deathbed statement to her mother that Innstetten had been justified in his action (425) is checked by the final exchange between her parents.[39] Her mother's musings on the contributing factors to Effi's fate elicit the ambiguity of Briest's refrain, and the final sentence of the novel opens rather than settles the issue.[40] The attempted "legitimation" of the institutional order which forms the causal progression of the plot in Fontane's novel is undercut one final time by the reference to an ultimate ambiguity of the proffered explanations. The level of conversation and dialogue in *Effi Briest* does not work to reinforce the narrative action but to challenge it in a manner which confronts the social logic with its own contingent conventionality.[41] It is an ambiguity inherent to the reality paradigm of the text, a phenomenon well-described by Berger and Luckmann as the final opacity of the perceived social world:

> Although the social stock of knowledge appresents the everyday world in an integrated manner differentiated according to zones of familiarity and remoteness, it leaves the totality of that world opaque. Put differently, the reality of everyday life always appears as a zone of lucidity behind which there is a background of darkness. As some zones of reality are illuminated, others are adumbrated.[42]

Effi's "fate," the sense of inevitability and opaque intangibility in the novel which is often commented upon, is the very nature of the social system composing the field of reference in the work. The friction between the causal linearity of the narrative progression and the problem of the necessity of the action in recurrent dialogue situations leaves the final conclusions to the reader. The social logic is countered by the inability of the characters to comprehend the totality of the social universe they inhabit. The sequential combination of incidents in the plot of the novel, the syntagmatic narrative pattern, is offset by the conversations, monologues, and dialogues, by the use of language to posit and simultaneously to challenge the validity of its own categories. The communicative structure of *Effi Briest* is characterized by a constitutive tension between the relatively transparent, logical course of the plot and the not entirely penetrable density of what I would term the paradigmatic level of the text.

The paradigmatic relations within a narrative system form the set of associations which are not connected in a linear pattern, as are the elements advancing the plot in most nineteenth-century novels, but which function by means of contrast and inference. Caution has been advised by Müller-Seidel and Ohl as to the advisability of speaking of "symbolism" in Fontane's works, and the categories of syntagmatic and paradigmatic levels of narrative is a productive alternative, at least in *Effi Briest*.[43] The terms themselves are derived from de Saussure's distinction between syntagmatic and associative relations in language, but they have been adapted for use in narrative analysis and are entirely appropriate for the communicative structure of Fontane's novel.[44] The straightforward causality of the plot, the coherent linkage of incidents from Effi's engagement to her death, produces an integrated pattern of comprehensible events. The narrative voice supports the pattern through an informal tone, a blend of personal and objective perspective, and the infrequent yet audible expression of sympathy for Effi, the most probable object of reader empathy as well.[45] Reuter contrasts the buoyant, sovereign character of narration in *Effi Briest* with the ponderous consequence of the narrated action, but a more important distinction is the manner in which the apparently natural, determined course of the narrative is countered by the indeterminate matrix of elements allowing multiple interpretation.[46]

The narrator in the work is unobtrusive but nevertheless present. Twice in the course of the story the interjection "arme Effi" appears (226, 424);[47] and in the passage detailing Gieshübler's first visit, the narrator's sentiment is incorporated into an ostensibly objective sentence: "Der armen jungen Frau schlug das Herz" (220). Such a blend is characteristic for the novel, and it is not limited to the title figure. The sentence describing Gieshübler's departure in the same scene is in clear sympathy with the sometimes awkward humanity of the endearing apothecary, whose fantasy would cast him as Cid offering Effi fealty: "Da dies alles aber nicht ging und sein Herz es nicht mehr aushalten konnte, so stand er auf, suchte nach seinem Hut, den er auch glücklicherweise gleich fand ..." (222).[48] The adverb "glücklicherweise" expresses the narrator's relief that Gieshübler is spared possible discomfiture, a reaction thereby suggested for the reader as well. At other points in the novel, the narrative voice assumes the tone of a specific character or strongly suggests a certain interpretation of events. An early example of the former strategy is the mixture of quoted speech and indirect reproduction of a character's tone in the opening scene as Frau von Briest greets the Jahnke twins and Hulda Niemeyer:

> Diese tat rasch ein paar Fragen und lud dann die Mädchen ein, ihnen oder doch wenigstens Effi auf eine halbe Stunde Gesellschaft zu leisten. Ich habe ohnehin noch zu tun ..." (173).

The "doch wenigstens" is clearly Frau von Briest's idiom. Similarly, when Effi enters her new home in Kessin for the first time and the text describes her welcome, in which Johanna "war der gnädigen Frau beim Ablegen von Muff und Mantel behilflich" (208), the "gnädig" is Johanna's "voice." An exact parallel is Roswitha's alacrity in assisting Effi upon her return from a walk:

> [Roswitha] ging, rasch abbrechend, auf das Haus zu, um der gnädigen Frau beim Umkleiden behilflich zu sein. Denn ob Johanna da war, das war die Frage. Die steckte jetzt viel auf dem "Amt" drüben, weil es zu Haus weniger zu tun gab und Friedrich und Christel waren ihr zu langweilig und wußten nie was (320).

The paragraph moves from objective narration to Roswitha's idiom, which incorporates Johanna's tone in the final clause.

In certain passages, the narrative voice reinforces a specific interpretation of narrated events. In an exchange between Crampas and Innstetten on an outing with Effi, there is a definite warning to the reader not to succumb to Crampas' point of view. Innstetten makes a statement which could appear to be a personal criticism of Crampas' carefree attitude. Such an interpretation, however, is explicitly countered:

> Crampas wurde einen Augenblick verlegen, weil er glaubte, das alles sei mit einer gewissen Absicht gesprochen, was aber nicht der Fall war. Innstetten hielt nur einen seiner kleinen moralischen Vorträge, zu denen er überhaupt hinneigte (279).

The passage is interesting because it serves a double function of reinforcing a specific perspective for the reader. It falls between two significant conversations in the novel. The one immediately preceding is Crampas' casual dismissal of the regulations restricting seal hunting with the remark "Alle Gesetzlichkeiten sind langweilig" (278), which meets with applause from Effi and disapproval from Innstetten. The narrative then undercuts Crampas' authority by emphasizing his misconception of Innstetten's remarks. At the same time, the final sentence establishes another example of Innstetten's pedagogical tendencies, preparing the reader for the analysis by Crampas in the following conversation with Effi.

A further instance of specific narrative emphasis is the description of Johanna and Roswitha and their respective positions within the Innstetten household. At the end of the passage, the text leaves no doubt in the reader's mind: "Noch einmal also: Beide Mädchen waren gleichwertig in Annies Augen" (366). A similar emphatic narrative statement is found at the end of Chapter 3. Frau von Briest's musings regarding Effi's unpretentious nature are corrected by the narrator in the final paragraph, which directly addresses the mother's assessment: "Das alles war auch richtig, aber doch nur halb" (185). The paragraph ends with sentences typical of the informal yet audible narrative voice in *Effi Briest,* phrases describing Effi's nature and also characterizing the constitutive tension in the narrative system itself:

> Ja, sie konnte verzichten, darin hatte die Mama recht, und in diesem Verzichtenkönnen lag etwas von Anspruchslosigkeit; wenn es aber ausnahmsweise mal wirklich etwas zu besitzen galt, so mußte dies immer was ganz Apartes sein. Und *darin* war sie anspruchsvoll (185).

The conversational tone of the passage is a feature of the buoyancy which Reuter designates as a dominant trait of the novel, and it is decidedly unpretentious. Such an "Anspruchslosigkeit" corresponds to the natural logic of the syntagmatic organization of the work. The contrastive realm, the paradigmatic level of inference and association, parallels "das Aparte" in Effi's nature, and the resultant ambiguity yields the opaque quality of the narrative system aptly termed "das Poröse" by Demetz.[49]

The intricate matrix of "symbols," recurrent motifs, and significant scenes in *Effi Briest* has been variously analyzed.[50] It is not my intent to undertake a further classification of such elements, but rather to indicate the narrative function of the very density of the level of the novel which defies definitive commentary. The most obvious illustration is the elusive Chinaman, which Fontane readily acknowledged as "ein Drehpunkt für die ganze Geschichte."[51] As in *Schach von Wuthenow*, the predominant strategy is the production of a textual referent through alternative versions within the narrative. The text offers no final clarification but leaves the reader to construe the significance of the Chinaman and his mysterious story. The nuanced ambiguity is a distinct contrast to the univocality of the narrative components in Auerbach's *Dorfgeschichte*, where the significance of such elements as the fir tree in *Befehlerles* is explicitly stated within the text. The narrative refraction in Fontane results in a reading process of continual modulation and refinement, and definitive interpretation is problematic. The forward movement of the plot, the comprehensible train of events supported by the narrative voice, is counteracted by the indeterminacy of meaning characteristic of the paradigmatic level of the text. The central image of the Chinaman and its web of associations within the narrative system contribute to an ambiguity in the field of reference of the work which corresponds to the ultimate opacity of the social universe as perceived by the characters inhabiting it.

Early in the novel, the image is connected to Effi's impression of Kessin as both "spießbürgerlich" and "ganz apart" (206), to her perception of the ambivalence of her new environment. For Effi, the figure also immediately evokes a sense of ominous intimidation: "was Gruseliges" (205). She has a similar reaction of "das Gruseln" while reading the story of the "weiße Frau" on the evening she is frightened by the apparition she believes to be the Chinaman (227). And Innstetten experiences the same sensation as he passes his former house on the way to the duel he feels compelled to fight: "Und das Gefühl des Unheimlichen, das Innstetten an Effi so oft bekämpft oder auch wohl belächelt hatte, jetzt überkam es ihn selbst, und er war froh, als sie dran vorüber waren" (378).

The uncanny aura surrounding the Chinaman and his unresolved tale holds no mystery for Crampas, who offers Effi a double explanation for Innstetten's partial encouragement of her fears: pride in being extraordinary and a pedagogical intent to control his wife (282-3). In reflecting upon Crampas' words, Effi rebels against her husband and his "Angstapparat aus Kalkül" (283). Later, she reveals her internalization of the constraints placed upon her and the conflict which ensues within her nature as she assimilates the phenomenon to the weight of her own conscience (315). In the conversation with Marietta Trippelli at Gieshübler's, the suggestion is made that such apparitions are connected to falsity of character (248), and Innstetten later admonishes Effi that the best defense is "eine reine Seele" (295). The motif of the Chinaman combines aspects of external restraint with individual perception and the inexplicability of the supernatural. The multifaceted image is variously perceived by the characters in the novel, and its elusive identity indicates the relative validity of all the themes which converge in it. The narrative function is parallel to that of Briest's refrain. It opens the text to questions for which no satisfactory answers are offered and lends the work a polyvalence which enables and encourages rereading. The centripetal effect of the narrative pattern in *Soll und Haben* and the *Dorfgeschichte* leaves the reader with no loose ends, as all aspects of the texts serve to reinforce the monolithic character of the reality paradigm constituting the field of reference of the work. In Fontane's *Effi Briest,* such a closed system is precluded by the reflective conversations and monologues and the paradigmatic level of the work. The "social logic" which dictates the inevitability of Effi's "fate" is countered by the opaque intangibility of the narrative elements which elude a one-dimensional reading and underscore the contingency of the social system determining the characters' lives and actions.

The Social Dynamics in Der Stechlin

Fontane's last novel does not correspond to the specific patterns of reading established for *Schach von Wuthenow* and *Effi Briest. Der Stechlin* (1898) does not present any single character for whom the constraints of the social environment preclude the attainment of a personal equilibrium within a socially approbated role. The formative tensions in the narrative are not provided by the friction between the syntagmatic movement of an integrated plot and the ambiguity of a paradigmatic level of inference and association. And although several of the figures in Fontane's final work display the same rigidity and restricted perception which contribute to the unfortunate train of events in the other two novels, there are no similarly tragic consequences. Müller-Seidel has repeatedly emphasized the ostensible lack of conflict in *Der Stechlin,* and Josef Hofmiller has appropriately described the work as initially appearing to be Fontane's simplest book but as actually being his most difficult.[52]

Fontane himself stresses the absence of an intricate plot and extensive narrative action in the work. His laconic synopsis in notes for a letter to Paul von Szczepanski characterizes the type of novel offered to readers of Szczepanski's periodical "Über Land und Meer" in 1897: "Zum Schluß stirbt ein Alter und zwei Junge heiraten sich – das ist so ziemlich alles, was auf 500 Seiten geschieht."[53] The contemporaneous reviews of the book, which appeared after the author's death, generally specified the anomalous aspect of a long novel without much action but recognized the value of Fontane's "Vermächtnis."[54] Twentieth-century scholars have pointed to the additive principle of organization underlying the narrative structure and to the predominance of ideational content carried by conversation.[55] Yet the potential effect of the communicative structure in *Der Stechlin* is similar to the reading experience in the two earlier novels, and the conventionality of the social universe and its relative validity are as perceptible to the reader of the more diffuse narrative as they are central to the reading of *Schach von Wuthenow* and *Effi Briest.* E.M. Forster's designation of the double allegiance of the novel to "the life in time and the life by values" is entirely applicable to Fontane's last work and reinforces the author's own defense of his novel as an example "nicht nur für die richtige, sondern sogar für die gebotene Art, einen Zeitroman zu schreiben."[56]

As in the other two works, the social system in *Der Stechlin* is stable yet not absolute. The fraying of the paramount reality and the fragility of the outward stability are more pronounced in the final novel, and yet it is an open potential and not a tenuous frailty. The finite plurality which differentiates Fontane's texts from the monolithic reality paradigm and authoritative narrative system of the *Dorfgeschichte* and *Soll und Haben* is nowhere more evident than in his last work. The plot is peripheral, and the non-escalating combination of narrative units juxtaposes varied spheres: the Stechlin estate, Kloster Wutz, the Barby residence and life in Berlin.[57] The recurrent point of orientation for a reader is the Stechlin estate and its surroundings, and yet the immutable center provided by the firm of T.O. Schröter in Freytag's text is missing. The constituent tensions in Fontane's narrative permeate every sphere, and it is the continual modification of all perspectives and definitions which distinguishes the communicative structure. The comprehensive pattern of organization and the individual narrative strategies result in an indeterminacy of meaning which encourages a reader to reconsider the text and to realize the complexity of the "Zusammenhang der Dinge" constituting Stechlin: the man, the lake, and the novel.[58]

The concern of German prose fiction in the second half of the nineteenth century with processes of integration is important in a consideration of *Der Stechlin.* In my preliminary definition of integration, I stressed the interrelation of individual unit and contextual system, the functional character of the component elements, and the necessary assimilation into a comprehensive entity. Such matters are of thematic import in Fontane's last novel, and they are integrally related to the narrative organization of the text and its interconnected spheres of action. When Dubslav von Stechlin receives a telegram announcing the arrival of his son Woldemar with two comrades Rex and von Czako, he expresses his misgivings regarding his imminent role as host:

> Aber wen laden wir dazu ein? So bloß ich, das geht nicht. Ich mag mich keinem Menschen mehr vorsetzen. Czako, das ginge vielleicht noch. Aber Rex, wenn ich ihn auch nicht kenne, zu so was Feinem wie Rex paß ich nicht mehr; ich bin zu altmodisch geworden (13).

Dubslav is aware of the difficulty of achieving the proper dinner table composition, a dilemma which is repeated in Chapter 26 when the von Barby sisters come to visit (231-233). His quandry has two dimensions: his sense of being old-fashioned and the disparate assortment of prospective guests in the immediate area. For the visit of Czako and Rex he invites the Gundermanns; on the subsequent occasion he excludes the mill-owner, whom Pastor Lorenzen labels as "ein Bourgeois und ein Parvenu, also so ziemlich das Schlechteste, was einer sein kann" (162). Dubslav's outmoded character traits are manifested mainly in his language. The narrative specifically designates his use of the word "Mantelsäcke" as old-fashioned (16), and he stresses his own distaste for the modern word "Lunch" (50-51) and later professes a preference for dated expressions such as "Schmöker" and "Schniepel" (291-292).[59]

Dubslav's sense of being behind the times is part of a larger thematic complex in the novel, the question of the old and the new.[60] The issue is multifaceted and is especially important in the elections in the district Rheinsberg-Wutz for a representative to the national Parliament. Dubslav is persuaded to run as the Conservative candidate, and he is defeated by the Social-Democrat Torgelow. The latter is an outsider who wins votes through empty promises, as Tuxen, "der alte Süffel von Dietrichsofen," abashedly admits when Dubslav encounters him following the election (186-187). A representative of the new political order, Torgelow proves to be a disappointment, and the local constable Uncke reports to Dubslav that neither his lower-class constituents nor his colleagues in Parliament are satisfied (338). But Dubslav, as a representative of the traditional order, would hardly have been a viable alternative, and Woldemar is just as glad that his father is not selected (151, 188). Neither do the other representatives of Dubslav's milieu inspire confidence in the vitality of the old order in the political realm. Von Molochow, von Kranzen, von Gnewkow, Baron Beetz, and Freiherr von der Nonne rather substantiate Lorenzen's comment, as reported by Dubslav: "Die aristokratische Welt habe abgewirtschaftet, und nun komme die demokratische" (47).[61] Yet Lorenzen's assessment itself is undercut by the negative imagery of decline, by the definition of culture as the trend, "daß immer weiter nach unten gestiegen wird" (47). In the elections in Rheinsberg-Wutz, there seems to be no clear solution to the conflict between the old and the new.

A similar ambivalence is evident throughout the text, and the possible coexistence of the old and the new which ensures the success of Dubslav's dinner parties is a central element in the finite plurality which marks the reality paradigm of the work. When Woldemar consults with his mentor Lorenzen, whom Rex estimates as one of the youngest, despite his age, the uncommon pastor advises against total allegiance to the new order: "Nicht so ganz unbedingt mit dem Neuen. Lieber mit dem Alten, soweit es irgend geht, und mit dem Neuen nur, soweit es muß" (27). Czako captures the essence of Lorenzen and the complex, uncertain stability of the social system underlying Fontane's text in a conversation with Rex: "Das Überlieferte ... ist doch sehr reparaturbedürftig, und auf solche Reparatur ist ein Mann wie dieser Lorenzen eben aus" (42). In the central dialogue between Melusine und Lorenzen in Chapter 29, the emphasis is on the necessary integration of the old with the new. Melusine explains her unwillingness to allow the ice covering the seismographic spot in Lake Stechlin to be disturbed:

> Ich habe mich dagegen gewehrt, als das Eis aufgeschlagen werden sollte, denn alles Eingreifen oder auch nur Einblicken in das, was sich verbirgt, erschreckt mich. Ich respektiere das Gegebene. Daneben aber freilich auch das Werdende, denn eben dies Werdende wird über kurz oder lang abermals ein Gegebenes sein. Alles Alte, soweit es Anspruch darauf hat, sollen wir lieben, aber für das Neue sollen wir recht eigentlich leben. Und vor allem sollen wir,

wie der Stechlin uns lehrt, den großen Zusammenhang der Dinge nie vergessen. Sich abschließen heißt sich einmauern, und sich einmauern ist Tod (251).

The extended passage merits quoting in its entirety because of its compact substance, which encompasses the central themes of the novel. The opacity is intimidating for Melusine, yet she expressly warns against losing sight of it.[62] The old and the new, that which exists and that which is in the process of coming into existence, claim equal importance, and a main accent is on the necessity of integrating the individual units into the comprehensive entity. Various modes of existence are presented within the novel, and the most viable among them correspond to Melusine's reading of the message of the lake. The obvious example of the dangers of self-isolation is Adelheid von Stechlin, deaconess (*Domina*) at Kloster Wutz, which has been aptly designated as being both geographically and ontologically the "vis-à-vis" to the Stechlin estate.[63] Dubslav reproaches his sister for being "petrefact" (263), and Melusine chooses the adjective "vorweltlich" in a conversation with her father (266). It is significant that her domain is not the fluidity of Lake Stechlin, but the crumbling cloister walls and a clock which habitually runs late. Woldemar's antediluvian aunt is noticeably disapproving of the mercurial and charming Melusine (247-8, 263-4, 354), and Graf Barby correctly diagnoses the suspicion with which Melusine is regarded by "alle beschränkten und aufgesteiften Individuen" (266). Adelheid's displeasure with Woldemar's choice of Armgard von Barby as a bride is based on her opposition to an extension beyond one's own sphere, a conviction which she defends in a letter to Woldemar (148-9) and in a conversation with her brother (263-4). There is no clearer contrast in the novel than that of Adelheid and Melusine, a contrast underscored in the text: "Sie waren eben Antipoden: Stiftsdame und Weltdame, Wutz und Windsor, vor allem enge und weite Seele" (354).

Yet the constellation of figures in the novel is not a static juxtaposition of those characters integrated into a broader community and those resolutely restricting their sphere. Fontane's narratives are not reducible to the schematic oppositions of the pattern of reading I suggested for Freytag and Auerbach. All characters are problematical, and the gentle humor with which the *Domina* is portrayed is far removed from Freytag's caricatures.[64] The correct proportion of "sich abschließen" and integration also appears to be a complex issue. If the rigidity of Kloster Wutz is undesirable, an exaggerated responsiveness to one's environment is equally dangerous. Dubslav likens the indecisive trait in most human beings to "Wetterfahnen" (166), and he collects weather vanes in his eccentric museum. Demetz designates the lake, the cloister walls, and the weather vanes as representing three alternative modes of existence,[65] and the reality paradigm circumscribed by such ambivalent possibilities still coincides with the functional social reality model of readers nearly a century later.

The dynamics of the social system in *Der Stechlin* encompass the temporal tensions between the old and the new and the intersection of the various spheres of narrative action. Dubslav's predicament concerning dinner invitations is brought about by the envisioned encounter of his local acquaintances with visitors from Berlin, whether Rex and Czako or Melusine and Armgard. The two visits to the Stechlin estate do produce some amusingly awkward situations, such as the extended conversation between Frau Gundermann and Czako on the topic of the rat population in certain areas of Berlin (30-1), but give rise as well to eloquent exchanges of consequence such as the consultation between Melusine and Lorenzen. The juxtaposition and interaction of the various spheres results in the relative position of each one, and the final effect is the possibility of communication and integration at all levels. Fontane's narrative is polysystemic in the sense of an interchange and mutual elucidation of tangential realms of action, and the resultant pattern of reading allows the perception of the contingent nature of all social systems.

The main spheres of Stechlin, Wutz, and Berlin are readily apparent. Despite all differences between the provincial and the cosmopolitan households, certain parallels are striking. Woldemar's diary entry in Chapter 12 outlines the similarity, which extends from personal characteristics of Graf von Barby and his father to "die gesamte Hausatmosphäre, das Liberale" (107). The meeting of the two men at the wedding is a success, and the union of Armgard and Woldemar is a solid one. The younger Stechlin has broadened his perspective through his regimental experience and his mission to England, and Armgard's preference for Elisabeth of Thüringen reveals her admirable aspirations (226). The main function of the contrasts and parallels among the constituent realms within the narrative structure, however, is not a conceivable synthesis but mutual respect and simultaneous existence, which precludes the exclusive validity of any single perspective. Fontane's narrative consists mainly of conversation, and one of the main rhetorical modes in the novel is elucidation. Since the main characters inhabit divergent spheres of experience, there is a continual need for explanations and mediations. The virtuoso use of language in *Der Stechlin* is characterized not only by the well-analyzed wit, irony, and sceptical modulation, but also by basic patterns of elucidation as a mode of mutual communication at all levels of the narrative.[66] The figures in Fontane's novel are not engaged in the authoritative type of discourse which composes Anton Wohlfart's "indoctrination" in conversations with Schröter or the confrontation between the peasants and the representatives of authority in *Befehlerles*. Neither are most of the dialogues dominated by attempts at self-justification and maintenance of a threatened existence, as is evident to the reader in Wilhelm Raabe's late novels. The dominant tone of discourse is one of curiosity and mutual respect, and the characters are differentiated by the degree to which they manifest it.

The novel itself begins with an extended passage of painstaking description, which serves to introduce the reader to the environs, household, and person of Dubslav von Stechlin. The immediate visit of Woldemar, Rex and Czako provides the occasion for further exposition combined with narrative action, as the morning program during their stay is a systematic orientation and a careful explanation of the components of life in Stechlin, from the school and the glass factory to the lake, the "pièce de résistance" (49). The entire program is repeated for the benefit of the von Barby sisters in the latter part of the novel with the additional "reading" of the lake by Melusine and the explanation of the museum. The initial visit of Woldemar, Rex, and Czako to Kloster Wutz requires further elucidation, as Woldemar attempts to describe the life of the *Domina* and her companions (72-4) and then subsequently finds himself explaining the various regiments to his aunt (90-93), much the same as he had attempted to illuminate the characters of his comrades, his life in Berlin, and his progress in choosing a wife to his father (44-46). His side-visit to Katzlers requires a special explanation to Rex and Czako in order to correct their misperceptions (66-69).

As Woldemar moves in all three spheres of action, he is involved in a great portion of the dialogue of elucidation. The section of the novel entitled "Nach dem Eierhäuschen" (Ch. 11-15) contains his further attempts to mediate between Stechlin and Berlin. He delineates the special qualities of Lake Stechlin for Graf von Barby and his daughters: "Er hat Weltbeziehungen, vornehme, geheimnisvolle Beziehungen" (124). At the end of the section, on the return from the outing to the "Eierhäuschen," Woldemar "explains" Lorenzen to his companions. His description of his friend and mentor as "ein Excelsior-, ein Aufsteigemensch," whose enthusiasm for the exemplary Portuguese writer João de Deus characterizes his own humanity, leads to the half-joking, half-serious alliance in the name of Lorenzen which concludes the section (143-6).[67]

The rhetoric of elucidation is not limited to the main figures in the novel. Hedwig, the *portier's* niece in Berlin, carefully explains the difficulties of finding a suitable position as a maid to Frau Imme, the coachman's wife (135-137). And the bilingual exchanges between Mr. Robinson, the Berchtesgadens' English coachman, and Herr and Frau Imme are a humorous paradigm of international understanding (127-8, 132-4). England opens the margins of discourse for Woldemar and the Barbys as well, as the latter offer advice for Woldemar's sojourn (199-204) and then form the audience upon his return (218-226).[68] Graf von Barby is absent for Woldemar's travel report, which is interrupted by Professor Cujacius' visit. The arrogant professor of painting provides the negative contrast to the communicative discourse of elucidation, as his apodictic statements preclude discussion and mutual enlightenment in much the same manner as Gundermann's inane comment reducing complex issues to water on the millwheels of the Social-Democrats (e.g., 23, 34).[69] A counter-example of non-enlightened, restricted discourse is the exchange between Cujacius and the volatile Wrschowitz (278-281).

The effect of the prevalent pattern of elucidation as a mode of mutual communication at various narrative levels is the effective forestallment of a single dominant set of explanations and definitions. No issue goes without background, subsidiary questions, or tangential aspects. Dubslav's conviction that there are no irrefutable truths (8) and the opening description of the *Junker* as one who "seinem ganzen Wesen nach überhaupt hinter alles ein Fragezeichen machte" (7) could be appropriately applied to the communicative structure of the novel itself. Reading Fontane's text involves the constitution of a fictional field of reference which integrates coexisting spheres. The narrative organization does not subsume all provinces of meaning under a single symbolic universe, as was the case with the dominant middle-class ideology in *Soll und Haben,* but implements the independence as well as the interdependence of the constituent spheres. The best example of a deviant sphere of experience is the incorporation of the figures of Agnes and her grandmother, "die Buschen." The latter is reputed to be a witch, and Dubslav consults her after taking a disliking to the impudent young substitute for the regular local doctor because of his Social-Democratic tendencies. He later summons Agnes to brighten his final days, knowing that her presence will rid him of the onerous ministrations of his sister Adelheid. Adelheid and Ermyntrud Katzler, *geb. Prinzessin* von Ippe-Büchsenstein, refuse to accept Agnes on her own terms. The *Domina* finds the child's red stockings an affront and a violation of social order.* The *Prinzessin,* who has renounced her lineage for a bourgeois marriage which she leads with a rigidly pious sense of duty and morality, resolves to reincorporate the wayward child into society by means of her pet project, an asylum for "sittlich zu Heilende" (345). As two of the most inflexible characters in the novel, it is not surprising that they are incapable of respecting an existence outside their realm of experience and control. Within the narrative structure, Agnes receives more tolerant treatment. The sincere despair of her grief at Dubslav's graveside allies her with the humanity

---

* Sie [die Strümpfe] sind ein Zeichen von Ungehörigkeit und Verkehrtheit ... ein Zeichen davon, daß alle Vernunft aus der Welt ist und alle gesellschaftliche Scheidung immer mehr aufhört (327).

which Lorenzen's eulogy, with its Terentian undertones, claims for Dubslav von Stechlin: "Nichts Menschliches war ihm fremd, weil er sich selbst als Mensch empfand und sich eigner menschlicher Schwäche jederzeit bewußt war ... Er war das Beste, was wir sein können, ein Mann und ein Kind" (351). The contrast is the following exchange between von Molchow and von der Nonne, two representatives of the old order, whose words are devoid of respect or emotion (352).[70]

The coexistence and interpenetration of divergent spheres of experience in *Der Stechlin* mark the finite plurality of the field of reference of the work. The comprehensive pattern of the narrative returns repeatedly to the Stechlin estate and its surroundings, but only in order to accentuate a mutable identity. Lake Stechlin, "der gleich mitrumort, wenn irgendwo was los ist" (49), offers only a relatively stable fulcrum in comparison with the monolithic center of Schröter's firm in *Soll und Haben.* The centripetal pattern of Freytag's novel and Auerbach's village tales is replaced by a "decentering," a return to a pivotal image which is itself of limited stability. Preisendanz suggests that the humor in Fontane's prose often functions as parabasis, as the intermittent interruption of the narrative, and that the humanity of his novels frequently lies in incidental details and anecdotes.[71] The statement is especially applicable to *Der Stechlin,* and the concept of parabasis is related to specific textual strategies as well as to the de-centering which distinguishes the comprehensive narrative pattern.

Since language is a fundamental factor in the reinforcement and stabilization of any given social reality, the attitudes towards language and the treatment of abstract concepts are indicative of the degree of rigidity of the reality paradigm itself. Dubslav's predilection for paradoxes and his scepticism concerning irrefutable truths (7-8) set the tone for a novel which lets no definition go unchallenged. As Dubslav states to Woldemar: "was bloß ein Wort ist, ist nie was Feines, auch wenn es so aussieht" (62). Such an attitude prevails in the text and extends from the *portier* Hartwig's refusal to accept the aura surrounding *Hagelversicherungssekretär* Schickedanz' death "drei Tage vor Weihnachten" as underlined in the burial service to the equivocal construing of heroism.[72] Dubslav declares that

127

"Heldentum ist Ausnahmezustand und meist Produkt einer Zwangslage" (25), and yet he is uncomfortable with Lorenzen's description of just such a singularly heroic incident. The pastor recounts the episode of Greely's decision on an expedition to the North Pole to shoot a comrade whose secret depletion of the meagre supplies threatens the survival of all the others. Dubslav's hesitant recognition of Lorenzen's admiration leaves the final import of the issue to the reader (319).[73] In the equivocal treatment of its own definitions, the text turns towards the reader for the final constitution of meaning.

Adelheid von Stechlin is uncomfortable with ambiguity, and she consistently attempts to establish clear boundaries and definitions. Her brother confronts her with the absurdity of her undertaking when she expresses strong disapproval of women who smoke, "Weil Rauchen männlich ist" (263). Since she herself slaughters geese, Dubslav concludes that slaughtering is therefore a feminine activity. The extrapolation of the logic of rigid categories is a humorous illustration of the contingency of established roles and definitions. The final conversation between Adelheid and Dubslav touches on a similar issue and exemplifies a basic principle of the narrative system in *Der Stechlin*. The *Domina* terms Agnes' red stockings a sign ("ein Zeichen"), and her brother counters: "Das sagt gar nichts, Adelheid. Ein Zeichen ist alles. Wovon sind sie ein Zeichen? Darauf kommt es an" (327). Dubslav again deflates his sister's indignation by extrapolation of her linguistic logic. She insists on the unequivocal reading of the stockings, and when she sets up a further one-dimensional equation, his laconic answer reveals the dangers of such correspondences:

[Adelheid]: "Ich aber wiederhole dir, diese roten Strümpfe, die sind ein Zeichen, eine hochgehaltene Fahne."
[Dubslav]: "Strümpfe werden nicht hochgehalten" (327).

The narrative tension in Fontane's novel consists partially of the lack of such correspondences and unambiguous signs.

In *Schach von Wuthenow,* the refraction of a concrete fact or specific event in a network of divergent perspectives determined the basic pattern of reader experience. In Fontane's last novel, the

"Lektüreanweisungsmuster" emphasizes the semioticity of all narrative elements and the fallacy of rigid definitions. Müller-Seidel is cautious in the use of "symbolism" as a descriptive expression for *Der Stechlin,* and Preisendanz rejects the term because the process of symbolization leads away from the realm of everyday experience which is the very import of the book.[74] Müller-Seidel's concept of "Kunstgegenstand" instead of symbol or allegory for such narrative elements as the lake does not adequately circumscribe their function. The indeterminacy of meaning is central to Fontane's narratives, as are the processes of perception and communication which lend meanings to signs, words, concepts, and activities. Like the elusive Chinaman in *Effi Briest,* concepts and objects in *Der Stechlin* are subject to continual modulation and refinement within the text, and the reader is left to construe any final significance. There is a loss of assumption of immediate comprehensibility, of the clear connection of sign and signified. Adelheid's interpretation of the red stockings is prompted by her own convictions and not by the object itself. The blossoms on Dubslav's favorite aloe plant in front of the house invariably elicit compliments from those unaware that the ostensible aloe blossoms are the product of another plant sharing the pot (7). Lake Stechlin is famed for its external connections and is not set into motion by itself; therefore it remains unclear to what extent it is "revolutionary" in character. It has been pointed out that Fontane's characters themselves are continually interpreting the "symbols" in the texts, and the processes of consensus and the lack of singular interpretations are typical for the semiotic level of the narrative, which exposes the contingency of its own "symbols," or signs and meanings.[75] The parabasis of Preisendanz' analysis of humor is the refusal of the text to establish fixed correspondences or a hierarchy of narrative elements. The text itself is composed of the processes of integration and communication and not of their results.

The narrative voice in *Der Stechlin* is similar to the conversational tone of the main character. The interpolated anecdotes resemble the tendency of the characters to comment parenthetically on their own statements, and the narrator also uses parenthetical asides, in order to elucidate and embellish the text. Bruno Hildebrandt finds a resultant unity of tone in the novel, which indicates an underlying stability of the narrated world.[76] It is a narrative strategy which contributes to the analysis of that stability as well, as the interpolations indicate the background, contradictions, and ancillary aspects of all issues. Dubslav's epistolary style is characterized by a tendency, "gern bei Nebensächlichkeiten zu verweilen und gelegentlich über die Hauptsache hinwegzusehen" (228). In *Der Stechlin,* the manner of integration of the "Nebensächlichkeiten" is exactly the main point. The narrative system in the novel is an open one, more so than in *Schach von Wuthenow* and *Effi Briest,* and the reality paradigm constituted in the reading of the text is concerned with the processes of the construction of social reality, with language and with the conventionality and temporality of social systems. The mutual elucidation of divergent spheres of narrative action and experience, the thematic complex of the old and the new, the semiotic level of the text, and above all the ambivalent stability of the central image of Lake Stechlin characterize the communicative structure of Fontane's final novel.

Despite the differences between *Der Stechlin* and the two earlier novels, the position of the reader regarding the field of reference actualized in reading the text is similar. In *Schach von Wuthenow,* the framework of reading and multiple interpretation results in the constant modulation and refinement of the varying perspectives, and the reading process effects the realization of the conventionality of the social universe accepted by the narrated characters. The tragedy in the novel is partially an outcome of the limited perception of the various figures, and the work ends with the dual epistolary optic which offers no final solution. In *Effi Briest,* the contingency of the social logic behind the syntagmatic narrative organization is exposed by the paradigmatic level of ambiguous elements such as the Chinaman and by the reflective conversations of the characters themselves, which leave open the question of the inevitability of Effi's "fate." The opaque totality of social reality and its force over the individuals finds a thematic variation in the ambiguous flux of the "Zusammenhang der Dinge" in the final novel. In *Der Stechlin*, the characters themselves exhibit an awareness of the finite plurality and conventionality of social reality. The refraction of all narrative elements in conversation and the central indeterminacy of meaning result in a text characterized as much by constitutive tensions as the more plot-oriented novels. The reading experience in all three works is not the reaffirmation of a dominant social system but the critical distance of analysis and comprehension.

IV. THE ELUSIVE CENTER: NARRATION AS DISORIENTATION

In turning from the sovereign yet sympathetic narrative voice in Fontane's novels to the first-person narratives of Wilhelm Raabe's Braunschweig trilogy, it is no longer feasible to consider the narrator as one element among many in the analysis of the texts. The figure writing the account in Raabe's late novels should be of main interest to a reader, both as a character in the narrated events and as a figure for whom the writing itself is a problematic "event." Of the Braunschweig trilogy, written after Raabe's move to Braunschweig in 1870, it is particularly *Stopfkuchen* (1891) and *Die Akten des Vogelsangs* (1896) which are important in my consideration of various aspects of German narrative in the second half of the nineteenth century. The earlier work, *Alte Nester* (1880), has a more mildly melancholic tone and is technically and thematically not as intriguing as the two later novels.[1] The narrative progression in the final works of the trilogy inverts the model of experience forming the field of reference in the initial segment of German Realism which I analyzed in *Soll und Haben* and the *Dorfgeschichte*. Anton Wohlfart, Mathes (*Befehlerles*), and Hans-Jörg (*Die Kriegspfeife*) all begin with certain illusions and, in the course of the narrative, become increasingly integrated into the dominant reality paradigm, which itself remains unchanged. In Berger and Luckmann's terms, the finite province of meaning, for example Anton Wohlfart's deference to the upper social strata, is incorporated into the paramount reality definition, in this case the prevailing matrix of middle-class values. The final state of narrative equilibrium aligns protagonist, narrative voice, and reader in affirmative recognition of such values.

Raabe's late novels offer a distinctly different reader experience. The story is "told" by a narrator whose existence and attitudes exemplify a solid bourgeois system of values and everyday routines. Even in *Stopfkuchen*, although the narrator has ostensibly fled the philistine environment of his youth to become a successful landowner in

South Africa, he retains the cultural pretensions and the penchant for the familiar neighborhood pub. At the center of the narrator's story is a protagonist who represents a challenge to the narrator's reality definition, and the process of narration is an attempt to come to grips with the challenge. Heinrich Schaumann in *Stopfkuchen* and Velten Andres in *Die Akten des Vogelsangs* may be regarded as "carriers of alternative reality definitions,"[2] and they effectively call into question the complacency of the respective narrators Eduard and Karl Krumhardt. The two works present an increasingly psychological treatment of the narrator, which Ohl has called the reflection of bourgeois self-definition upon its own presuppositions.[3] The result is a dual role for the reader, as two patterns of reading are established. The friction between them is what the novel is all about. The first pattern relates the elements of narrator, reader, and central figure of concern. The narrator assumes empathy on the part of the reader regarding the subject of the narrative. In *Die Akten des Vogelsangs*, Krumhardt designates his role as that of "Protokollist," and the reader then becomes judge and jury in assessing Velten Andres' aberrant existence. The readers are addressed as "die geehrten Herren und Damen auf dem Richterstuhl des Erdenlebens."[4] The readers are allowed to judge, yet it is assumed that we are all within the same legal system as the narrator. We are all defending "the laws of the land" — Krumhardt's carefully preserved bourgeois values. Such a pattern of reading places narrator and reader equidistant from the subject and leaves the reader at the same level of inadequacy in dealing with Velten as the narrator, who states: "Ich bin eben in seinem Leben über nichts im Dunkel geblieben als — über ihn selber" (318).

The broader pattern of reading involves the elements of reader, text, and thematic field of reference. The reader of Raabe's text is not restricted to the perspective of the narrator but "reads" the process of narration as well. In *Stopfkuchen,* a reader can perceive the manner in which Schaumann dominates the narrator as the latter attempts to recuperate his sense of identity after Schaumann's own narrative has relativized the bases of his previously complacent existence. In the later novel, the outcome of the "case" of Velten Andres is not entirely clear. Although Anna Krumhardt and the narrator's children, representing order and continuity, have the final word, their mode of existence has been called into question, and there is an awareness of the fragility and of the price paid for complacency. The constitutive narrative tensions, which are fixed in binary oppositions in the works by Freytag and Auerbach and which result in the narrative refraction and indeterminacy of meaning in Fontane's novels, are located in the process of writing itself in Raabe's late novels. Assessments of the disastrous effect of the story upon the narrator as a collapse of the accustomed system of values or a massive identity crisis are perhaps overstated.[5] Total disillusionment would be too strong of a term, as would radical disintegration. The process of narration in *Stopfkuchen* and *Die Akten des Vogelsangs* is best characterized as disorientation, as the gradual relativization of the narrator's purported stance.

In the novels by Fontane, the linear plot movement was found to be increasingly peripheral to the import of the works. In the two Raabe texts, the attempt to establish a coherent plot would be difficult. Martini has appropriately designated the main difficulty in interpretations of Raabe's more complex narratives as the necessity of separating for analysis the interrelated layers of the texts.[6] The temporal structure in *Stopfkuchen* consists of the time of narration, which is the thirty days of Eduard's sea voyage from Hamburg to Cape Town, the narrated account of the recent visit to his hometown, and the more distant past of his childhood, which is rendered in his own reminiscing and in Heinrich Schaumann's version.[7] *Die Akten des Vogelsangs* actually begins with the end, with the letter marking the final episode of the narrated material. Yet it is the end of the narrative, the letter and Krumhardt's final visit to Berlin, which marks the beginning of narration. The letter, designating the incipient moment of the narrative process, therefore belongs on the opening page of the novel and signals to the perceptive reader that the dynamics of narration are as important as the narrative itself.[8]

In *Soll und Haben* and the *Dorfgeschichte,* the univocality of the texts was partly a result of the reinforcement of the story by the authoritative narrative discourse. In the refraction of narrated event in the perspectives of individual characters in Fontane's novels, there was an expansion of the narrative system and increased reader involvement in constituting the field of reference of the texts. Nevertheless, the occasional narratorial interpolations, such as "arme Effi," revealed the narrator's unequivocal sympathies. Despite the occasional assumption of a restricted perspective, such as the "surmise" concerning the topic of conversation in Frau von Carayon's salon, the narratives never worked against the narrator as is the case in Raabe's first-person novels. The figures of Eduard and Karl Krumhardt are anxious to retain the legitimacy of their carefully established existence, a legitimacy extending to the concepts and primary figures of their earliest socialization. Their narrative re-encounter with the past results in a growing disorientation within the present. The inadequately socialized figures of Heinrich Schaumann and Velten Andres confront the narrators with the contingent character of their own lives. The reality paradigm which is valorized at one level of the text by the narrator is called into question by the comprehensive pattern of narration. When Claude David states that the amusing and clever form of presentation in *Stopfkuchen* is only peripherally associated with the theme of the work, he is neglecting the manner in which the narrative structure results in a pattern of reading in which the disorientation encompasses reader as well as narrator.[9] The reader is not presented with a monolithic reality paradigm as in the pattern of reading established for Freytag and Auerbach, but is rather left to integrate the various elements in constituting the field of reference of the texts. Barker Fairley has stated that it is necessary to read *Stopfkuchen* from front to back and then again from back to front in order to know it, and his advice is not entirely facetious.[10] There is no recurrent point of orientation for the reader, and recurrent narrative elements are as often emptied of meaning as they are tendered as reliable guides. A recent study of *Stopfkuchen* postulates the novel as a discourse on the proper perception of reality,[11] and it is the problematic aspect of perceiving one's social environment and the related question of the possibility of structuring and living a justifiable individual existence which are of central concern in all three novels of the Braunschweig trilogy.

The tendency in scholarship on Raabe's late works to emphasize the positive nature of the aberrant figure and the inherent criticism of the "philistine," bourgeois existence is not sufficient for the complexity of the central concerns and the continued realistic level of the works.[12] The constitutive tensions in the texts are not bipolar but in a more fundamental sense centrifugal.[13] Erich Weniger's study of word frequencies in Raabe's works finds the top group composed of the concepts "Dasein-Leben-Welt-Erde-Zeit-Zeitlichkeit-Säkulum-Existenz" and discovers a tension within that semantic field.[14] The course of the narrative and the process of narration in *Stopfkuchen* and *Die Akten des Vogelsangs* expose the tenuousness both of past presuppositions and present alternatives. The "outsider" figure is not necessarily the "essential human being," as Hermann Meyer has termed him, but a mixed character.[15] The manipulative abilities of Heinrich Schaumann border on cruelty, and the "victory" of Velten Andres, described by Krumhardt as Velten's "siegreich gewonnener Prozeß gegen meine, gegen *unsere* Welt," is a hollow one (295). The "Lektüreanweisungsmuster," the pattern relating the elements of reader, text, and thematic field of reference, results in the mutual relativization of all perspectives. The narrators in *Stopfkuchen* and *Die Akten des Vogelsangs* are challenged, but their concerns are not totally refuted. Separate analyses of the two related novels will serve to substantiate the manner in which the communicative structure of the texts exposes the contingency of the presumably stable social system without denying its necessity.

The Force of Narrative Inertia: Stopfkuchen

Stopfkuchen has been variously termed Raabe's best novel, his most inaccessible text, his most personal book, his most subjective work, the shortest "Bildungsroman" ever, and the narrative which demonstrates Raabe's humor at its deepest.[16] The plethora of superlatives suggests a fascination with the work among Raabe scholars, a fascination by no means indicative of a critical consensus concerning the interpretation or even identification of the main elements of the text. The invariably quoted passage in which the title figure emphasizes his reliance on "Anschauung" instead of "Begriff" as an epistemological principle,* read by Ohl as an ironic allusion to Schopenhauer, is taken quite seriously by Dierkes and Eisele in their analyses.[18] For David, the revelation of Störzer as the murderer is relatively unimportant; for Gisela Warnke, Störzer is a central figure in the narrative.[19] Martini has captured the basis for such discrepancies in his remark that every statement made about *Stopfkuchen* requires an immediate qualifying statement of the opposite.[20] The text itself appears to elicit conflicting readings.

Ambiguity and conflict are inherent features of the middle novel of Raabe's Braunschweig trilogy. The work is concerned with questions of perception and authority, and at a basic level the central issue is whose narrative it actually is. Problems of identity and orientation are raised in the opening pages, and the primary elements of the reality paradigms constituted in realist narrative of the nineteenth century are at stake. Continuity and temporality, the interrelation of individual and social world, the force of convention and the transmission of values: the degree and manner of integration of the social system in Raabe's text leave all such issues problematic. The communicative structure of *Stopfkuchen* includes the divergent reality definitions of narrator, townspeople, and protagonist, as well as the complex structure and strategies of the narrative system itself.[21] The text begins and ends with a question, and a main distinction between the pattern of reading in Raabe's Braunschweig trilogy and the highly-directed narratives of Auerbach and Freytag is that the answer is left to the reader. There is no unquestioned, cohesive system of meanings and values at the center of *Stopfkuchen,* and the indeterminate nature of the narrative contributes to the polyvalence of its realism.

The novel is divided into thirty-two segments, and an intermingling of the various temporal levels is often found within individual segments. It is left to the reader to separate and order the various elements. The most remarkable example of transition between the

---

* Ich war feist und faul, aber doch nun gerade, euch allen zum Trost, noch vor meiner Kenntnisnahme des Weisen von Frankfurts bester Table d'hote ein Poet ersten Ranges. Der Begriff war mir gar nichts, ich nahm alles unter der Hecke weg, mit dem Sonnenschein des Daseins warm auf dem Bauche, aus der Anschauung![17]

narrated point in time and the present time of narration is Eduard's interpolated comment in the narrative present as he is remembering in detail his embarrassed response as a youth to Schaumann's exhortation that he should look off into the distance and enjoy the view while Schaumann took leave from Valentine Quakatz:

> Als ich wieder aufsehe, ist weiter nichts vorgefallen, als daß *die Jahre hingegangen sind* und daß die langen Wogen des großen Meeres unter dem Schiff weiterrollen und es gegenwärtig gutmütig, ohne zu arges Rollen, Schütteln und Schüttern weitertragen, dem Kap der Guten Hoffnung zu (49; original emphasis).

The following section reverts to the past, but only half-way, to the more recent past of Eduard's visit to Schaumann and Valentine in the Rote Schanze, which was the final event of a journey back to his hometown from his present in South Africa. As the waves carry him toward the resumption of his present identity, the sequence of narrated events is non-linear and works against a progressive integration of narrative units. The reader is required to shift back and forth, and the result is a lack of facile orientation within the text.

Already the subtitle of the work, "Eine See- und Mordgeschichte," is misleading and yet appropriate. Any genre expectation of adventure on the high seas is left unfulfilled; as Eduard states near the end: "Etwas Besonderes ist auf dem Schiffe nicht vorgefallen und scheint auch nicht passieren zu sollen" (145). The murder is rather an inadvertent homicide, and it is the delaying tactics of Schaumann's method of revelation of the culprit as well as the details of his technique of detection which are important. A reader expecting an adventure "Krimi" would be forced to revise such a genre orientation, and yet the main title and the double subtitle indicate precisely the principal points of the narrative: the figure of *Stopfkuchen,* rendered in the derisive nickname which indicates his aberrant position within society, the murder committed by Störzer, and the unsettling process of narration for Eduard on his sea-voyage home. "Reading" the title of the work is a process of being confronted with one's own unreflected genre assumptions and then reconstructing the applicability of "Eine See- und Mordgeschichte" to the text as it stands.

The opening narrative segments continue the strategy of adapting traditional narrative structures in a manner congruent with the underlying thematic concerns of the work. The initial section is a presentation of the narrator's credentials, a topos traceable back to medieval epic. Eduard emphasizes his culture and education, despite his position as a wealthy emigrant to South Africa. The use of the impersonal "man" in the opening pages has a similar function of claiming authority for the individual voice:

> Nachdem man also seinen Berechtigungsgrund, im alten Vaterlande mitzusprechen, wo gebildete Leute reden, auf den Tisch gelegt hat, kann man hoffentlich weitergehen (8).
>
> Natürlich könnte man hier Gedanken, Gefühle, Stimmungen und Anmerkungen aus der Tiefe des deutschen Herzens, Busens und Gemütes heraus noch recht erklecklich weiter, und zwar ins Behaglichste ausmalen; man tut es aber nicht, sondern bemerkt nur das Notwendige (12).

The passages expressly evoke specific narrative conventions, yet it would be misleading to read the first passage, for example, solely within established genre traditions. The apparent relief of the initial entry "Wieder an Bord! – " (7) has been mentioned in studies of *Stopfkuchen*,[22] and the initial sections evince a defensive, semi-apologetic tone which is important for Raabe's narrative as it betrays the unease of Eduard the narrator with his "Seegeschichte." The discussion of the problem of orienting oneself to the night sky in the other hemisphere (9) is followed by Eduard's self-assertion as one who lights a cigar in the face of the infinite heavens:

> denn das leuchtet doch auch und der Mensch auf Erden ist darauf angewiesen, gegen alles und also auch gegen das "Übermaß der Sterne" zu reagieren.
> Jaja, und wenn man auch noch ein Deutscher älterer Generation ist, so bleibt man doch am liebsten bei dem Nächstliegenden, dem angenehmen Abend, der guten Gesellschaft und was sonst so dazu gehört, wenn man sich auch, der Abwechselung wegen, einmal auf "Siriusweiten" in das Glitzern und Flimmern überm Kopfe davon entfernt. Und das ist unser gutes Erdenrecht (9-10).

The use of "man" in the passage is connected with an attempted self-justification through identification with a collective tendency. It is apparent that Eduard is anxious to establish his identity in the initial entries in his sea-journal, and the reflective question early on in the text underscores the concern: "Wie kommen Menschen dahin, wo sie sich, sich besinnend, zu eigener Verwunderung dann und wann finden?" (7). The more general query grows out of a literary allusion in which the specific question is how a shepherd in Arcadia came to desire an estate on the Cape of Good Hope.[23] The connection to Eduard, the South African landowner, is clear, and Eduard's reality definition and his sense of self are a principal topic of the novel, as they are called into question by the encounter with his childhood comrade Heinrich Schaumann, whom he as well as the other children called Stopfkuchen. It is necessary to characterize the reality paradigm valorized by Eduard and the manner in which it is relativized by Schaumann's existence even before the latter's revelation of Störzer as the murderer of Kienbaum. The postman Störzer, Eduard's friend and childhood mentor, had allowed suspicion to rest on the recluse Quakatz, whose daughter and property Schaumann had long coveted and finally attained, and Schumann's disclosure of the truth at the fortuitous juncture of Störzer's death and Eduard's visit home confronts Eduard with the inauthenticity of his presumably reliable guide. Since Eduard's tentative response to the questions raised at the outset of the narrative had been that Störzer was responsible for the course his life had taken (7), the revelation has repercussions beyond the disturbance of a childhood memory.

Eduard distinguishes himself from the other inhabitants of the town he grew up in, and it is a differentiation which is significant for his perception of himself in relation to his social environment. He prides himself on his broader horizons, on his home in South Africa where he claims to be a personal friend of the President (8). The source of such a distinctive identity was Störzer, who shared his penchant for geography, nourished by the travelogues of François Le Vaillant, in Störzer's idiom "Levalljang." Eduard also makes a claim for distinction as having been a friend of Schaumann, separated from the other townspeople and children who taunted the fat youth mercilessly. Yet his own narrated account betrays the fictitious nature of his selected recollections. Despite the ironic designations such as "Busenfreund" (125), "bester Freund" (140, 147), and "liebster Freund" (66) granted Eduard by Schaumann and his wife Valentine, the latter forgets his name totally at one point (104). When Eduard is asked to recall Schaumann's motto in his childhood, he is unable to reproduce the "Friß es aus und friß dich durch" which a friend would well have retained (114). Schumann expressly connects him with the other townspeople from whom Eduard is so anxious to distinguish himself:

> Na, Eduard, du bist auch mit einer von meinen Jägern gewesen, wenn auch keiner von den allerschlimmsten: (82-3)
> Den biederen Buren Klaas Baster wirst du wahrscheinlich allmählich auch gefunden haben und ihn in sentimentalen afrikanischen Stimmungen an den Busen schließen; aber den biederen Heinrich Schaumann hast du jenerzeit auch nicht gefunden, sondern ihn nur mit den übrigen von uns als Stopfkuchen unter der Hecke belassen (116).
> Hast du nicht mit den Wölfen geheult, so hast du mit den Eseln geiahet, und jedenfalls bist auch du mit den andern gelaufen und hast Stopfkuchen mit seiner unverstandenen Seele gleichwie mit einem auf die gute Seite gefallenen Butterbrot auf der Haustürtreppe, auf der faulen Bank in der Schule und am Feldrain vor der Roten Schanze sitzenlassen (66).

The passages warrant quoting at length because they contain the motifs which mark Schaumann's alternative reality definition and its challenge to Eduard. The recurrent phrase "unter der Hecke liegen" and the Rote Schanze, the property which Schaumann inherited from Quakatz, are generally regarded as symbolic elements of prime significance in the novel.[24] Stopfkuchen's nickname derives from his prodigious appetite which was coupled even in his earliest childhood with a propensity to avoid physical exertion. He refers to himself as "immer etwas schwach, nicht nur von den Begriffen, sondern auch auf den Füßen" (637). In school he had been an unsuccessful pupil, scorned by the insensitive teacher Blechhammer, and his studies came to an abrupt end when he returned to his hometown and followed the assessment offered him in the pub "Goldener Arm" that his actual goal through all the years had been the Rote Schanze (135-6). The passage alluding to Schopenhauer (117) opposes his mode of perception ("aus der Anschauung") to the orientation towards concepts ("Begriff") of his social environment. Stopfkuchen's isolation "unter der Hecke" signifies his refusal to conform, his avowal of his own self as his life's ideal (82). At the same time, it directly negates the bases of Eduard's self-identity. Schaumann characterizes himself as a "Hinhocker" in comparison to Eduard as "Weltwanderer" (61). The adage painted over Schaumann's house door astounds Eduard, as it seems hardly applicable to Stopfkuchen, "dieser behaglichste aller Lehnstuhlmenschen" (75). The motto reads:

Da redete Gott mit Noah und sprach: Gehe aus dem Kasten (75).

Schaumann later coins the phrase "Herdenkasten" (96), and the position of his Rote Schanze in relationship to the town and its inhabitants signifies the manner in which his mode of sedentary existence with its philistine accouterments of pipe and "gutbürgerliche Küche" has brought him farther from the mediocrity of the townspeople than Eduard's South African adventure. The middle section of the novel is occupied by Stopfkuchen's account of his conquest of the Rote Schanze, his goal since earliest childhood. Once the object of scorn and abuse at the hands of the townspeople as Quakatz and his daughter were social pariahs, the Rote Schanze under Stopfkuchen's rule reassumes the position which had defined its earlier history, when Prince Xaver of Saxony used its dominant location to bombard the town during the Seven Years' War. Schaumann reconstructs and rehabilitates both property and owner, and his paleontological studies, initiated through the discovery of a remarkable fossil, earn him acclaim and respect. His wedding banquet is a subtle form of revenge on the solid burghers of the town, as they all flock to a feast of reconciliation with the man they reviled for so long as Kienbaum's murderer. Yet it would be an overly superficial reading to designate the wedding as solely a human gesture of reconciliation.[25] Schaumann compares it to washing one's spear in the entrails of the enemy (142-3). He also decidedly includes Eduard in his category of the adversary:

Du bist auch so einer von denen, die sich stündlich gratulieren, daß sie nicht der Mörderbauer von der Roten Schanze oder Heinrich Schaumann sind.
Da verkennst mich aber riesig, Heinrich.
Gar nicht, Eduard; ich kenne euch nur. − Alle kenne ich euch, in- und auswendig (28).

The undermining of Eduard's sense of self and his relation to his social environment by the protagonist in his sea-narrative extends beyond Schaumann's refusal to recognize Eduard's distinction between himself and the other townspeople. Schaumann's question in conversation with his South African visitor echoes the initial question of Eduard's journal: "Woher stammen im Grunde des Menschen Schicksale, Eduard?" His answer is: "Gewöhnlich, wenn nicht immer aus *einem* Punkte" (62; original emphasis), and he sets up an equation of Eduard and Störzer with himself and the Rote Schanze:

> Du läufst mit Störzern, Eduard, und ich liege vor der Roten Schanze — jeder nach seinem Geschmack (28).
> Dich, lieber Eduard, haben Störzer und M. Le Vaillant nach dem heißen Afrika gebracht, und mich haben meine schwachen Verstandeskräfte und noch schwächeren Füße im kühlen Schatten von Quakatzenhof festgehalten. Eduard, das Schicksal benutzt meistens doch unsere schwachen Punkte, um uns auf das uns Dienliche aufmerksam zu machen" (62-3).

The apparent equality of all members of the equation Eduard : Störzer = Schaumann : Rote Schanze wanes with the exposure by Stopfkuchen of the figure of Störzer. The extended narrative account by Schaumann of his conquest of the Rote Schanze is followed by the stroll into the town and the seemingly casual revelation that Störzer had been the murderer of Kienbaum. The extent of Störzer's connection to Eduard's social identity is especially evident in the narrator's initial designation of the faithful and diligent postman as "verantwortlich" for his present South African existence (7) and in a parallelization within his nocturnal musings before he visits Schaumann: "ich lag im Bett in den Heiligen Drei Königen als Gatte, Vater, Grundbesitzer und großer Schafzüchter am Oranjefluß und lief zu gleicher Zeit mit dem Landbriefträger Störzer als zwölfjähriger Schuljunge" (25). Berger and Luckmann analyze social integration at an individual level as consisting of the performance of discrete, individual actions as part of a perceived, subjectively meaningful universe whose meanings are socially articulated and shared, and the analysis is an appropriate description of the significance of Störzer within the novel.[26] Not only is he a model civil servant whose daily path of duty carried him the equivalent of five tracings of the earth's circumference, but there is no better profession to signify recurrent, quotidian patterns of reality than a postman. Stopfkuchen's exposure of the erratic conduct of the paragon of reliable social responsibility erodes Eduard's perception of reality and is a main factor in the disorientation of the narrator. As they leave Störzer's house after Schaumann has indicated at Störzer's coffin that the postman "killed cock robin," Eduard suffers a "Betäubung durch einen halben Welteinsturz" (164).[27]

Yet the catastrophe is not irreparable, and the disorientation results neither in Eduard's abdication of narrative authority nor in his repudiation of his definition of his social environment and his position within it. Schaumann's manipulation of Eduard and his usurpation of the narrative voice for a great portion of *Stopfkuchen* emphasize the ambivalence and conflict within the field of reference of the text. A closer examination of the dynamics of narration reveals the elasticity of the narrator and his strategies of recuperation.

The studies of Raabe's novel which grant Stopfkuchen a totally positive evaluation seem to adhere to Dubslav von Stechlin's dictum "Wer am meisten red't, ist der reinste Mensch."[28] Eduard warns the reader early in the text about the protagonist's garrulousness: "Er wird sehr häufig auf diesen Blättern das Wort haben" (11), and the prediction proves correct. Eduard designates the owner of the Rote Schanze as a "Selbstredner" who answers his own questions (62), and he asserts, "Es war gegen den Menschen nicht anzuerzählen" (115). Fairley has proposed an alternative subtitle for the novel which reflects the domination of the title figure: "Stopfkuchen, and how he talked the others down,"[29] and Guardini's early essay on the work suggested that the reaction of most readers is initial discomfiture and eventual resignation and submission to Schaumann's monologue, leaving the reader in a parallel position to Eduard and Valentine.[30]

Stopfkuchen himself points to the connection between his character and his manner of discourse: "Ich bin ein wenig breit — auch in meiner schöne-Geschichten-Erzählungsweise" (183). The inertia of the lethargic owner of the Rote Schanze includes his ability to dominate his partners in conversation and discussion through his unshakeable adherence to his own agenda. In the case of his wife Tine, it is a domination which has transformed the angry daughter of Quakatz into a calm, good-humored matron. Stopfkuchen's interaction with Eduard is a more ambivalent manipulation, and it is difficult to agree with Meyer's assessment that Schaumann's delay in revealing the truth about Kienbaum's murderer is a positive pedagogical tactic to inculcate in Tine and Eduard a sense of the priority of human values.[31] His refusal to allow his wife to accompany them into the town on an errand of importance to her as the daughter of Quakatz, whose name is finally to be cleared of guilt, emphasizes his orientation toward Eduard more as an adversary than as a pupil to be enlightened. He cleverly chooses a specific path into town along the wall of the Rote Schanze. Eduard is uncertain as to the reason for his chosen route (157), but it occurs to him that they could stop by Störzer's house, which is right on their way, and pay final respects to the guide of his youth (158-9). Stopfkuchen's response: "Wenn du meinst? ... Ich bin ganz zu deiner Verfügung," is highly ironic, as it is clear to the reader by the end of the narrative that his choice of a route into town was hardly coincidental. His revelatory gesture and brief statement at Störzer's coffin (162) and the ensuing extended tale in the Goldener Arm are calculated and effective. Schaumann trivializes his revelation to Eduard: "da habe ich dem guten alten Kerl doch noch eine nette Erinnerung an die alte gemütliche Heimat mit aufs Schiff gegeben" (167). The narrative itself, Eduard's thirty-day attempt to come to grips with the encounter with his childhood comrade, belies the purported unimportance of the incident.

Schaumann's manipulation of his environment is evident as well in his technique of detection of Kienbaum's murderer. It was certainly his astute powers of observation as "Schau-mann," congruent with his principles of the primacy of "Anschauung" over "Begriff" which led him to notice that Störzer failed to assist in the burial rituals for Quakatz, but it was his "assistance" to the pastor in formulating the eulogy which set up the opportunity. In relating the incident to Eduard, Schaumann's transposition of pronouns is significant: "Ich räusperte mich – nein, er räusperte sich und sprach: 'Nun sieh mal, christliche Gemeinde, da liegt er – mausetot!' " (171). Eisele's analysis of the novel designates Heinrich Schaumann as a "Diskurs-Täter,"[32] and the denomination is appropriate for the manner in which Stopfkuchen refuses to be deflected from his own line of discourse. Even when he grants his wife the opportunity to relate a portion of his conquest of the Rote Schanze (103 ff), he interrupts, corrects, and takes credit for her very words.* It is an inertia which overwhelms the listeners and commands the reader for a great portion of Eduard's sea-journal and Raabe's narrative.

As he embarks upon his diliatory narrative before completing the story of Kienbaum's murder, Stopfkuchen suggests that his audience of Tine and Eduard will have to evaluate his tactics of narration for themselves:

> Also bleiben wir noch ein wenig in der Idylle, ehe wir von Kienbaum, und wie er zu Tode kam, weiterreden. Nachher magst du ja selber beurteilen, ob du deine, seine, oder meine Geschichte für die wichtigere hältst (96).

At the end of Raabe's novel, the reader must resolve the same issue, and it is not entirely clear that Stopfkuchen prevails. If inertia can designate the single-minded sluggishness of Heinrich Schaumann and his emblem of the giant sloth, it is applicable as well to the uniform, repetitive motion of the narrator Eduard's existence. Following the devastating revelation and detailed account by Schaumann, Eduard's decision is to return as rapidly as possible to South Africa. He reports the self-reflection leading to the decision:

> Wie wäre es denn, wenn du den Kopf aus der Geschichte zögest, Eduard und dein Teil daran sofort mit auf das Schiff nähmest?
> Mit *dem* Wort oder vielmehr Gedanken stand ich bereits nicht mehr auf dem festen Boden des Vaterlandes, ich stand wieder auf meinen Seebeinen, auf den beweglichen Planken über dem großen Gewoge des Ozeans, und es blies mir ein sehr erfrischender Meerwind ins Gesicht (200).

Eduard's strategies of recuperation include the recovery of his "sea-legs" and the reestablishment of the equation Eduard : Störzer = Stopfkuchen : Rote Schanze. In his nocturnal musings following Schaumann's revelation, he appropriates Stopfkuchen's phrase and refers to himself as being "unter *meiner* Hecke" (196; original empha-

---

*   Das Wort traktieren hat sie von mir, Eduard (112). Das Wort Geschmack hat sie von mir, Eduard (112). Genügsamkeit hat sie von mir (112).

sis). He gradually equates himself with his former schoolmate: "So wahrscheinlich bald nach Mitternacht hatte ich mich ganz in des Dicken Stelle, das heißt seine Haut versetzt" (197). The motive that he imputes to Stopfkuchen for the day's events is the desire to demonstrate, "daß man auch von der Roten Schanze aus aller Philisterweltanschauung den Fuß auf den Kopf setzen kann" (197). The adverb "auch" indicates that Eduard has retained the claim for himself as well, and the recuperation is evident in his parting thoughts upon settling into his railroad coupé:

> Ja, im Grunde läuft es doch auf ein und dasselbe hinaus, ob man unter der Hecke liegenbleibt und das Abenteuer der Welt an sich herankommen läßt oder ob man sich von seinem guten Freunde Fritz Störzer und dessen altem Le Vaillant und Johann Reinhold Forster hinausschicken läßt, um es draussen auf den Wassern und in den Wüsten aufzusuchen! (204).

Under the rubric of the "Satz vom zureichenden Grunde" (197), Eduard manages to develop adequate defenses to incorporate the events and revelations of his visit home into his existing reality paradigm.[33] A main tactic is the valorization of Valentine Schaumann, geb. Quakatz who occupies his thoughts more than her husband or Kienbaum and Störzer (197). She and the Rote Schanze become the "Grund" for Schaumann's behavior, and it is a basis of family and property with which Eduard can identify. Throughout his sea-journal he emphasizes Tine, actually taking her hand at one point (130). Even as he assumes Stopfkuchen's "Leibesumfang" in his thoughts (197), he assimilates the aberrant figure to his own existence, and the phrase "unter *meiner* Hecke" refers to his bed in the hotel, the same bed where he had lain as "Gatte, Vater, Grundbesitzer" (25) before the encounter with Stopfkuchen. Heinrich Schaumann as "Gatte" and "Grundbesitzer" is within the realm of Eduard's comprehension, and the inertia of his narrative is the orientation toward that identity.

Yet Eduard's standpoint is not the sole narrative perspective within the complex communicative structure of Raabe's text. *Stopfkuchen* is dominated by the title figure for a great portion of the work, and Valentine Schaumann and Störzer himself take over the narrative voice at specific points. Eduard's recuperation at the end of his sea-journal may be observed by a reader without being shared. Raabe's novel raises more questions than it answers, and the pattern of disorientation includes particular textual strategies as well as a basic undermining of the narrator by the process of narration. The manner in which specific narrative elements are introduced and expanded is a main example. In the opening pages of the text, mention is made of certain items before it is clear to the reader what the referent is. An explanation eventually follows, and the items become structuring elements for sections of the narrative, but their position and value within the text shift, leaving the reader without reliable points of reference.

"Brummersumm" appears in the second segment of the novel as a position of orientation within the narrated action. Following the initial establishment of the narrator's credentials, the scene is set as "auf dem Heimwege von Brummersumm" (8-9). The reader has to figure out what is meant by the name, and the probable surmise is affirmed by the explicit naming at the beginning of the third narrative segment of the "Krug zum Brummersumm" (12). A substantial passage of description and elucidation of the meaning of this particular *Kneipe* for the narrator follows. Yet an ambivalence characterizes the remarks made about the "deutscher Spießbürger in seiner Kneipe" (12), and it is the ambivalence of the narrative itself. Similarly, the significant name and figure of Le Vaillant is first introduced in unrecognizable form, in Störzer's rendering of "Levalljang" (18). The second time it is mentioned, it is specified further as a book (19), and the full title and explanation follow only with the third reference (20-21). The subsequent course of the narrative works to empty the travelogue and the figure of the postman who so respected it of the clearly positive significance attached to them by the narrator at the outset.

The significance of individual narrative elements varies within the course of the story, and the necessary integration of elements within the field of reference of the text must be accomplished by the reader. There is a tension at all levels of the text, encompassing basic questions of narrative authority and individual textual strategies. Raabe's *Stopfkuchen* is a complex narrative, in which the standpoints of both the bourgeois narrator and the isolated aberrant figure are problematical.

Isolation, Integration, and Compromise:
Die Akten des Vogelsangs

The final novel in Raabe's Braunschweig trilogy well illustrates the dialectic reversal within German Realism postulated by Helmuth Widhammer, the shift from affirmative narrative to unflinching, often melancholy criticism.[34] Although *Stopfkuchen* has received more extensive critical attention, *Die Akten des Vogelsangs* provides a more radical scrutiny of the accepted patterns of quotidian reality valorized at one level of the text, and the reading experience is actually more complex than in the early work. The narrator's recuperation, the final inertia of Eduard in *Stopfkuchen,* is less convincing and yet more urgent in the later novel. Karl Krumhardt as narrator is specifically aware of the tenuous nature of his own carefully constructed existence, and his attempt to incorporate the challenge presented by the eccentric figure of Velten Andres forms the fabric of Raabe's narrative. Unable to dismiss the childhood friend and his increasingly incongruous behavior either as a pathetic or as a humorous aberration, Krumhardt's preoccupation with Andres is of a different variety than Eduard's sea-journal. In *Stopfkuchen,* it is the exposure of personal illusions which composes the narrative, and the title figure undercuts Eduard's complacency but is moderated by the ambivalence of his manipulative character and the humorous portrayal of the philistine traits of life in the Rote Schanze.

In *Die Akten des Vogelsangs,* the issues go much deeper than a personal tension between narrator and protagonist. There is a system of values at stake, and the communicative structure of the text emphasizes both the necessity and the contingency of Karl Krumhardt's mode of existence. As the unsuccessfully socialized individual, Velten Andres effectively hinders the desired legitimation of the existing social-institutional order. Berger and Luckmann have outlined the manner in which the paramount reality will attempt to integrate any deviant or problematic sector in order to reestablish the continuity of everyday routines, and it is such a process which forms a main focus of Raabe's novel.[35] In the narrative pattern characteristic of *Soll und Haben* and Auerbach's *Dorfgeschichte,* the deviant sector or finite province of meaning is ultimately reincorporated into the predominant system of values, which is reaffirmed by the story, the narrative voice, and the general pattern of reading. In Raabe's novel, such an integration is not achieved, and the thematic issues of continuity and change, community and individual identity, isolated self and the necessary compromise of bourgeois existence remain unresolved. Felix Wassermann has suggested that *Die Akten des Vogelsangs* retains a vitality for the modern reader,[36] and the potential realistic level of the text consists of the continued congruence, at least partial, between the field of reference actualized in reading the work and a modern reader's contextual, historical field of reference. The centrifugal force of Raabe's narrative, the incomplete coextension of individual and social role and the increasing disorientation of the narrator, mark *Die Akten des Vogelsangs* as a novel with critical concerns appropriate for the twentieth century as well. The narrative situation has been compared with that of Thomas Mann's *Dr. Faustus*,[37] although such an assessment must be amended to account for the more trenchant analysis of German society in the later work and for the diminished effectuality of the narrator's attempts to come to grips with his subject matter. Yet the final novel of Raabe's Braunschweig trilogy, in its thematic concerns and narrative structure, extends the parameters of German Realism into the realm of the modern novel.

Wassermann's essay on *Die Akten des Vogelsangs* establishes a discrepancy between the work and its initial context of reception, but there is actually a fundamental congruence between the pattern of social integration evident in the novel and the historical situation of the reception in the 1890s.[38] As I outlined in my initial chapter, by the end of the century growing pessimism regarding the compatibility of personal needs and social dictates was evident, and bureaucratic centralization and increasing rationalization restricted both the situation of the middle classes and the mobility of the individual. The reality paradigm composing the field of reference of Raabe's novel of 1896 is appropriate for the context of its appearance. The private sphere is no longer a determinant compositional unit within the social system but a defensive realm of escape. Retreat is evident both in the aberrant existence of Velten Andres and also in the ostensible security of Karl and Anna Krumhardt and their children.

Mutter Andres admonishes Karl: "Bleib du ruhig auf deinem Weg und halte die Welt aufrecht: nicht bloß hier im Vogelsang, sondern auch für den Vogelsang" (312). Yet the circle of family, the carefully circumscribed identity of Oberregierungsrat Dr. jur. K. Krumhardt, is rather a realm of retreat. It stands as a refuge from the pressures of Karl's professional responsibilities, as Anna contrasts her husband's work with the family (215). And the presuppositions underlying it are threatened in the course of Krumhardt's narrative, revealing the precarious position of the personal sphere. Anna Krumhardt's initial reaction to the letter bearing the news of Velten's death is to withdraw into the security of family:

> Ich für meinen Teil werde morgen diesen unheimlichen Brief bei hellem Tageslicht lesen. Jetzt ist er mir wie ein Stein auf den Kopf gefallen, und ich gehe zu den Kindern. Die Mädchen sind eben aus dem Theater nach Hause gekommen. Das ist in diesem Augenblick meine einzige Rettung nach dieser Lektüre ... Der Himmel bewahre sie uns vor zu viel Einbildungskraft und erhalte ihnen einen klaren Kopf und ein ruhiges Herz (216).

The family, specifically the leitmotif of the children, functions within the narrative as a defense against the excesses of Velten Andres' challenge. Anna stresses the centrality of "unser geregeltes Dasein und unsere Kinder" (220) and resolves to prevent their possible development in the direction of her husband's childhood friends Velten Andres and Helene Trotzendorff. Karl Krumhardt finds the transition between his idyllic home and his friend's unconditional destruction of all earthly possessions a jarring one:

> ein anderer Übergang aus meinem ruhigen, behaglichen Heim, von dem Kamin, wo mein Weib mit ihrem Kindchen an der Brust auf niedrigem Schemel leise ihr Wiegenlied sang, zu dem Ofen im Vogelsang, vor dem der wunderliche Freund sich frei machte – (300).

The final page of the novel belongs to "Das Haus, die Frau und die Kinder" (408), to the fragile recuperation of the narrator.

Velten Andres' mode of existence, however, not only represents a challenge to the Krumhardt's "geregeltes Dasein" but is itself an escape from the exigencies of the surrounding society. If Andres were merely an exception to the novel's system of values, Helmer's assessment of a bipolar structure would be appropriate.[39] But just as both the narrator's private realm and the protagonist's chosen manner of life represent a certain retreat from the pressures of the society they inhabit, so also are both part of the basic bourgeois ideology of individualism which became ever more problematic in the latter half of the nineteenth century and has remained so into our own era.[40] For Anton Wohlfart and the characters in Auerbach's village tales, self-realization is compatible with integration into established social patterns, and the resultant assimilation is mutually beneficial for society and individual. The constraint of social roles which is evident in Fontane's novels recurs in Velten Andres' refusal to assume a role dictated to him by society. The opportunities opened to him after his rescue of a fellow pupil belonging to the upper social strata bear no productive results, and Andres persists in referring to himself as a vagabond and wanderer (326), a tramp and a "Landstreicher" (328), one outside of established social categories. Krumhardt says of Velten that he inhabited his own world, "die nur sehr selten mit der – unsrigen übereinstimmte" (294), and that he was "ein Herr in einem Reich, das leider auch nicht sehr von dieser Welt war" (261). Yet his consistent refusal to become anyone other than himself, to integrate himself into a society whose presuppositions he does not share is within the tradition which Born describes for mid-century German society as middle-class individualism and self-determination.[41] It is this tradition and this era which are approaching an end in the 1890s. Velten's failure, or the hollowness of a victory synonymous with acquiescent denial, calls into question the compromises made by those around him. Karl Krumhardt's attempt to defuse the potentially disruptive influence of Velten's existence for his own carefully nutured reality is indicated in his insistence upon the orderly, objective form of documentation for his narrative. Appropriately for a doctor of jurisprudence, Krumhardt refers to his account as "die Akten," and the terminology alone expresses the desire to integrate the deviant or problematic sector into established, quotidian categories. Velten Andres is not simply the outsider in a bipolar constellation of opposition but a challenge from within to the system of values which emphasizes the integration of individual development and social continuity.

"Die Akten" and "die Kinder" are recurrent elements in Raabe's text, and their function within the narrative is an example of the communicative structure of the work. As in *Stopfkuchen,* the position and value of specific narrative elements shift in the course of the novel, leaving the reader to mediate and draw conclusions. In the segment of the narration recounting the death of the old neighbor Hartleben, his own parents' move to Berlin and their subsequent death, Krumhardt interposes a strange reflective passage comparing life to a play in which the actors on stage frequently cannot hear the director's signal for a change of scene (333). Suddenly, and without consternation, they find themselves in a different setting, and only seldom does anyone stop to realize and question what is happening. The lack of conscious perception is characterized as "ein schweres Eintrittsgeld, das man für die Tragikomödie des Daseins zu erlegen hat" (334). The rare moments of reflection in "dem ewig wechselnden und ewig gleichen Schauspiel" are eerily uncomfortable: "Wie aus einem unbekannten schauerlichen Draußen haucht das vor den Theaterlichtern einen fremd und kalt an" (334). The passage is a self-characterization of the process of narration for Karl Krumhardt and of the pattern of reading of Raabe's text.[42] The recurrent narrative elements in *Die Akten des Vogelsangs* are more specifically organized and interconnected than in *Stopfkuchen,* and the central component common to all of them is a sense of relationship. As an abstract concept, relationship is a question of form, of the connection between two or more items. The issue of orientation which is of vital concern for narrator and reader in Raabe's Braunschweig trilogy entails the task of establishing and maintaining perceptible relationships among narrative elements, and the recurrent concepts of *Akten, Nachbarschaft, Kinder,* and *Eigentum* circumscribe the complex field of reference in the final novel of the series.

Krumhardt's attempt to document the existence of his childhood friend Velten Andres, to relate to it on his own terms by compiling *Akten,* is the endeavor of a self-conscious narrator to distance himself from the material he is recounting. The narrative technique in *Die Akten des Vogelsangs* is a concatenation of reminiscence and reflection, in the course of which the narrator is forced to relinquish his assumed stance of objectivity and to admit his acute involvement with the narrated material. Krumhardt establishes himself at the outset as the recorder of documents in the case of Helene Trotzendorff and Velten Andres and consistently emphasizes such a role through the terms *Akten* and *aktenmäßig*. However, beginning with the twelfth narrative segment (261), a gradual shift becomes apparent. The first sentence of the section, which immediately follows the significant episode of the shooting stars, uses only the pronoun "er." There is no doubt as to who is meant, and from this point on, the narration becomes Velten's story. The remaining two-thirds of the novel consist of Krumhardt's attempts to come to grips with Velten. In an allusion to Lessing, Krumhardt asserts at one point that he is writing Velten's story because he "kann nicht länger mit ihm unter einem Dach wohnen" (358). He finds himself losing his self-composed, business-like style of writing as he works on the Vogelsang "case." The piles of documents on his desk, i.e., his carefully constructed identity as a jurist, threaten to cave in on him (270), and the originally postulated objective case of Andres vs. Trotzendorff becomes Velten's "Prozeß gegen meine, gegen *unsere* Welt" (295). The documentary form fails to achieve the orderly relationship to his subject matter which Krumhardt seeks. And *Akten* and *aktenmäßig*, originally introduced as positive terms of orientation for both narrator and reader, gradually lose their function as the means to achieve clarity and order.

A second motif or recurrent narrative element which is established as a supposedly fixed unit of orientation and then undercut is *Nachbarschaft*. The term is introduced early in the novel as an ideal which is rapidly becoming extinct. The passage of time not only brings outward changes, such as the replacement of Hartleben's garden with a canned-goods factory or the reduction of the once green and pleasant suburb of Vogelsang to the token hedge of the stubborn Frau Andres, but also the disappearance of certain values. *Nachbarschaft* is strongly connected by Krumhardt to "*unserer* Zeit, als die Stadt noch nicht das 'erste Hunderttausend' überschritten hatte" (219, original emphasis). Krumhardt describes for the reader the surface tensions and quarrels in the Vogelsang community, but he staunchly defends the existence of *Nachbarschaft* as a positive element in his past. Yet the recurrent theme is a contributing factor to the relativization of values in the text, as the past ideal is itself exposed as questionable. There is a subtle undermining of the myth of the past idyllic community, and the more comprehensive pattern of reading reveals deeper tensions within the values which the narrator assumes to be shared by himself and the reader. The fourth narrative segment begins with the exclamation "Die Nachbarschaft!" and speaks proudly of "Unsereinem, der noch eine Nachbarschaft hatte" (218). In this section Krumhardt introduces the families composing the Vogelsang community. The ideal of *Nachbarschaft* is, however, relativized by the unconscious hierarchy of residency which he sets up, based on inheritance (his family), purchase (Andres), and "Mietwohnung" (Trotzendorff). Krumhardt's unreflected adherence to the hierarchy contributes to his status as an unreliable narrator and undercuts his defense of *Nachbarschaft* as the harmonious past existence. The basic thematic structure of the tension between the preservation of certain values and the threat to them is augmented by the relativization of past idylls and values. For the reader, the effect is similar to that of the *Akten* motif: the shift in reliability of a recurrent narrative element.

The motif of *Nachbarschaft* is connected to the issue of the old and the new, of temporality and the costs of progress. The Vogelsang suburb, where the birds actually sang (219, 240), falls victim to industrialization. The "Hungerwinkel" grows up, and the green areas are limited to the cemetery, of which Krumhardt sadly but realistically states: "wo wir, meine Kinder, mein Weib und ich, wo Velten Andres und Helene Trotzendorff nicht ihre Ruhestätten ... finden werden" (240). A further, related motif of *Kinder* is struck here, and it is equally fraught with issues of temporality, continuity, and relationship. The motif of children also fluctuates within the novel. The portrayal of the narrative present begins and ends with an emphasis on Krumhardt's children, on his family as continuity and reassurance. Initially Krumhardt says to his wife Anna of the letter with the news of Velten's death: "Dich und deine Kinder geht es nur recht mittelbar was an" (215). Later, however, they are not only a separate sphere but a bulwark in Krumhardt's struggle to validate his existence: "Was aber würde erst sein, wenn ich auch nicht mein liebstes Weib, meine lieben Kinder gegen diesen 'verlorengegangenen', diesen — besitzlosen Menschen mir zu Hülfe rufen könnte? —" (295). By the end of the novel, the implications of Velten Andres' challenge for his children have become clear to the narrator. After almost losing his son to typhoid fever, Krumhardt resumes his chronicle on his son's account (385).[43] In the final pages, Helene Trotzendorff Mungo urges that he write up the story for his children and store it in his house archives, albeit somewhat removed from his personal family papers (403-4). Krumhardt's response indicates his awareness of the relationship between the ostensibly distanced chronicle and his own family history:

> Diese Blätter beweisen es, daß ich — diesmal ein wenn auch treuer, doch wunderlicher Protokollführer — nach ihrem Willen getan habe, doch abseits von meinen und der Meinigen Lebensdokumenten werden sie nicht zu liegen kommen. Die Akten des Vogelsangs bilden ein Ganzes, von dem ich und mein Haus ebensowenig zu trennen sind wie die eiserne Bettstelle bei der Frau Fechtmeisterin Feucht und die Reichtümer der armen Mistreß Mungo (404).

The fluctuation in the function of *Kinder* within the text, from separate sphere to integral component, focuses the reader's attention on the extended theme of children, parents, and the necessity and hazards of adequate and protective parenting. The entire novel could be read as depicting the interrelated paths of three childhood friends who grew up with various degrees of parental presence, and the divergence is reflected in their respective wishes as children upon the shooting stars and in the paths their lives take. Karl Krumhardt's father was, with the exception of the disciplinary efforts of neighbor Hartleben, the only stern male father figure in the Vogelsang community, and his portrait still hangs above the narrator's desk (217). For Krumhardt's father, basic values were self-evident, and his speech is correspondingly marked by tautology: "hier in meinen vier Pfählen bleibt Verstand Verstand, Sinn Sinn, Unsinn Unsinn und Schund Schund" (244). Karl's fascination with Velten, which even assumes the form of envy of the other (295), reveals the degree to which his father's stable perspective on the world has become less certain in the transmission. The question is left open whether even the most careful parenting can ensure continuity and transmission of values.

The other two children from the Vogelsang, Helene Trotzendorff and Velten Andres, lacked the stern paternal discipline, and the significant episode of the wishes made by the three friends on shooting stars illustrates the differences. In a scene dominated by Velten, each of the three utters a characteristic wish which is later attained. But the manner of later fulfillment is undercut in such a way as to relativize the basis of each individual existence. Helene's wish, "daß es für mich wieder so wird, wie ich es drüben gehabt habe in Amerika als Kind" (259), is bountifully fulfilled in her luxurious life as Mistress Mungo. Yet in her letter to Krumhardt she can only refer to herself as "Die wilde Törin" and announce her intention to become Velten's "Erbnehmerin" in an existance diametrically opposed to her own (213-14).[44] Velten's wish is more complex, and in living out the existence implied in it, he not only exposes the untenable aspect of that existence but also calls into question the compromises made by those around him:

"Dem seligen Diogenes seine Tonne wünsche ich mir," lachte Velten Andres. "Den Heckepfennig, den Däumling und das Tellertuch des Rolandsknappen, den Knüppel-aus-dem-Sack, das Vergnügen, Persepolis in Brand zu stecken, und ein friedliches Ende auf Salas und Gomez" (260-1).

Velten attains the desired elements, from the fairy-tale existence of varied identities and occupations to the asceticism of Diogenes, the victorious autodafé and the isolated death.[45] As in the episode of the dramatization of Cornelius Nepos' biography of Alcibiades which almost sets Hartleben's garden on fire (223 ff), Velten Andres takes his literary and historical allusions seriously. But the self-destructive manner in which he attains his wishes undercuts greatly the admirable consistency of his achievement.

Krumhardt's wish is the most prosaic, and I would designate his comfortable existence with a secure profession and home as the extended fulfillment of his childhood wish for success in his exams (259). Nevertheless, the reader witnesses in his narration the questioning of that complacency. Velten's systematic destruction of all his belongings after his mother's death has been described as the point in the novel where Krumhardt's fascination changes to a sense of being threatened by his friend's mode of existence.[46] Krumhardt watches Velten use the household inherited from his mother as fuel through an entire winter and even assists him in the process (372-3). Velten speaks of an immense fatigue, and Krumhardt finds himself unable to defend his own "Besitzfreudigkeit" against the "*Eigentumsmüdigkeit*" with which he is confronted (375, original emphasis).

Eigentum is also a recurrent narrative element, particularly in the second half of the novel as the issues of continuity and security become ever more problematic. Hartleben first uses the word to describe what the sale of his property means to him (316). He compares his loss with Mutter Andres' emotions as Velten departs for America, thereby connecting the questions of *Eigentum* and parenting. The narrator and Anna use the term for each other (343, 348, 384), and it is also applied to their first child (345, 347, 383). In reference to the children of Leon des Beaux it designates their severance from the family tradition: "das Eigentum ihrer Vorfahren väterlicher Seite hat kaum noch Bedeutung für sie" (386). *Eigentum* refers to more than material property; it carries the sense of "ownness," of standing in relation to someone or something.[47] It is in this sense that Helene Trotzendorff, the materially wealthy Widow Mungo, proclaims at the end of the novel that her only *Eigentum* is the memory of her final moments with Velten (405). It is the same sense of relating to external elements that Velten seeks to negate in deliberately ridding himself of all possessions. Krumhardt comprehends the motivation of Velten's attempt to free himself, "nicht von den Sachen, sondern von dem, was in der Menschen Seele sich den Sachen anhängt" (370). Andres wishes to die "vollkommen ernüchtert. So eigentumslos wie möglich" (351). In his quest to retain Helene by travelling to America, Velten had experienced the fragility of the tie which he had thought to be so strong. He returns to free himself in order to negate the most vulnerable *Eigentum* which he possesses: "ein leicht bewegtes Herz."

While at the Trotzendorffs in America, Velten is struck by four lines from an ode by Goethe to Behrisch, and the verse is an important motif in the final section of the novel. Velten's attempt to divest himself of all *Eigentum* includes a desire to become emotionless as well as propertyless. The lines from Goethe serve as a guide, and once again Velten Andres takes his literature seriously:

159

Sei gefühllos!
Ein leicht bewegtes Herz
Ist ein elend Gut
Auf der wankenden Erde (352).

The function of the motif has been excellently analyzed by Joachim Müller, who outlines the structural and thematic functions.[48] Velten's attempt to orient himself on a literal reading of Goethe is decidedly unsuccessful. Nevertheless, his efforts are unsettling to Karl Krumhardt's sense of the security of his own life and family. Müller juxtaposes "wankende Erde" with another line in which Velten speaks of heating through the winter "mit meinem hiesigen Eigentum an der wohlgegründeten Erde" (371), i.e., with the inheritance which to the community represents stability and a bourgeois identity. The stability ("wohlgegründet" versus "wankend") is a matter of perspective, and Velten's perception of the instability relativizes the perceived stability of the established society. The interpretation emphasizes the manner in which Velten Andres represents a challenge to the priorities and values which Krumhardt defends. In his final farewell to Helene Mungo, Krumhardt characterizes the world with Velten's term of "wankend" (404) and then finds himself unwilling or unable to visit Leon des Beaux in his family idyll. After the reencounter with Velten Andres, this idyll, so close to his own existence, is no longer beyond all question: "Es war mir wirklich unmöglich, seinem Lebensbehagen jetzt die rechte Teilnahme entgegenzubringen" (407).

Although the stability of Krumhardt's complacent existence is undermined by Velten Andres, I still would not designate the latter as the positive, critical pole. In keeping with the manner in which all positions and elements in the novel are continually shifting, his position is undercut as well. The most striking illustration is in the scene depicting the culmination of Velten's destruction of all material possessions in the plundering by invitation of the remnants of his household by the community. After the long winter of burning most of his mother's possessions as heating fuel, he now dispenses the rest among neighbors and passers-by. The grotesque aspect of such a frenzied disavowal of all *Eigentum* and the ultimate negativity of the calculated endeavor to diminish the risks of any relationship "auf der wankenden Erde" are emphasized by the presence of the member of the "Théâtre-Variété," the local freak show. Among them is German Fell, the missing link or "Affenmensch." As he leaves, he salutes Velten as a comrade who has also climbed too high and become inextricably entangled in the tree of life, from which neither of them would ever again return to "bürgerlich festen Boden" (381).[49] The image and motif of "verklettern" are connected to an early childhood episode in which Helene Trotzendorff climbs beyond her abilities, and Velten is unable to rescue her. In recounting the episode to Leon des Beaux, he states, "diesen Baum und, was dran hing und hängt, werde ich bei keiner Lebens-, Haupt- und Staatsaktion mehr los: es ist das erstemal gewesen, daß ich des Menschen Unzulänglichkeit auf dieser Erde auch an mir in Erfahrung gebracht habe" (300). On the afternoon where he has ostensibly completed his self-emancipation from such inadequacy by ridding himself of all *Eigentum,* of all relationships of "ownness," the statement of German Fell serves to emphasize the futility of that effort. A distorted reflection of Velten's existence on the fringe of society, the "Affenmensch" foreshadows the necessary decline of Velten's existence from that day on when he wishes him "einen recht guten Abend, und nicht bloß für den heutigen Tag" (381).

For Karl Krumhardt, Velten's course of action following his mother's death is a decided challenge to the Krumhardt's security of home and family, and the recurrent memory is troubling:

> jedesmal waren dann meine vier sicheren Wände drohend, beängstigend auf mich eingerückt, es war mir bänglich und asthmatisch zumute geworden, ich traute auch dem zierlichen Stuck des Plafonds nicht, ich fühlte mich dann jedesmal recht unbehaglich in meinen vier Pfahlen und im Erdenleben überhaupt (366).

The figure of Velten Andres relativizes the perceived stability of the established social reality and the Krumhardts' integrated position within it. Velten's position proves to be untenable, while Krumhardt's defense tends to be uninspiring and not entirely convincing. In his study of reminiscence as a narrative technique in Raabe's works, Pascal concludes that there is no real danger for Karl Krumhardt's existence.[50] The assertion may be partially valid, as the novel gives Anna and the children the final word. Yet the point is that their mode of existence has been called into question, that the narrator and his wife are aware of the fragility and the price paid for complacency. In the final analysis, there is no invariable, totally justified perspective represented within the text. The communicative structure and the interwoven themes of the novel destabilize all representations of endurance.[51] For the reader, both the isolation of Velten and the integrated existence of the Krumhardts are undercut. The necessity of Karl's compromise is underscored by the untenability of Velten's solution. Yet the lack of comprehension and the lack of a social identity for Andres indicate the only partial validity of a society which excludes him. There is definitely the sense of a necessary continuity, of a durability rooted in the Karl and Anna Krumhardts. Near the end, Krumhardt states the fact expressly, but not without a certain, sad irony: "Der Menschheit Dasein auf der Erde baut sich immer von neuem auf, doch nicht von dem äußersten Umkreis her, sondern stets aus der Mitte. In unserem deutschen Volke weiß man das auch eigentlich im Grunde gar nicht anders" (404). The course of his *Akten,* the narrative attempt to come to grips with such a necessary insight, suggests strongly that the regenerative durability, the continuity "aus der Mitte," is not without its price. For the reader, the tenuousness of even such modest continuity is emphasized through the communicative structure which subverts all elements of certain orientation.

With one exception, no figure in the novel retains a position not undercut at some level by the narrative itself. The unity of cherished tradition and prosaic, economically productive diligence represented in the coexistence of the "historischen Traumstübchen der Geschwister des Beaux" (290) with the successful tailoring enterprise is lost in the following generation.[52] Leon's children are severed from the family tradition.[53] Leonie's life as a *Diakonissin* relieves but does not alter the social ills of her age, and her ascetic, childless existence mirrors the peripheral quality. Even their childhood "Märchenwinkel" (287) was only the remembrance of the past, much the same as Krumhardt's conservation of the past idyll of *Nachbarschaft.* Similarly, Mutter Andres is a character built on illusions and the attempted preservation of the transient. She is characterized by her

"Sonnenlächeln," which is the result of her viewing the world as beautiful through an act of will (222-3). She preserves her share of the former *Nachbarschaft* by retaining her house and garden while apartments and factories spring up around her. She is, however, aware of her own illusions with the exception of her belief in Velten, which the Vogelsang community and the reader see all too clearly as self-deception.[54]

Only one figure remains in an unambivalent connection to *Eigentum,* and she is presented unequivocally within the narrative structure. When Karl Krumhardt returns to Berlin, he finds Velten's landlady unchanged and records: "Die Frau Fechtmeisterin Feucht allein von uns allen hatte ihr Eigentum noch vollständig beisammen" (391). Yet this amazing woman is ninety years old and represents the end of an epoch.[55] Her continuity can hardly reverse the ambivalent fragility otherwise so apparent but only emphasize its prevalence. In representing the close of an era, her figure underscores the transiency and the changes brought with time. And the era which is drawing to an end forms the system of values which is at stake. All three novels in the "Braunschweig Trilogy" focus on questions of continuity and tradition and the possibilities for individual development within a restrictive social environment. Such issues became increasingly complex in the nineteenth century, and the communicative structure of *Die Akten des Vogelsangs* embodies the tensions. The disorienting pattern of reading reinforces the thematic concerns, and the dual role afforded the reader manifests the degree to which Realist narrative had become problematic by the 1890s.

Eduard's recuperation in *Stopfkuchen,* his ability to transfer the character and challenge of Heinrich Schaumann into terms of his own reality definition and to assimilate the aberrant figure to his own existence, eludes Karl Krumhardt. Leon des Beaux manages to screen out portions of his childhood no longer congruent with his staid and settled adult identity, but for Krumhardt the presence of Velten Andres and the ambivalent challenge of the latter's isolation to his social identity as a well-established lawyer and family man cannot be so easily ignored. The reader is offered the role of participant in Krumhardt's identity and system of values. The pattern of reader involvement which aligns narrator and reader in regarding the aberrant figure is, however, counteracted. Yet the complementary pattern of reading the narrator's struggle to retain his bearings, the troubling disorientation of *Die Akten des Vogelsangs*, does not result in a refutation of Krumhardt's position. And it is the tension between the two patterns of reading which carries the import of the novel. The reader participates both in sharing the parameters of Krumhardt's situation and in challenging them. The communicative structure of Raabe's late novels is characterized by shifting narrative and temporal perspectives and by recurrent elements and motifs which are variable in significance. *Akten, Nachbarschaft, Kinder, Eigentum,* originally introduced as positive points of orientation for both narrator and reader, fluctuate. The property of relationship conveyed by each one becomes suspect, and the final assignment of weight accorded each is left to the reader. The motto for *Die Akten des Vogelsangs,* taken from the poem "An meinen alten Freund Peter Schlemihl" by Adalbert von Chamisso, well characterizes the pattern of narration in Raabe's Braunschweig novels:

> Die wir dem Schatten Wesen sonst verliehen
> Sehen Wesen jetzt als Schatten sich verziehen.
> Peter Schlemihl (212)

The obvious literary allusion is to Chamisso's novella *Peter Schlemihls wundersame Geschichte* (1814) with its related themes of existential and social identity. Chamisso's novella has elicited as many varying interpretations as Raabe's novel, and some of the disputed issues are similar. Beyond the literary-historical echoes, the lines reverberate at a crucial juncture in the novel as Krumhardt wrestles with the pervasive disorientation, "dem stolz-ruhigen Schatten gegenüber, der so wesenhaft Velten Andres in meinem Dasein hieß" (345). The motto thus depicts Krumhardt's difficulties in compiling his *Akten,* in maintaining his orientation.

The lines describe the difficulties of reading Krumhardt's account and Eduard's sea-journal as well. The orientation offered by the narrator loses its substantive reliability in the process of reading, and the communicative structure of *Stopfkuchen* and *Die Akten des Vogelsangs* is well characterized by the elusive fading away of substance to shadow. Raabe himself placed the motto in the context of his entire literary production in a letter to Paul Gerber of November 8, 1895: "Auf der Buchausgabe werden sie ein Wort aus dem Peter Schlemihl finden, welches vierzig Jahre nach der 'Chronik der Sperlingsgasse' nicht ohne Grund am Schlusse einer so langen litterarischen Lebensarbeit steht."[56] The forty years span not only Raabe's literary production, but also the eventful second half of the nineteenth century and the literary period we designate as Realism. In reading Raabe's late novels it is evident how complex Realist narrative had become. Krumhardt's and Eduard's representations of the reality they perceive can no longer be reaffirmed by the reader. In contrast to the univocality of *Soll und Haben* in 1855 or the earlier *Dorfgeschichten,* the lack of coincidence of narrative statement and narrated action, the elusive nature of specific concepts, and the mutual relativization of the various reality definitions contribute to a pattern of disorientation for both narrator and reader in Raabe's "Braunschweig Trilogy." The integration of the dominant reality structure, which is presupposed in Freytag and Auerbach and analyzed in Fontane, is revealed as increasingly fragile. Raabe's final novels convey a sense of the intricacy and contingency of both reality and its representation. Since the pattern of reading partially opposes the reality paradigm specifically valorized at one level of the text by the narrator, the works can retain a congruence with a reader's frame of ordinary experience nearly a century later. It is the writing and reading of Karl Krumhardt's *Akten* and Eduard's sea-journal, and not only their content, which constitutes the multifaceted Realism of Wilhelm Raabe.

V. THE EXTENDED PERSPECTIVE: REALISM AND READER EXPERIENCE

Specific analyses of a limited number of texts can hardly yield a sufficient basis for a conclusive typology of the prose fiction of nineteenth-century German Realism. Nevertheless, the three patterns of reader experience exemplified in works at mid-century by Berthold Auerbach and Gustav Freytag, in novels by Theodor Fontane, and in the late novels of Wilhelm Raabe illustrate three distinct modes of literary communication, and the implications of each, as well as the similarities and contrasts among them, contribute to the ongoing critical discussion of realist prose. In a survey of scholarship on German Realism, Ulf Eisele suggests that the entire question of realism in literature is a paradigm for the difficulty of establishing definitive concepts in literary history, as it is an area where it is almost impossible to avoid basic issues of the relationship of literature to external reality and questions of diachrony and synchrony.[1] Since the concern with reception aesthetics was originally an attempt to deal with such issues as well as to mediate between formalistic textual analysis and a consideration of the interaction between a literary work and its varying historical contexts, the theoretical orientation towards the reader as an integral component in the constitution of a literary work is a viable approach to questions of realism and narrative prose in the epoch designated as nineteenth-century German Realism. The necessary companion volume to the present study would be a reception history of the novels and stories considered, in order to complement the concentration on intrinsic textual analysis. In the chapter on *Soll und Haben* and the *Dorfgeschichte,* I suggested the outlines of such a reception history, as it was essential to establish a parallel pattern for the novel and the village tales, despite the differences between their historical contexts of origin.

The designation of a single communicative structure common to Auerbach's tales of the *Vormärz* and Freytag's novel of 1855 illustrates the incipient typology of realist narrative in my work. In coordinating the analysis of the social system available in the text with the structures and strategies of the narrative system, a pattern of reading is obtained which is characteristic of works by two separate authors. The contrast between the pattern of reading in the works by Auerbach and Freytag and the texts by Fontane or the novels by Raabe demonstrates the disparate character of narrative prose within the epoch generally termed German Realism. Designating the reader, or the intersection of reader and literary text, as the locus of realism accounts for the diversity and also retains the connection between literature and external reality and enables both diachronic and synchronic analysis of the works and their status as "realistic" texts. The realistic dimension of a novel is the congruence between the functional social reality model of a reader's environment and the field of reference or reality paradigm constituted in the reading process. As the historical context of generations of readers changes, so also will the status of a particular text as a realistic narrative. In order for a work to retain a realistic dimension, it must enable the constitution of a sufficiently broad field of reference, allowing noncontemporaneous readers to experience a sense of familiarity.

The implications of such a definition of realism extend beyond the delimitation of a literary epoch in the nineteenth century. Within that period, however, the focus on the reader and on a recognition of the familiar in a novel was prevalent. Fontane's dictum that a novel should tell a story, "an die wir glauben können," exemplifies the concern with *vraisemblance,* with the contiguity of narrated experience to the reader's external realm of experience.[2] Yet the credibility of narratives in the latter half of the nineteenth century does not remain constant for successive generations of readers, as the variegated history of reception for Freytag's *Soll und Haben* illustrates. The possible field of reference constituted in reading Freytag's novel is a narrow, overly-determined one, and the realistic dimension of the text is correspondingly limited. The *vraisemblance* of the novel which formed the center of realism discussions in the 1850s does not display the vitality of the works by Fontane and Raabe.

The reasons for the limited realism of Freytag's novel, and the main bases of distinction between the narrative pattern characteristic of *Soll und Haben* and the *Dorfgeschichte* and the reading experience afforded by Fontane's and Raabe's novels are found in the degree of integration within each pattern. My original definition of integration as the incorporation of individual unit into encompassing system is applicable to the communicative structure of a literary text and also to the functioning of a work within the context of reception. The analysis of narratives by Auerbach and Freytag which composes my second chapter outlines the highly integrative function of the texts, the manner in which the reader is led to reaffirm the values set forth. The communicative structure works to draw the reader into the text, integrating the individual reader into an already established system. The field of reference constituted in the reading process is overdetermined and a reader has little leeway in actualizing the textual directives. The social system is presented by the texts as a monolithic entity, and the narrated characters are assimilated into the comprehensive order. In Berger and Luckmann's terms, a unified symbolic universe is all-pervasive, and the lives of individual figures are defined and contained by the matrix of socially established roles and meanings.

The cohesive social system in the pattern of reading common to Auerbach and Freytag is coupled with a narrative structure which is authoritative and ultracoherent. The narrative progression is the alternation of the perturbance of a stable system and the constitution of a state of equilibrium, with the final establishment of a comprehensive and cohesive order. The intermediary tensions are provided by well-defined binary oppositions, and a reader is consistently oriented toward the positive elements. The persistent narrative voice contributes to the cohesive communicative structure and reinforces the basic univocality of the works. Within *Soll und Haben* and the village tales there is no distance to the dominant social order which is valorized by the texts, and the reading experience is channeled to reaffirm the fictive field of reference as given. The congruence with a reader's external reality is of limited duration, as the reception history of the *Dorfgeschichte* and Freytag's novel illustrates. Acclaimed as realistic texts while the social order they propounded was in the ascendancy, they cannot sustain the congruence in a historical context which diverges from their era of origin.

The tensions in Fontane's novels are of a different variety. A critical distance to the prevailing social order is incorporated into the communicative structure of the texts, and the integration of the social system is no longer complete. The individual characters in the works analyzed in my third chapter are not always successfully assimilated into the social universe they inhabit, and the institutional order itself, carried by language and rituals of social interaction, is a restricting as well as an enabling force. The reality paradigm characteristic of *Schach von Wuthenow, Effi Briest* and *Der Stechlin* is stable yet not absolute in its authority as apprehended by a reader. The narrative structure is more complex and less directed than in Freytag's novel and Auerbach's stories. There is no single authoritative perspective within Fontane's texts, and the binarism of the initial pattern of reading is replaced by formative tensions and variable interpretations, which incorporate a critical distance to all narrated events. The "social logic" which appears to dictate the characters' lives and the course of the narrative is undercut and its conventionality exposed. The communicative structure is distinguished by the continual modification of all perspectives and definitions. Iterative patterns in the texts result in variation rather than singular reinforcement, and an indeterminacy of meaning, a lack of univocality, accounts for the vitality of Fontane's novels. Modern readers may not experience a total correspondence of the narrated world to their own, but the distance to that narrated world, the partiality and contingency of the social system, is part of the field of reference of Fontane's novels and a factor in the continued realistic dimension of the works.

The fraying of the paramount reality and the fragility of the outward stability in the novels analyzed in my third chapter are especially evident in *Der Stechlin*. Yet even in Fontane's late novel, it remains an open potential, and the "Zusammenhang der Dinge" is complex and mutable yet resilient. In the final pattern of narrative the resilience itself is threatened. The novels of Wilhelm Raabe's Braunschweig trilogy are first-person narratives, and the process of narration is the gradual relativization of the secure existence of the narrator. The reality paradigm valorized at one level of the text is undercut by the comprehensive pattern of narration. Questions of perception and authority and the issue of legitimation of an outwardly stable social system are central to the pattern of narrative analyzed in my final chapter. The elements of reader, text, and thematic field of reference form a complex communicative structure which links Raabe's works, especially the final novel in the trilogy, to modern narrative techniques. *Die Akten des Vogelsangs* raises more questions than it answers, and there is no final integration of the divergent reality definitions. The compromise inherent in the narrator's position appears a necessary one, yet it is sharply called into question by the protagonist who so fascinates and unsettles the narrator. Similar to most novels in the latter half of the nineteenth century, the main issues are questions of continuity and temporality: in E.M. Forster's terms "the life in time and the life by values."[3] Within the final novel, the integration and transmission of the dominant reality structure is revealed as increasingly fragile and conventional. The process of both novels of Raabe's Braunschweig trilogy which I have considered in detail is a scrutiny and partial betrayal of the quotidian, routinized reality. A reader is not integrated into the text but led to observe the constitution of the reality paradigm composing the field of reference of the work through the focus on the process of narration itself.

The original impetus in selecting three patterns of realist narrative from German prose fiction of the nineteenth century was a focus on the process of reading and the contextual production of meaning in a literary work. The intersection of text and reader was assumed to construct the world which a "realistic" text is so often thought to reflect or describe. The major portion of the analyses which I have offered are formalistic in character and involve description and evaluation of repetitive structures within the selected narratives and the examination of the social reality constituted in the text. The designation of three distinct patterns of possible reader experience on the basis of consideration of internal narrative structure and questions of content indicates the implications of a theoretical orientation toward the reader in considering the issue of realism in narrative prose. In a century concerned with integration as an underlying principle of social composition, the degree of integration evidenced by a narrative text is related to its function within a social-historical context. The highly integrated narratives of Freytag and Auerbach exercised an affirmative function within their original contexts of reception. Fontane's and Raabe's novels, in relativizing or partially opposing a unified reality paradigm, are less affirmative, and their identity as realistic texts can remain for successive generations of readers. The question remains, and it is a central one for discussions of realism in literature, whether the continued realistic dimension of a text is not related to its critical function. Within the scope of the narratives considered in the present study, it is the distance to a specific reality paradigm which ensures the polyvalence of a text as realistic. The link between literary work and external reality, and the locus of the realistic dimension, is the reader, and the reading experience of a work is guided and delimited by the communicative structure. Further analyses such as the ones in the preceding chapters are necessary to do justice to the disparate character of German Realism and to continue to probe the more basic questions concerning realism and reader experience.

NOTES

Chapter I: The Altered Perspective

1 Lucien Goldmann, *Pour une sociologie du roman* (Paris: Gallimard, 1964). English version: *Towards a Sociology of the Novel*, trans. Alan Sheridan (London: Tavistock, 1975). A succinct definition of realism is offered at the end of the section on the *nouveau roman*: "creating a world whose structure is analogous to the essential structure of the social reality in which the *œuvre* has been written" (p. 149).

2 Erich Auerbach, *Mimesis,* trans. Willard Trask (Princeton: Princeton University Press, 1968), p. 518.

3 Two standard examples of such an assessment: Auerbach, pp. 452-453, 516-519; Georg Lukács, *Die Grablegung des alten Deutschland* (Reinbek bei Hamburg: Rowohlt, 1967), pp. 12, 21-27.

4 "Verklärung" (transfiguration) is an unavoidable concept in a consideration of German Realism. Perhaps the best brief definition is that established by Wolfgang Preisendanz: W. Preisendanz, "Voraussetzungen des poetischen Realismus in der deutschen Erzählkunst des 19. Jahrhunderts," in *Formkräfte der deutschen Dichtung von Barock bis zur Gegenwart*, ed. Hans Steffen, Kleine Vandenhoeck-Reihe, 196S (Göttingen: Vandenhoeck and Ruprecht, 1963), pp. 187-210; rpt. in *Begriffsbestimmung des literarischen Realismus,* ed. Richard Brinkmann, Wege der Forschung 212 (Darmstadt: Wissenschaftliche Buchgesellschaft, 1969), pp. 453-479. In Brinkmann especially pp. 468-9. Hugo Aust's Metzler volume has a section on "Verklärung" which gives references ranging from the nineteenth century's own versions of the concept to its variations in later scholarship: Hugo Aust, *Literatur des Realismus,* Sammlung Metzler, M157 (Stuttgart: Metzler, 1981), pp. 42-46.

5 The term "poetischer Realismus" first appears in Schelling, in the 1802 "Vorlesungen über die Methode des academischen Studium," although it is generally associated with Ludwig. Aust gives a survey of the use of the term (Aust, pp. 26-28). Preisendanz, "Voraussetzungen" also gives a short and clear treatment of the term "poetischer Realismus."

6 Richard Brinkmann, *Wirklichkeit und Illusion. Studien über Gehalt und Grenzen des Begriffs Realismus für die erzählende Dichtung des neunzehnten Jahrhunderts* (Tübingen: Max Niemeyer, 1957); Hubert Ohl, *Bild und*

Wirklichkeit. Studien zur Romankunst Raabes und Fontanes (Heidelberg: Lothar Stiehm, 1968); Wolfgang Preisendanz, *Humor als dichterische Einbildungskraft*, 2nd ed. (Munich: Fink, 1976).

7   Gerhard Kaiser, "Realismusforschung ohne Realismusbegriff," rev. of *Bild und Wirklichkeit*, by H. Ohl, *Deutsche Vierteljahrsschrift für Literaturwissenschaft und Geistesgeschichte* 43 (1969), p. 159. Heinz Schlaffer's review of Ohl contains a similar criticism: Heinz Schlaffer, rev. of *Bild und Wirklichkeit*, by Hubert Ohl, *Zeitschrift für deutsche Philologie*, 89 (1970), pp. 287-295.

8   Werner Hahl, "Gesellschaftlicher Konservativismus und literarischer Realismus. Das Modell einer deutschen Sozialverfassung in den Dorfgeschichten," in *Realismus und Gründerzeit*, ed. M. Bucher, W. Hahl, G. Jäger and R. Wittmann, v. I (Stuttgart: Metzler, 1976), pp. 48-95.

9   Hermann Kinder, *Poesie als Synthese. Ausbreitung eines deutschen Realismusverständnisses in der Mitte des 19. Jahrhunderts* (Frankfurt am Main: Athenäum, 1973); Hartmut Steinecke, *Romantheorie und Romankritik in Deutschland: Die Entwicklung des Gattungsverständnisses von der Scott-Rezeption bis zum programmatischen Realismus*, 2 vol. (Stuttgart: Metzler, 1975); Helmuth Widhammer, *Realismus und klassizistische Tradition: Zur Theorie der Literatur in Deutschland 1848-60*, (Tübingen: Niemeyer, 1972). The second volumes of Steinecke and *Realismus und Gründerzeit* contain valuable collections of excerpts from essays, journals, etc. Another useful collection of excerpts is: Helmuth Widhammer and Hans-Joachim Ruckhäberle, eds., *Roman und Romantheorie des deutschen Realismus* (Kronberg, Czechoslovakia: Athenäum, 1977). There is also a relevant Metzler volume: Helmuth Widhammer, *Die Literaturtheorie des deutschen Realismus 1848-1860*, Sammlung Metzler, 152 (Stuttgart: Metzler, 1977). See also: Kenneth Bruce Beaton, "Gustav Freytag, Julian Schmidt und die Romantheorie nach der Revolution von 1848," *Jahrbuch der Raabe-Gesellschaft* (1976), pp. 7-32; Ulf Eisele, *Realismus und Ideologie. Zur Kritik der literarischen Theorie nach 1848 am Beispiel des "Deutschen Museums"* (Stuttgart: Metzler, 1976); Mark Gelber, "Die literarische Umwelt zu Gustav Freytags *Soll und Haben* und die Realismustheorie der *Grenzboten*," *Orbis Litterarum*, 39 (1984), pp. 38-53; Hans-Wolf Jäger, "Gesellschaftliche Aspekte des bürgerlichen Realismus und seiner Theorie. Bemerkungen zu Julian Schmidt und Gustav Freytag," *Text und Kontext*, 2, Heft 3 (1974), pp. 3-41; Friedrich Sengle, "Zur näheren Bestimmung des programmatischen Realismus und zu seiner Abgrenzung von den Richtungen der Biedermeierzeit," in his *Biedermeierzeit. Deutsche Literatur im Spannungsfeld zwischen Restauration und Revolution 1815-1848*, Vol. I (Stuttgart: Metzler, 1971/2), pp. 257-291.

10 Theodor Fontane, *Sämtliche Werke*, ed. Kurt Schreinert (Munich: Nymphenburger Verlagshandlung, 1963), v. XXI:1, pp. 214-230.

11 T.E. Carter, "Freytag's 'Soll und Haben': a Liberal National Manifesto as a Best-seller," *German Life and Letters*, 21 (1967-8), pp. 320-29; Mark H. Gelber, "Teaching 'Literary Anti-Semitism': Dickens' *Oliver Twist* and Freytag's *Soll und Haben*," *Comparative Literature Studies*, 16, Nr. 1 (1979), pp. 1-11; Leo Löwenthal, "Gustav Freytag," in *Festschrift zum 80. Geburtstag von Georg Lukács*, ed. F. Benseler (Neuwied: Luchterhand, 1965), pp. 392-401; Hans Mayer, afterword, *Soll und Haben* (Munich: Hanser, 1977), pp. 837-844; Jeffrey L. Sammons, "The Evaluation of Freytag's *Soll und Haben*," *German Life and Letters*, 22 (1968-9), pp. 315-324; Michael Schneider, "Apologie des Bürgers. Zur Problematik von Rassismus und Antisemitismus in Gustav Freytags Roman "Soll und Haben," *Jahrbuch der deutschen Schillergesellschaft*, v. 25, pp. 385-413; Hartmut Steinecke, "Gustav Freytag: *Soll und Haben* (1855). Weltbild und Wirkung eines deutschen Bestsellers," in *Romane und Erzählungen des bürgerlichen Realismus. Neue Interpretationen*, ed. Horst Denkler (Stuttgart: Reclam, 1980), pp. 138-152; Joachim Worthmann, *Probleme des Zeitromans* (Heidelberg: Carl Winter Universitätsverlag, 1974), pp. 91-99. Mayer contrasts the novel to Keller; Sammons suggests the mendacity. Regarding the question of anti-Semitic elements in the novel, Michael Schneider also urges caution with the term in his book-length study: Michael Schneider, *Geschichte als Gestalt. Formen der Wirklichkeit und Wirklichkeit der Form in Gustav Freytags Roman "Soll und Haben"* (Stuttgart: Akademischer Verlag Hans-Dieter Heinz, 1980), pp. 112-141. For additional analyses of the novel, see my next chapter.

12 Helmut Kreuzer, "Zur Theorie des deutschen Realismus zwischen Märzrevolution und Nationalismus," in *Realismustheorien*, ed. Reinhold Grimm and Jost Hermand (Stuttgart: Kohlhammer, 1975), pp. 48-67. Here p. 48.

13 Widhammer, *Realismus und klassizistische Tradition*, p. 71.

14 Fritz Martini, *Deutsche Literatur im bürgerlichen Realismus 1848-1898*, 4th ed. (Stuttgart: Metzler, 1981), pp. 974-985, esp. pp. 982-985.

15 Horst Steinmetz, "Der vergessene Leser: Provokatorische Bemerkungen zum Realismusproblem," in *Dichter und Leser*, ed. F. van Ingen, E. Kunne-Ibsch, H. de Leeuwe, F. Maatje (Groningen: Wolters-Noordhoff, 1972), pp. 113-133; *Bürgerlicher Realismus*, ed. Klaus-Detlev Müller (Königstein, Cz.: Athenäum, 1981), pp. 20-21. Roman Jakobson's essay of 1921 should also be mentioned as it considers the category of "Wahrscheinlichkeit" and its relation to reader experience as distinct from other definitions of realism. Jakobson's essay, however, had no immediate effect on scholarship. Roman Jakobson, "Über den Realismus in der Kunst," in *Russischer Formalismus*, ed. Jurij Striedter (Munich: Fink, 1971), pp. 373-391.

16 Horst Steinmetz, "Die Rolle des Lesers in Otto Ludwigs Konzeption des 'Poetischen Realismus'," in *Literatur und Leser*, ed. Gunter Grimm (Stutt-

gart: Reclam, 1975), pp. 223-239; Leo Lensing, *Narrative Structure and the Reader in Wilhelm Raabe's "Im Alten Eisen"* (Bern: Peter Lang, 1977). Also: Lilian Hoverland, "Die Rolle des Lesers in der deutschen Novellistik des 19. Jahrhunderts," *Akten des VI. Internationalen Germanisten-Kongresses Basel 1980 (Jahrbuch für Internationale Germanistik,* Reihe A, Bd. 8,3), eds. H. Ruppland and H.-G. Roloff (Bern: Lang, 1980), pp. 409-414. Hoverland's analyses are more traditional. Elsbeth Hamann's lengthy study of *Effi Briest* purports to do justice to "dem sich zwischen Autor, Werk und Leser ergebenden kommunikativen Beziehungsgefüge" (p. 31), but at the same time insists on a "produktionsorientierte Betrachtungsweise" and emphasizes authorial intention: Elsbeth Hamann, *Theodor Fontanes "Effi Briest" aus erzähltheoretischer Sicht unter besonderer Berücksichtigung der Interdependenzen zwischen Autor, Erzählwerk und Leser* (Bonn: Bouvier, 1984).

17 Aust, *Literatur des Realismus,* pp. 19-22, 61-66.

18 D.W. Fokkema and Elrud Kunne-Ibsch, *Theories of Literature in the Twentieth Century* (London: C. Hurst, 1977), p. 136.

19 Wolfgang Iser, *Die Appellstruktur der Texte. Unbestimmtheit als Wirkungsbedingung literarischer Prosa,* Konstanzer Universitätsreden, Nr. 28 (Constance: Universitätsverlag, 1971); English version: "Indeterminacy and the Reader's Response in Prose Fiction," in *Aspects of the Narrative,* ed. J. Hillis Miller (New York: Columbia University Press, 1971), pp. 1-45; also anthologized in *Rezeptionsästhetik: Theorie und Praxis,* ed. Rainer Warning, Uni-Taschenbücher, Nr. 303 (Munich: Fink, 1975), pp. 228-252. W. Iser, *Der implizierte Leser: Kommunikationsformen des Romans von Bunyan zu Beckett,* Uni-Taschenbücher, Nr. 163 (Munich: Fink, 1972); English version: *The Implied Reader* (Baltimore: Johns Hopkins Press, 1974). W. Iser, "The Reading Process. A Phenomenological Approach," in *New Literary History* 3 (1971/2), pp. 279-299; later German version: "Der Lesevorgang. Eine phänomenologische Perspektive," in Warning, pp. 253-276. W. Iser, "Die Wirklichkeit der Fiktion — Elemente eines funktionsgeschichtlichen Textmodells," in Warning, pp. 277-325; English version in *New Literary History* 7 (1975), pp. 7-38. W. Iser, *Der Akt des Lesens: Theorie ästhetischer Wirkung,* UTB 636 (Munich: Fink, 1976); English version: *The Act of Reading* (Baltimore: Johns Hopkins, 1978). W. Iser, "Interaction between Text and Reader," in *The Reader in the Text. Essays on Audience and Interpretation* (Princeton: Princeton University Press, 1980), pp. 106-119.

20 Hans-Robert Jauß, "Literaturgeschichte als Provokation der Literaturwissenschaft," in his *Literaturgeschichte als Provokation,* (Frankfurt am Main: Suhrkamp, 1970), pp. 144-207. The best English version of the essay is in the volume *Toward an Aesthetic of Reception,* trans. T. Bahti (Minneapolis: University of Minnesota Press, 1982). Also relevant are the following:

"Racines und Goethes Iphigenie. Mit einem Nachwort über die Partialität der rezeptionsästhetischen Methode," in Warning, pp. 335-400; originally in *Neue Hefte für Philosophie* (1973), pp. 31-46. H.-R. Jauß, *Ästhetische Erfahrung und literarische Hermeneutik I: Versuche im Felde der ästhetischen Erfahrung* (Munich: Fink, 1977); English version: *Aesthetic Experience and Literary Hermeneutics,* trans. M. Shaw (Minneapolis: University of Minnesota Press, 1982).

21 Gunter Grimm, "Einführung in die Rezeptionsforschung," in *Literatur und Leser,* pp. 11-84. For an extensive discussion of the practical and theoretical possibilities of reception aesthetics see volume 2 of the Proceedings of the Ninth International Congress of Comparative Literature, held 1979 in Innsbruck: *Literary Communication and Reception,* Actes du neuvième Congrès de l'Association Internationale de Littérature Comparée, eds., Z. Konstantinović, M. Naumann, H.-R. Jauß (Innsbruck: Verlag des Instituts für Sprachwissenschaft der Universität Innsbruck, 1980). For a critical and thorough survey of work in the field see Robert C. Holub, *Reception Theory: A Critical Introduction* (London: Methuen, 1984).

22 René Wellek has provided two useful summaries of Mukařovský's influence: R. Wellek, "The Literary Theory and Aesthetics of the Prague School," in his *Discriminations* (New Haven: Yale University Press, 1970), pp. 275-303, and his foreword to Jan Mukařovský, *The Word and Verbal Art,* trans. J. Burbank and P. Steiner (New Haven: Yale Univ. Press, 1977), pp. vii-xiii. Also available in English are the following: J. Mukařovský, *Aesthetic Function, Norm and Value as Social Facts,* trans. M. Suino (Ann Arbor: Dept. of Slavic Languages and Literature, Univ. of Michigan, 1970), and *Structure, Sign and Function,* trans. J. Burbank and P. Steiner (New Haven: Yale Univ. Press, 1978). For the German forum of discussion the following was of major importance: J. Mukařovský, *Kapitel aus der Ästhetik,* (Frankfurt am Main: Suhrkamp, 1970), esp. the essays "Ästhetische Funktion, Norm und ästhetischer Wert als soziale Fakten" (pp. 7-112) and "Die Kunst als semiologisches Faktum" (pp. 138-147).

23 Götz Wienold, "Textverarbeitung. Überlegungen zur Kategorienbildung in einer strukturellen Literaturgeschichte," in *Sozialgeschichte und Wirkungsästhetik,* ed. P.U. Hohendahl (Frankfurt am Main: Athenäum, 1974), pp. 97-134.

24 It should probably be pointed out that the degree of "partiality" of textual determination varies greatly from one variation to the next. For Ingarden, for example, reading is a reconstitution in the sense of *Nachvollziehen* rather than a constitutive process. (Ingarden, "Konkretisation und Rekonstruktion" in Warning, pp. 42-70). Hugo Aust has taken a quotation from H. Steinmetz as an example of the other extreme: "daß Dichtung 'eigentlich nie als das geschriebene Werk' existiere" (Aust, p. 21). He has

distorted Steinmetz' statement by removing it from the context of his essay ("Der vergessene Leser," p. 122). For Steinmetz the reading process is characterized by an interaction between a given, albeit not totally determined, textual structure and the reader's own personal experience. The question of realism for Steinmetz concerns the degree to which the reader finds an agreement between the "Romanwirklichkeit" and "persönliches Realitätsgefühl." What Steinmetz neglects to clarify, however, is the sociohistorical context of the reader's sense of "reality."

25 Charles W. Morris, *Foundation of the Theory of Signs*, Int. Encyclopedia of Unified Science Vol. 1, Nr. 2 (Chicago: University of Chicago Press, 1938), specifically on pragmatics, pp. 29-42.

26 The difference in linguistics between models which view the recipient as either "decoding" a message or participating in the process of producing meanings is parallel to the distinction in reception aesthetics between reconstitution of textual directives and a constitutive process of reading.

27 Heinrich Plett, *Textwissenschaft und Textanalyse*, UTB 328 (Heidelberg: Quelle und Meyer, 1975); Elisabeth Gülich and Wolfgang Raible, *Linguistische Textmodelle: Grundlagen und Möglichkeiten*, UTB 130 (Munich: Fink, 1977). A selected bibliography is found in the series *Papers in Textlinguistics*, Nr. 35; Jürgen Bredenmeier and Käthi Dorfmüller-Karpusa, "Textlinguistik – Texttheorie. Einführungen, Monographien/Sammelbände, Periodica, Reihen (Auswahlbibliographie)," in *Text, Kontext, Interpretation: Einige Aspekte der texttheoretischen Forschung*, eds., J.S. Petöfi and K. Dorfmüller-Karpusa (Hamburg: Helmut Buske, 1981), pp. 286-291.

28 A separate literature exists concerning the question of fictionality in literary texts. The issue is of course relevant for works which are "realistic". Five of the most valuable contributions for the purposes of my study are: Johannes Anderegg, *Fiktion und Kommunikation: Ein Beitrag zur Theorie der Prosa* (Göttingen: Vandenhoeck und Ruprecht, 1973); Siegfried J. Schmidt, "Fictionality in literary and non-literary discourse," *Poetics*, 9 (1980), pp. 525-546; S.J. Schmidt, "Ist Fiktionalität eine linguistische oder eine texttheoretischen Kategorie," in *Textsorten*, eds., E. Gülich and W. Raible (Frankfurt am Main: Athenäum, 1972), pp. 59-71, also in S.J. Schmidt, *Elemente einer Textpoetik* (Munich: Bayerischer Schulbuchverlag, 1974), pp. 71-87; John Searle, "The Logical Status of Fictional Discourse," *New Literary History*, 6 (1975), pp. 319-332; *Funktionen des Fiktiven*, ed. W. Iser, Poetik und Hermeneutik, 10 (Munich: Fink, 1983).

29 In an application of categories from Anderegg and Searle to realist narrative, Peter Demetz has suggested that it is the unique character of a work of fiction, the reader's unwillingness to accept a substitute, which separates fiction from a factual text. Reducing narratives to formulas and summaries without considering the mode of manifestation as well denies such a quality.

To illustrate with an absurd exaggeration: imagine working from Fontane's own paraphrase of *Stechlin*: "Zum Schluß stirbt ein alter und zwei junge heiraten sich." Peter Demetz, "Über die Fiktionen des Realismus," *Neue Rundschau,* 88 (1977), pp. 554-567.

30 Such criticism is also heard within linguistic scholarship. An example is H. Rieser and J. Wirrer's critique of Teun A. van Dijk. They point out the insufficiency of formal analysis without contexts of reception, for which they envision interdisciplinary research. Hannes Rieser and Jan Wirrer, "Zu Teun van Dijks 'Some Aspects of Text Grammar.' Ein Beitrag zur Textgrammatik-Literaturdiskussion," in *Probleme und Perspektiven der neueren textgrammatischen Forschung* I, ed. Projektgruppe Textlinguistik Konstanz (Hamburg: Helmut Buske, 1974), pp. 1-80, esp. p. 31. Siegfried J. Schmidt seems ambivalent on the concept, using the term *homo linguisticus* as differentiated from a concrete recipient (*Rezipient*) and even speaking of a *homo communicativus.*

31 The difference between text-linguistics and text-theory is stated very simply in S.J. Schmidt, *Texttheorie,* 2nd ed., UTB 202 (Munich: Fink, 1976), p. iv. A similar distinction is made in Plett's establishment of two origins of text-theory: linguistics and the social sciences (Plett, pp. 11-12). The concept of "kommunikatives Handlungsspiel" is detailed in Schmidt, *Elemente einer Textpoetik,* esp. 48 ff, 77 ff; also in *Texttheorie,* pp. 43-50. In an article published in 1978 Schmidt relinquishes the term for the new concept of "komplexe Voraussetzungssituation." The initial designation, however, seems more applicable: S.J. Schmidt, "Some Problems of Communicative Text Theories," in *Current Trends in Textlinguistics,* ed. W. Dressler (Berlin/ NY: de Gruyter, 1978), pp. 47-60, esp. 52-3. The semantic-semiotic differentiation is stated most clearly in: S.J. Schmidt, "Text und Bedeutung," in *Text, Bedeutung, Ästhetik,* ed. S.J. Schmidt (Munich: Bayerischer Schulbuch-Verlag, 1970), pp. 43-79, esp. pp. 60-64. See also: Gerhart Wolff, "Wittgensteins Sprachspiel-Begriff. Seine Rezeption und Relevanz in der neuen Sprachpragmatik," *Wirkendes Wort,* 30 (1980), pp. 225-240.

32 Iser's concept of indeterminacy would be an example of a corresponding term, as would Mukařovský's statement that the aesthetic function is "empty," a principle of organization and re-arrangement of historically variable non-aesthetic values. (*Kapitel aus der Ästhetik,* p. 103).

33 Henry J. Schmidt, "Text-Adequate Concretizations and Real Readers: Reception Theory and Its Applications," in *New German Critique,* 17 (Spring 1979), pp. 157-169.

34 Quoted in Grimm, "Einführung ...," p. 59.

35 Grimm, p. 75.

36 The futility of the Restoration period is well outlined in Theodore S. Hamerow, *Restoration, Revolution, Reaction: Economics and Politics in Germany, 1815-1871* (Princeton: Princeton University Press, 1958). The most concise summary of the fundamental changes in the century is Karl-Erich Born, "Structural Changes in German social and economic development at the end of the nineteenth century," accessible in English in *Imperial Germany*, ed. James J. Sheehan (New York: New Viewpoints [Franklin Watts], 1976), pp. 16-38. Cf. also: Hans Motteck, *Wirtschaftsgeschichte Deutschlands: Ein Grundriß*, Bd. II: *Von der Zeit der französischen Revolution bis zur Zeit der Bismarckschen Reichsgründung* (Berlin/GDR: VEB Deutscher Verlag der Wissenschaften, 1964).

37 Social estate is a rendering of the German *Stand*. Bramstedt expresses "ständische Gesellschaft" (also "Standesgesellschaft") with the English "Society based on status" or "Estates System." Ernest K. Bramstedt, *Aristocracy and the Middle-Classes in Germany: Social Types in German Literature 1830-1900*. (Chicago: Univ. Chicago Press, 1964), p. 9.

38 Born, p. 35.

39 Fritz Stern, *The Failure of Illiberalism: Essays on the Political Culture of Modern Germany* (New York: A. Knopf, 1972).

40 Bramstedt, pp. 118-19.

41 Cf. *Deutsche Sozialgeschichte: Dokumente und Skizzen*, Bd. II *1870-1914*, eds. Gerhard A. Ritter und Jürgen Kocka (Munich: C.H. Beck, 1974), p. 67.

42 Böhme outlines the roots of this phenomenon even in the *Vormärz*: Helmut Böhme, *Prolegomena zu einer Sozial- und Wirtschaftsgeschichte Deutschlands im 19. und 20. Jahrhundert* (Frankfurt am Main: Suhrkamp, 1968), esp. pp. 26-40. Born uses the concept of "feudalization" of the *Großbürgertum* (Born, p. 25). The troublesome relationship between the aristocracy and the middle classes is a central theme of Bramstedt's book, as the title indicates. A further English treatment of the theme, albeit cursory, is found in portions of Eda Sagarra, *Tradition and Revolution, German Literature and Society 1830-1890* (London: Weidenfeld & Nicholson, 1971), esp. pp. 5-10 and 251-269.

43 Hajo Holborn, *A History of Modern Germany*, v. 3 *1840-1945* (New York: A. Knopf, 1969), p. 161.

44 The disparate social situations may explain the inapplicability of Arnold Hauser's *Social History of Art* for Germany, despite his analyses of the English, Russian and, especially, French culture of the period. In Russia it is, of course, the intelligentsia which provides the vehicle of cultural production. Such an analysis is, however, also inapplicable to Germany.

45 A concentration on the development of the middle class by no means intends to deny the existence of other segments of German society. Within the framework of the present study, it is the middle-class segment which is dominant.

46 See *Realismus und Gründerzeit,* pp. 120-7 and Hans Rosenberg, "Political and Social Consequences of the Great Depression of 1873-1896 in Central Europe" in Sheehan, pp. 39-60.

47 Two revealing excerpts from Max Weber regarding the dangers of an increasing "Alleinherrschaft bureaukratischer Lebensideale" which he terms "eine Parzellierung der Seele" are anthologized in *Deutsche Sozialgeschichte,* pp. 82-83 and 380-381. The latter deals with the turn of the century and characterizes the civil servants as "Bürgerliche mit feudalen Prätensionen."

48 Rosenberg and (in great detail) Helmut Böhme, *Deutschlands Weg zur Großmacht* (Cologne: Kiepenheuer & Witsch, 1966), p. 341 ff.

49 Romance is defined as "fictitious narrative in prose or verse; the interest of which turns upon marvellous and uncommon incidents." The definitions are from Scott's essay on Romance for the Encyclopedia Britannica (Supplement to the Fourth Edition, 1824, vi, 435). Quoted from *Sir Walter Scott on Novelists and Fiction,* ed. Ioan Williams (London: Routledge and Kegan Paul, 1968), p. 1.

50 The motto originally comes from Julian Schmidt, *Geschichte der deutschen Literatur im 19. Jahrhundert.*

51 The most well-known parallel between the natural and the social realm is found in the preface to *Bunte Steine* (1853). The story *Granit* from that collection illustrates the interconnection of the natural environment with human affairs. The forest in the grandfather's story is a populated, "humanized" forest, and the surroundings of his walk with his grandfather serve to emphasize the reintegration into the family. *Der Nachsommer* (1857) in its entirety underscores the complementary compatibility of human ethos and natural environment.

52 Peter Demetz, *Formen des Realismus: Theodor Fontane, Kritische Untersuchungen* (Frankfurt: Ullstein Verlag, 1973, originally Munich: Carl Hanser, 1964), p. 100 ff.

53 E.M. Forster, *Aspects of the Novel* (New York: Harcourt, Brace & World, 1927), pp. 28-29; Ian Watt, *The Rise of the Novel* (Berkeley: University of California Press, 1957), p. 24.

54 Peter Berger and Thomas Luckmann, *The Social Construction of Reality: A Treatise in the Sociology of Knowledge* (New York: Doubleday, 1966, rpt. Garden City: Anchor Books, 1967).

55 Roger Fowler, *Linguistics and the Novel* (London: Methuen 1977), p. 70.

56 Fowler, p. 123.

57 Robert Weimann, *Structure and Society in Literary History: Studies in the History and Theory of Historical Criticism* (Charlottesville: University of Virginia, 1976).

58 Peter Demetz suggests a similar importance for repetitive structures in "realistic" literature. Demetz, "Fiktionen des Realismus."

59 Gülich and Raible, *Linguistische Textmodelle*, p. 189.

Chapter II: Cohesion and Integration

1 The studies by W. Hahl in *Realismus und Gründerzeit*, K. Beaton, H.-W. Jäger, H. Kinder, H. Steinecke, H. Kreuzer, H. Widhammer and J. Worthmann have already been mentioned, as well as the English articles by T.E. Carter, J.L. Sammons, and M. Gelber (Chapter I, notes 8, 9, 11, 12). The *Dorfgeschichte* and *Bauernroman* have been the subject of four books since 1974, including a Metzler volume (U. Baur, J. Hein, P. Mettenleitner, and P. Zimmermann). There have also been earlier studies on both Freytag and Auerbach. The section on Freytag in W. Kockjoy's study of the *Kaufmannsroman* is interesting within the framework of the present discussion: Wolfgang Kockjoy, *Der Deutsche Kaufmannsroman* (Straßburg: Universitätsbuchdruckerei Heitz & Co., 1932), esp. pp. 63-77. The publication history and documentation of the astounding vitality of *Soll und Haben* is accessible in the Carter article, in Michael Kienzle, *Der Erfolgsroman* (Stuttgart: Metzler, 1975), pp. 44-53, in Peter Heinz Hubrich, *Gustav Freytag's "Deutsche Ideologie in 'Soll und Haben' "* (Kronberg, Cz.: Scriptor, 1974), pp. 31-44, and in Claus Richter, *Leiden an der Gesellschaft. Vom literarischen Liberalismus zum poetischen Realismus* (Königstein/Cz.: Athenäum, 1978), pp. 209-214. Hahl documents Auerbach's popularity and "rezeptionsgeschichtliche Schlüsselstellung;" and the excerpts from essays, journals, reviews, etc., in the second volumes of Steinecke's *Romantheorie und Romankritik in Deutschland* and *Realismus und Gründerzeit* are useful for tracing the reception of both Freytag's novel and Auerbach's tales. Bettelheim gives further publication statistics and excerpts (all of them favorable) from contemporary reviews: Anton Bettelheim, *Berthold Auerbach* (Stuttgart/ Berlin: Cotta'sche Buchhandlung Nachfolger, 1907), pp. 128-168. Also, Bettelheim, *Biographenwege* (Berlin: Paetel, 1913), p. 119. Bettelheim's devotion to Auerbach may color the statistics or excerpts somewhat, as is

obvious in the five sections on Auerbach in *Biographenwege*. Additional scholarship on Auerbach and Freytag is listed in section 4 of the Selected Bibliography.

2 F. Rhöse emphasizes the "ungebrochenen bildungsbürgerlichen Liberalismus" behind Auerbach's writings: "daß das gesamte literarische Werk auf den theoretischen Positionen basiert, die in den vierziger Jahren ausgebaut und dann nur leicht modifiziert wurden." Franz Rhöse, *Konflikt und Versöhnung* (Stuttgart: Metzler, 1978), pp. 161-175. W. Hahl offers a concise interpretation of the poetic and political liberalism in *Schrift und Volk* and its position in Auerbach's work: Werner Hahl, *Reflexion und Erzählung* (Stuttgart: Kohlhammer, 1971), pp. 209-213. H. Kinder (*Poesie als Synthese*, pp. 115-139) also emphasizes the continuity of Auerbach's liberal orientation and its connection to the tradition of humanism marked by Schiller, Goethe, Lessing, and Spinoza. P. Zimmermann, referring to *Ludwig* Auerbach, is overly superficial in postulating Auerbach's renunciation of his liberalism after 1848 (Zimmermann, p. 21). For a detailed analysis, see my "Berthold Auerbach: The Dilemma of the Jewish Humanist from *Vormärz* to Empire," *German Studies Review*, 6 (1983) pp. 399-420.

3 Bettelheim, *Berthold Auerbach*, pp. 324-349 (chapter entitled "Im neuen Reich"). The critical comment concerning Bismarck "als Ausbund junkerlicher Hoffart" is on page 291.

4 Kinder, p. 116 n.

5 Mettenleitner, pp. 45-49.

6 In a letter to K.E. Franzos in 1881. Quoted in: M.J. Zwick, *Berthold Auerbachs sozialpolitischer und ethischer Liberalismus* (Stuttgart: Kohlhammer, 1933), p. 108.

7 23. November 1880, Letter 697, *Berthold Auerbach. Briefe an seinen Freund Jakob Auerbach*, ed. Fr. Spielhagen (Frankfurt/Main: Literarische Anstalt Rütten und Loening, 1884), v. II, p. 442.

8 The point is well argued in Rhöse, p. 174 and in: Margarita Pazi, "Revolution und Demokratie im Leben und Werk von Berthold Auerbach," in *Revolution und Demokratie in Geschichte und Literatur. Festschrift für Walter Grab*, eds. J. Schoeps and I. Geiß (Duisburg: Walter Braun, 1979), pp. 355-374.

9 Bettelheim, *Berthold Auerbach*, p. 239.

10 Hans Lindau, *Gustav Freytag* (Leipzig, Hirzel, 1907), p. 165.

11 Lindau, pp. 280-286; Bettelheim, *Berthold Auerbach*, pp. 328-330. An analysis of Freytag's relationship to the Crown Prince, who later reigned briefly as Frederick III, would counter any attempt to dismiss Freytag too quickly

as being solely on the side of the ultimately illiberal forces in Germany. The Crown Prince was an intriguing figure, with definite liberal associations at mid-century and on into the constitutional dispute.

12 Lindau has an appendix of Freytag's comments on Bismarck which includes many critical remarks. Lindau, pp. 410-432. Also (p. 278): "Freytag's Stellung zu Bismarck ist die des theoretisierenden Zartgefühls gegenüber einer bisweilen rauhen, aber mit genialer Zweckmäßigkeit sich betätigenden Willensmacht." The comment charcterizes both Freytag *and* Lindau!

13 See also Widhammer: "Schon Mitte 1848 vertritt Freytag die Unionspolitik der späteren Gothaer: die Paulskirche mit ihren zentralistischen Bestrebungen sei nur ein Umweg zur deutschen Einheit, die als 'freie Vereinigung der deutschen Völker' [Freytag in the *Grenzboten*, 1848] unter Preußens Führung gedacht wird." H. Widhammer, *Realismus und klassizistische Tradition*, p. 29. Further details are furnished by Kienzle, pp. 5-8; Hubrich, pp. 16-31; Richter, 231-233.

14 The most thorough examples of a link to the agrarian sector are: Hahl, *Realismus und Gründerzeit*, pp. 65-93, and U. Baur, *Dorfgeschichte – Zur Entstehung und gesellschaftlichen Funktion einer literarischen Gattung im Vormärz* (Munich: Fink, 1978), pp. 47-58.

15 Both Hahl and Baur stress the point, although examining the agrarian sector as well.

16 See also Hahl, *Reflexion und Erzählung*, pp. 209-213. An analysis such as Winterscheidt's, which locates the concept of *Volk* solely "im romantisch-biedermeierlichen Denken" is too hasty. Friedrich Winterscheidt, *Deutsche Unterhaltungsliteratur der Jahre 1850-1860* (Bonn: Bouvier, 1970), p. 186. Most secondary sources stress the connection to the liberal cause.

17 Theodor Fontane, *Sämtliche Werke*, v. XXI:1, p. 224. The review appeared in 1855.

18 Robert Giseke: "*Soll und Haben*. [...] Eine Charakteristik." (Rez. G. Freytag: *Soll und Haben*, Leipzig, 1855). In: *Novellen-Zeitung*, 3. Folge, Jg. 1 (1855), S. 311-318. Excerpted in *Realismus und Gründerzeit*, v. II, pp. 336-40, esp. p. 338.

19 The review originally appeared in the *Augsburger Allgemeine Zeitung*, 1855 and is reprinted in an article by R. Leppla: "Berthold Auerbachs Besprechung von *Soll und Haben*," *Gustav Freytag Blätter*, Nr. 28 (1969), pp. 2-7.

20 An anonymous review in the *Neue Münchener Zeitung*, 1855, reprinted in Felix Dahn, *Bausteine*, 3. Reihe (Berlin, 1882), S. 9-14. Quoted here from Rhöse, p. 132.

21 Quoted by Bettelheim, *Berthold Auerbach*, p. 167.

22 Karl Hagen, "Berthold Auerbachs *Schwarzwälder Dorfgeschichten,*" *Jahrbücher der Gegenwart* (1844), S. 810-817. Quoted from *Realismus und Gründerzeit,* v. II, pp. 152-4.

23 In Bettelheim, *Berthold Auerbach,* pp. 158-9.

24 Ferdinand Kürnberger, "Ein Votum über die Literatur der Dorfgeschichten," *Österreichisch-Kaiserlich-Privilegierte Wiener-Zeitung,"* 1848. Quoted here from *Realismus und Gründerzeit,* v. II, p. 163.

25 Quoted by Steinecke, v. I, p. 196.

26 Steinecke, v. I., p. 192. Also in Mettenleitner, p. 356 and Bettelheim, *Biographenwege,* pp. 164-5.

27 *Realismus und Gründerzeit,* p. 339.

28 Quoted by Ulf Eisele, *Realismus und Ideologie,* p. 101.

29 Hermann Marggraff: "Ein Roman 'der das deutsche Volk bei seiner Arbeit sucht' " (Rez. G. Freytag *Soll und Haben,* Leipzig 1855) in *Blätter für literarische Unterhaltung* 1855. Quoted here from *Realismus und Gründerzeit,* v. II, p. 340.

30 A review appearing in *Abendblatt* to the *Neue Münchener Zeitung* 1857. Quoted in Rhöse, pp. 133-134.

31 Karl Gutzkow, *Liberale Energie: Eine Sammlung seiner kritischen Schriften,* ed. Peter Demetz (Frankfurt: Ullstein, 1971), p. 337 (original emphasis).

32 Gutzkow, p. 253. The quotation is from an earlier essay of Gutzkow's, which appeared in 1835 in *Phönix.* His *Soll und Haben* polemic, however, illustrates the continuity of his attitudes as expressed in the quoted passage.

33 Steinecke's conclusion of a dominant tone of resignation among the middle classes in the 1850s is hardly tenable. Even the passages he quotes document the economic self-confidence. Steinecke, v. I, p. 201 ff.

34 Gutzkow, p. 339.

35 Julian Schmidt, "Schiller und der Idealismus" *Grenzboten* 17/4 (1858). Quoted from *Realismus und Gründerzeit,* p. 95.

36 Julian Schmidt, *Geschichte der deutschen Literatur im 19. Jahrhundert,* Bd. 3 (Leipzig, ²1855). Quoted from Eberhard Lämmert, ed. *Romantheorie in Deutschland 1620-1880* (Cologne/Berlin: Kiepenheuer and Witsch, 1971), p. 327.

37 Schmidt, "Schiller und der Idealismus," p. 95.

38 Fontane, "Unsere lyrische und epische Poesie seit 1848," in his *Sämtliche Werke* v. XXI:1, pp. 7-34.

39 Gustav Freytag, *Soll und Haben,* ed. Hans Mayer (Munich/Vienna: Hanser, 1977), p. 10. All further references to the novel will be to this edition, and page references will appear in the text.

40 Berthold Auerbach, "Schrift und Volk," vol. 20 of *Berthold Auerbachs gesammelte Schriften* (Stuttgart/Augsburg: Cotta, 1858), p. 104.

41 Auerbach, *Schrift und Volk,* p. 108. Reference to the "notwendiges geschichtliches Gesetz" underlying the *Volksschrift* and the portrayal of "volkstümlicher Zustände" is from page 107.

42 Auerbach, *Schrift und Volk,* p. 238.

43 Kinder, p. 123.

44 Kinder, p. 171, referring to *Die Grenzboten.*

45 Widhammer, *Literaturtheorie,* p. 57.

46 Widhammer, *Literaturtheorie,* p. 57. Widhammer labels Freytag "Der Wirkungsästhetiker des Programms par excellence," a conclusion he had reached in his earlier *Realismus und klassizistische Tradition,* p. 122.

47 Berger und Luckmann, pp. 124-126. Since their treatise forms one of the bases of investigation in the present study, it seemed expedient to adopt their definition of ideology, which is flexible and also appropriate for the context of discussion.

48 Eisele's study of Prutz's *Deutsches Museum,* to take a slightly different example, is a densely argued, extremely perceptive analysis of the consequences of Hegelian "Identitätsdenken," the immanent character of the rational essence within contingent reality, for the entire question of literary realism in Germany. Unfortunately, Eisele grants the sphere of literary theory an autonomy which diminishes the weight of his conclusions. He characterizes the basis of his analysis early in the book: "Die literaturtheoretische Dimension muß dem, was man den historischen Kontext nennt, erst entrissen werden." Eisele, *Realismus und Ideologie,* p. 3. It is necessary to connect the historical context, the literary-theoretical or programmatic dimension and the literary works as literature.

49 Dieter Kafitz, *Figurenkonstellation als Mittel der Wirklichkeitserfassung: dargestellt an Romanen der 2. Hälfte des 19. Jahrhunderts* (Kronberg/Cz.: Athenäum, 1978); Michael Schneider, *Geschichte als Gestalt. Formen der Wirklichkeit und Wirklichkeit der Form in Gustav Freytags Roman "Soll und Haben"* (Stuttgart: Akademischer Verlag Hans-Dieter Heinz, 1980).

50 Berger and Luckmann, p. 96.

51 Berger and Luckmann, p. 98.

52 Rhöse, p. 162.

53 Berger and Luckmann, p. 99.

54 The most relevant books by Barthes in the present context are: *Le Degré Zéro de L'Ecriture* (Paris: Edition du Seuil, 1967); *Éléments de Sémiologie* (Paris: Editions du Seuil, 1964); *Mythologies* (Paris: Editions du Seuil, 1957); and *S/Z* (Paris: Editions du Seuil, 1970). I will quote from the following English versions: *Writing Degree Zero. Elements of Semiology*, trans. A. Lavers and C. Smith (Boston: Beacon, 1967); *Mythologies*, trans. A. Lavers (New York: Hill and Wang, 1972); *S/Z*, trans. R. Miller (New York: Hill and Wang, 1974). The passage referred to here is from *S/Z*, p. 156.

55 Baur lists the original publication of all village tales. Baur, p. 276.

56 Hahl, *Realismus und Gründerzeit*, v. I, p. 61.

57 Berthold Auerbach, *Gesammelte Schriften*, v. I (Stuttgart/Augsburg: Cotta, 1857), p. 170. All further references to the two stories will be to this edition, and page references will appear in the text.

58 Mettenleitner's designation of the segments as only "lose verbunden" is superficial. Peter Mettenleitner, *Destruktion der Heimatdichtung: Typologische Untersuchungen zu Gotthelf – Auerbach – Ganghofer* (Tübingen: Tübinger Vereinigung für Volkskunde E.V. Tübingen Schloß, 1974), p. 217.

59 It should be noted that Auerbach's rendering of the village dialect in the tales is partially oriented toward his middle-class readers. Baur has chosen the apt designation "Auerbachsches Bauernhochdeutsch" with reference to Walter Henzen, *Schriftsprache und Mundarten* (Bern, 1954); Baur, p. 111.

60 Hahl, p. 61. A further example of liberal demands is the criticism of the legal practice of closed hearings on page 161 in the story.

61 Baur interprets the passage as an "Erziehungsprozeß" which allows the village boy to regard a part of his ordinary environment in a new "artistic" perspective. His interpretation does not contradict the change in perspective postulated here. Baur, p. 108.

62 The refusal, and the entire speech of Buchmaier are of course representative of the "political" dimension of the story as connected to the *Vormärz* opposition to arbitrary authority.

63 Hahl, p. 61. The thesis itself is valid, as outlined in the first section of this chapter.

64 The pipe is expressly designated as a sign of social identity in *Tolpatsch*, another of the early stories. The sexual implications are readily apparent and support the interpretation of deviance, willful and harmful self-assurance, and final recuperation within the socially accepted institution of marriage.

65 Fontane, *Sämtliche Werke,* v. XXI:1, p. 218.

66 Lindau, p. 165.

67 Kafitz, pp. 71-72.

68 Already Fontane criticized the foreshortening of the realms of the Jews and the aristocracy in order to emphasize the middle-class, as much as he was in sympathy with the *Idee* of the novel: Fontane, *Sämtliche Werke,* v. XXI-1, pp. 227-230.

69 All treatments of the novel agree on the question. Stockinger modifies the simple "Verherrlichung des Bürgertums" in a differentiated analysis of the text as an answer to the legitimation crisis of liberalism in the 1850s, but his revised assessment of the nobility still corresponds to bourgeois ideology of the period: Ludwig Stockinger, "Realpolitik, Realismus und das Ende des bürgerlichen Wahrheitsanspruchs. Überlegungen zur Funktion des programmatischen Realismus am Beispiel von Gustav Freytags 'Soll und Haben'," in *Bürgerlicher Realismus,* ed. Müller, pp. 174-202.

70 Bramsted suggests the reason for the anachronism was Freytag's close acquaintance with such businesses, and he also points to the continued suitability of that type of firm for the middle-class consciousness in the 1850s: Bramsted, pp. 116-118. The model for Schröter's company is generally agreed to be the Breslau firm of Th. Molinari: Bramsted, p. 117. See also Kienzle, p. 22, and Helmut Schwitzgebel, "Gustav Freytags 'Soll und Haben' in der Tradition des deutschen Kaufmannsromans," *Gustav-Freytag-Blätter,* 24 (1980), pp. 3-12; 25 (1981), pp. 3-11; 26 (1982), pp. 3-13.

71 There have been several analyses made of the Jewish figures in *Soll und Haben* which call attention to the figure of Bernhard as anomalous and attempt to circumscribe Freytag's stance on Jewish questions during his lifetime: Kockjoy, pp. 75-77; Kienzle. pp. 36-38; Kafitz, pp. 74-75; Hubrichs, pp. 118-123; Schneider, pp. 136-139; Gelber, "Teaching 'Literary Anti-Semitism' ..." and his article "An Alternate Reading of the Role of the Jewish Scholar in Gustav Freytag's *Soll und Haben,*" *Germanic Review* 58 (1983), pp. 83-88. Discussions with Mark Gelber on the issue have been helpful. See also his dissertation, "Aspects of Literary Anti-Semitism: Dickens' *Oliver Twist* and Freytag's *Soll und Haben*" Diss. Yale University 1980.

72 Kafitz, p. 72.

73 Berger and Luckmann, pp. 25-6.

74 Berger and Luckmann, p. 130.

75 Berger and Luckmann, p. 138.

76 Carter, p. 321.

77 Berger and Luckmann, p. 96.

78 Herbert Kaiser bases his entire analysis of the novel on the "Poesie des Geschäfts." Herbert Kaiser, *Studien zum deutschen Roman nach 1848* (Duisburg: Walter Braun, 1977), pp. 57-106. See also E. McInnes, " 'Die Poesie des Geschäfts.' Social Analysis and Polemic in Freytag's *Soll und Haben*," in *Formen realistischer Erzählkunst, Festschrift für Charlotte Jolles,* ed. J. Thunecke (Nottingham: Sherwood Agencies, 1979), pp. 99-107.

79 Kaiser, p. 88.

80 On the connection to *Technik des Dramas*: Kaiser, pp. 95-103; Paul Ulrich, *Gustav Freytags Romantechnik,* Beiträge zur deutschen Literaturwissenschaft, Nr. 3 (Marburg: N.G. Elwert'sche Verlagsbuchhandlung, 1907). On the ties to the *Grenzboten*, among others: Steinecke, v.I, pp. 204-225; Helmut Kreuzer, "Zur Theorie des deutschen Realismus zwischen Märzrevolution und Naturalismus," in *Realismustheorien,* eds. J. Hermand and R. Grimm (Stuttgart: Kohlhammer, 1975), pp. 48-67; Rhöse, pp. 117-145, and Mark Gelber, "Die literarische Umwelt zu Gustav Freytags *Soll und Haben* und die Realismustheorie der *Grenzboten*," *Orbis Litterarum,* 39 (1984), pp. 38-53.

81 John L. McHale, *Die Form der Novellen "Die Leute von Seldwyla" von Gottfried Keller und der "Schwarzwälder Dorfgeschichten" von Berthold Auerbach* (Bern: Paul Haupt, 1957). Mettenleitner compares Gotthelf, Auerbach and Ganghofer, and Baur treats numerous authors of the *Vormärz*.

82 Jonathan Culler, *Structuralist Poetics* (Ithaca: Cornell Univ. Press, 1975), p. 224.

83 Barthes, *S/Z*, p. 156. Also there: "The moral law, the law of value of the readerly, is to *fill in* the chains of causality; for thus each determinant must be, insofar as possible, determined, so that every notation is intermediary, doubly oriented, caught up in an ultimate progression" pp. 181-2.

84 John Lyons, *Introduction to Theoretical Linguistics* (Cambridge: Cambridge Univ. Press, 1968), pp. 127, 470-472. Also: Roman Jakobson and Morris Halle, *Fundamentals of Language,* 2nd ed. (1956; rpt. The Hague: Mouton and Co., 1971). The use of the term in the present context is restricted to the heuristic definition established for it.

85 Schwitzgebel refers to Schröter as "der Fixpunkt, nicht der Endpunkt," and the point is well-expressed: Schwitzgebel, Teil 2 (1981), p. 10.

86 Sammons, p. 320.

87 Such an avoidance of direct authorial interpolation is in accordance with Auerbach's criticism of Romantic narration and "Tendenzdichtung." See

Schrift und Volk, especially the rejection of irony and the call for "ein völliges Zurücktreten des Autors" (pp. 50-51).

88 Berthold Auerbach, *Gesammelte Schriften,* I (Stuttgart/Augsburg: Cotta, 1858) p. viii.

89 Ibid., pp. v-vi.

90 McHale terms this paralleling "Seelengemeinschaft." McHale, p. 74.

91 Auerbach, *Schrift und Volk,* p. 147.

Chapter III: Convention and Narrative Refraction

1 Reuter's two-volume monograph refers to a second, definitive renaissance, following a previous revival of interest in the 1920s. Preisendanz and Jolles write of a new beginning in the 1950s, and Brinkmann's study of Fontane and summary-reports on current scholarship by Paulsen and Skreb specify a "Fontane-Renaissance." Documentation and interpretation of the intensified critical interest in Fontane is available in the volume by Tontsch, who designates the 1960s as the period of a Fontane renaissance. Betz points to the coincidence of interest in Fontane in the 1960s and the research in literary sociology and popular literature. The three main editions are published by the Nymphenburger Verlagshandlung (1959 ff), Hanser Verlag (1962 ff) and Aufbau Verlag (1969 ff). Frederick Betz, "Fontane Scholarship, Literary Sociology, and *Trivialliteraturforschung,*" *Internationales Archiv für Sozialgeschichte der deutschen Literatur,* 8 (1983), pp. 200-220; Richard Brinkmann, *Theodor Fontane: Über die Verbindlichkeit des Unverbindlichen,* 2nd ed. (Tübingen: Max Niemeyer Verlag, 1977), p. 11; Charlotte Jolles, *Theodor Fontane,* 3rd. ed., Sammlung Metzler, 114 (Stuttgart: Metzler, 1983), p. 136; Wolfgang Paulsen, "Zum Stand der heutigen Fontane-Forschung," *Jahrbuch der deutschen Schillergesellschaft,* 25 (1981), pp. 474-508; Wolfgang Preisendanz, "Vorwort," in *Theodor Fontane,* ed. W. Preisendanz, Wege der Forschung, 381 (Darmstadt: Wissenschaftliche Buchgesellschaft, 1973), pp. vii-xiii; Hans-Heinrich Reuter, *Fontane* (Munich: Nymphenburger Verlagshandlung, 1968), II, pp. 908-919; Zdenko Skreb, "Forschungsbericht − Fragen zum deutschen Realismus: Fontane," *Jahrbuch der Raabe-Gesellschaft* (1979), pp. 155-185; Ulrike Tontsch, *Der "Klassiker" Fontane: ein Rezeptionsprozess* (Bonn: Bouvier, 1977), pp. 104-119. Also of interest is U. Tontsch, "Fontane im Lesebuch," in *Fontane aus heutiger Sicht,* ed. H. Aust (Munich: Nymphenburger Verlagshandlung, 1980), pp. 282-294.

2 Walter Müller-Seidel, *Theodor Fontane: Soziale Romankunst in Deutschland* (Stuttgart: Metzler, 1975), pp. 3-4.
3 Peter Härtling, "Theodor Fontane: 'Der Stechlin'," *Die Zeit,* 9. Mar. 1979, p. 49, cols. 1-5.
4 Rainer Werner Fassbinder, "Gehabtes Sollen — gesolltes Haben," *Die Zeit,* 18. Mar. 1977, p. 15, cols. 1-4, here col. 4. Fassbinder clearly states the aim of his project several times in the article and emphasizes the critical distance repeatedly: "das Erkennen bestimmter Werte und Haltungen als geschichtlich gewordene, kann an Hand einer Neubesichtigung von 'Soll und Haben' geleistet werden." Other pertinent articles in the controversy include the following: Hans Mayer, "Ist Gustav Freytag neu zu entdecken," *Frankfurter Allgemeine Zeitung,* 26. Feb. 1977, p. 23, cols. 1-5. (parallels the afterword to his edition of Freytag's novel); "Tragischer Itzig," *Der Spiegel,* 7. Mar. 1977, p. 193, cols. 1-2; p. 194, col. 3; Hans C. Blumenberg, "Die Angst des Intendanten," *Die Zeit,* 25. Mar. 1977, p. 14, col. 1; Theodor Eschenburg, "Gustav Freytag und der Antisemitismus," *Frankfurter Allgemeine Zeitung,* 9. Apr. 1977, p. 21, cols. 1-5.
5 Christian Braad Thomsen, "Interview with Fassbinder (Berlin 1974)," in *Fassbinder,* ed. Tony Rayns (London: British Film Institute, 1976), pp. 45-55, here p. 45. Also: Helmut Schanze, "Fontane Effi Briest: Bemerkungen zu einem Drehbuch von Rainer Werner Fassbinder," in *Literatur in den Massenmedien: Demontage von Dichtung?,* ed. F. Knille, K. Hickethier, W.-D. Lützen, Reihe Hanser, 221 (Munich: Hanser, 1976), pp. 131-138; Nikola Hoeltz, "Fontane — mediengerecht?," *Kürbiskern,* 2 (1979), pp. 91-104; Joachim Biener, "Zur Aneignung von Fontanes Epik durch Film und Fernsehen," *Fontane-Blätter,* 4, Heft 8 (1981), pp. 713-728; Jürgen Wolff, "Verfahren der Literaturrezeption im Film, dargestellt am Beispiel der Effi-Briest-Verfilmungen von Luderer und Fassbinder," *Der Deutschunterricht,* 33, Heft 4 (1981), pp. 47-75; William R. Magretta, "Reading the Writerly Film: Fassbinder's *Effi Briest* (1974)," in *Modern European Filmmakers and the Art of Adaptation,* ed. A. Horton and J. Magretta (New York: Frederick Ungar, 1981), pp. 248-62. Magretta's article is very relevant to my analysis. He utilizes Barthes's theoretical framework and follows Fassbinder's understanding of Fontane as seeing the audience "producing a text" (p. 250).
6 Victor Lange, "The Reader in the Strategy of Fiction," in *Expression, Communication and Experience in Literature and Language: Proceedings of the XII Congress of the International Federation for Modern Language and Literature,* ed. R.G. Popperwell (London: Modern Humanities Research Association, 1973), p. 98. The specific reference is to Balzac.
7 Peter Demetz, *Formen des Realismus: Theodor Fontane* (1964; rpt. Frankfurt/Main: Ullstein, 1973), pp. 120-125.

8 "Resignation" seems a perennial category of Fontane scholarship. Karl Richter, *Resignation: Eine Studie zum Werk Theodor Fontanes*. (Stuttgart: Kohlhammer, 1966), on the societal restriction placed on Fontane's characters esp. 25-39 and (on *Effi Briest*) pp. 45-51. Richter differentiates between those who act unconsciously in accord with fixed social norms and the figures who choose to acquiesce. Joachim Remak, *The Gentle Critic: Theodor Fontane in German Politics 1848-1898* (Syracuse: Syracuse University Press, 1964), pp. 34-5, using *Irrungen, Wirrungen* as an example. Remak finds a consistency between Fontane's literary production and his political views. Richard Brinkmann, in an often-quoted phrase, distinguishes the "critical contemporary" from the "conciliatory author." Brinkmann, "Gesellschaftskritik: Der strenge Zeitgenosse, der versöhnliche Dichter," in his *Theodor Fontane*, pp. 27-38. "Resignation" is also a theme for J.P. Stern, "Realism and Tolerance: Theodor Fontane," in his *Re-Interpretations* (New York: Basic Books, 1964), pp. 300-347, esp. p. 339. Also: Walter Müller-Seidel, "Gesellschaft und Menschlichkeit im Roman Theodor Fontanes," *Heidelberger Jahrbücher*, IV (1960), pp. 108-127; rpt. in *Theodor Fontane*, ed. W. Preisendanz, pp. 169-200; on resignation esp. pp. 194-5. A carefully considered repudiation of "resignation" is offered in Hanni Mittelmann's study of selected female figures: Hanni Mittelmann, *Die Utopie des weiblichen Glücks in den Romanen Theodor Fontanes* (Bern: Lang, 1980).

9 Berger and Luckmann, p. 79.

10 Berger and Luckmann, p. 60.

11 Berger and Luckmann, p. 64.

12 The following are a few of the important treatments of the issue: Mary-Enole Gilbert, *Das Gespräch in Fontanes Gesellschaftsromanen*, Palaestra, 174 (Leipzig: Mayer and Müller, 1930); Hubert Ohl, "Welt als Gespräch," in his *Bild und Wirklichkeit: Studien zur Romankunst Raabes und Fontanes* (Heidelberg: Lothar Stiehm, 1968), pp. 156-199; Ingrid Mittenzwei, *Die Sprache als Thema: Untersuchungen zu Fontanes Gesellschaftsromanen*, Frankfurter Beiträge zur Germanistik, 12 (Bad Homburg v.d.H.: Gehlen, 1970); Fritz Martini, *Deutsche Literatur im bürgerlichen Realismus 1848-1898*, pp. 767-770; Wolfgang Preisendanz, *Humor als dichterische Einbildungskraft: Studien zur Erzählkunst des poetischen Realismus*, 2nd ed. (Munich: Fink, 1974), pp. 230-237; Demetz, 112-116; Brinkmann, pp. 127-154 ("Das Gespräch als menschliche Realität"). One of the most succinct and appropriate descriptive phrases for the function of language and social interaction in Fontane's works is Ohl's adaptation of a phrase of Friedrich Beißner's: "dialogische Facettierung der erzählten Welt." Ohl, p. 176.

13 Conrad Wandrey, *Theodor Fontane* (Munich: Beck, 1919), p. 155; Demetz, p. 134; Reuter, II, pp. 602, 609, 640; Martini, p. 765; Mittenzwei, p. 50;

Pierre-Paul Sagave, ed., *Schach von Wuthenow*, by Theodor Fontane (Frankfurt/Main: Ullstein, 1966), p. 117.

14 The alternative titles which Fontane considered are also significant in assessing the importance of the historical setting: "1806," "Vor Jena," "Et dissipati sunt," "Gezählt, gewogen und hinweggethan," "Vor dem Niedergang (Fall, Sturz)," "Vanitas Vanitatum:" Jolles, p. 68. Müller-Seidel and Reuter give summaries of Fontane's interest in the exact period, and an extensive treatment is found in the articles by Berend and Sagave and in the latter's documented edition of the text. Eduard Berend, "Die historische Grundlage von Theodor Fontanes Erzählung 'Schach von Wuthenow'," *Deutsche Rundschau*, 50 (1924), pp. 168-182; Pierre-Paul Sagave, " 'Schach von Wuthenow' als politischer Roman," in *Fontanes Realismus: Wissenschaftliche Konferenz zum 150. Geburtstag Theodor Fontanes in Potsdam: Vorträge und Berichte*, ed. H.E. Teitge and J. Schobeß (Berlin/GDR: Akademie Verlag, 1972), pp. 87-94; Sagave, ed., *Schach von Wuthenow*, pp. 113-152; Müller-Seidel, *Theodor Fontane*, pp. 132-138; Reuter, II, pp. 596-601. See also the appropriate section in Verchau's book and the useful volume of materials in the Reclam series: Ekkhard Verchau, *Theodor Fontane. Individuum und Gesellschaft* (Frankfurt am Main: Ullstein, 1983), pp. 150-156. Walter Wagner, ed., *Theodor Fontane: Schach von Wuthenow. Erläuterungen und Dokumente* (Stuttgart: Reclam, 1980). Garland gives a good English commentary on the historical connections: Henry Garland, *The Berlin Novels of Theodor Fontane* (Oxford: Clarendon Press, 1980), pp. 29-44.

15 Benno von Wiese, "Theodor Fontane: 'Schach von Wuthenow'," in his *Die deutsche Novelle von Goethe bis Kafka* (Düsseldorf: August Bagel, 1962), II, pp. 236-260, here pp. 237-238; Reuter, II, p. 602; Sagave in *Fontanes Realismus*, pp. 93-4; Müller-Seidel, *Theodor Fontane*, p. 149.

16 Wandrey's interpretation suffers from this error. His assessment of the psychological inconsistency of the title character leads him to fault the strategies of narrative refraction which carry the very import of the work. Wandrey, pp. 157-163.

17 Theodor Fontane, *Sämtliche Werke* (Munich, Nymphenburger Verlagshandlung, 1959), v. II, p. 274. All further references to the novel will be to this edition and will be given in parentheses in the text.

18 Gilbert, pp. 70-71; von Wiese, *passim;* Ohl, pp. 162-165; Demetz, pp. 136-137; Mittenzwei, p. 51.

19 On the "Nachgespräch" and its function in Fontane's novels: Demetz, pp. 124-5.

20 Demetz, pp. 122-123.

21 Mittenzwei, p. 55.

22 H.R. Vaget has published a cogent analysis of Chapter 14: H. Rudolf Vaget, "Schach in Wuthenow: 'Psychographie' und 'Spiegelung' im 14. Kapitel von Fontanes 'Schach von Wuthenow'," in *Monatshefte,* 61 (1969), pp. 1-14.

23 Müller-Seidel, p. 138.

24 Mittenzwei overlooks the passage and designates Victoire's defense of the Poles as the first opposition to Bülow, which allows her to draw a frame for the novel in the parallel to the opposition of the final letters. Mittenzwei, p. 53. Her conclusion could be modified to apply to the more general opposition of personal and political perspectives.

25 Georg Lukács gives a good example of the tendency to equate Bülow with Fontane's own standpoint. Georg Lukács, "Der alte Fontane," in his *Die Grablegung des alten Deutschland,* pp. 120-156, here pp. 151-153.

26 Müller-Seidel, *Theodor Fontane,* p. 143. Von Wiese misses the narrative function and reads the passage as a paradox. von Wiese, p. 243.

27 Fontane, *Sämtliche Werke,* II, p. 385 *(Schach von Wuthenow).* All further passages quoted in this section are from *Effi Briest* and refer to volume VII of the Nymphenburger edition. Page references will be given in parentheses in the text.

28 Roy Pascal, *The German Novel* (Toronto: University of Toronto Press, 1956), p. 188.

29 Martini's analysis repeatedly emphasizes the irrational forces underlying the story, and his own language of interpretation is characterized by adjectives, nouns, and verbs which establish the irrational as a final level of the novel, an explanation in itself, as the "Offenheit zur unbegrenzten Möglichkeitsfülle des Lebens": "Der klar geordnete Ablauf innerhalb der alltäglichen Realität wird zum Irrationalen transparent." Martini, p. 791. Brinkmann refers to "fate" as calling Effi from her state of childlike innocence and finally releasing her again. Brinkmann, p. 80. Reuter is more perceptive in his connection of fate to social forces and declares the feminine lot to be a social paradigm in itself. Reuter, II, pp. 636, 641-7. His analysis of *Effi Briest* is marred by the harshly overstated reduction of marriage to an exchange of property, an analysis prompted more by his own political convictions than by Fontane's novel. Reuter, II, pp. 682-3. Müller-Seidel's more subtle analysis of the secular, social character of marriage in the nineteenth century, which he labels "eine gesellschaftliche Veranstaltung schlechthin," is more appropriate. Müller-Seidel, p. 354. Thomas Degering's comparison of *Effi Briest* and *Madame Bovary* offers a brief examination of society as fate, connecting it mainly to the leitmotif of "ein weites Feld." Thomas Degering, *Das Verhältnis von Individuum und Gesellschaft in Fontanes "Effi Briest" und Flauberts "Madame Bovary"* (Bonn: Bouvier, 1978), pp. 79-81.

Helen E. Chambers offers few new interpretative insights, but her study provides background and sees a definite role for fate: Helen E. Chambers, *Supernatural and Irrational Elements in the Works of Theodor Fontane* (Stuttgart: Akademischer Verlag Hans-Dieter Heinz, 1980), pp. 185-214. See also: Heinz Schlaffer, "Das Schicksalsmodell in Fontanes Romanwerk. Konstanz und Auflösung," *Germanisch-Romanische Monatsschrift,* N.F. 16 (1966), pp. 392-409.

30 The best example of her rigidity is the exchange with Roswitha following the discovery of the letters (383-385). Jost Schillemeit indicates the manner in which Johanna's language in the segment parallels Innstetten's arguments concerning the necessity of his actions. Renny Harrigan examines the function of Johanna as a contrast figure to Roswitha, especially in this scene. For Mary-Enole Gilbert, Roswitha is "ganz Natur" and Johanna "ganz Form." Reinhard Thum's treatment offers the interesting opposition of blondes and brunettes in the novel, exemplified by Johanna and Roswitha. The point is a bit strained in the application to Innstetten as a mixture of types. Fassbinder's casting of the role of course destroys any such typology. Jost Schillemeit, *Theodor Fontane: Geist und Kunst seines Alterswerkes* (Zürich: Atlantis, 1961), pp. 84-5; Renny Harrigan, "The Portrayal of the Lower Classes and the Petty Bourgeoisie in Theodor Fontane's Social Novels," Diss. Brown 1973, pp. 134-143; Mary-Enole Gilbert, "Fontane's 'Effi Briest'," *Der Deutschunterricht,* 11, H. 4 (1959), pp. 63-75; Reinhard H. Thum, "Symbol, Motif and Leitmotif in Fontane's 'Effi Briest'," *The Germanic Review,* 54 (1979), pp. 115-124, here pp. 119-120.

31 Berger and Luckmann, p. 64. Michael Minden's application of Adorno's concept of tact to *Effi Briest* resembles portions of Berger and Luckmann's analyses: Michael Minden, " 'Effi Briest' and 'Die historische Stunde des Takts'," *Modern Language Review,* 76 (1981), pp. 869-879. An example of common ground is the statement: "The world and language of tact have the ability to circumscribe, order, and contain immediate experience, but they are also liable to do violence to such experience."

32 Mittenzwei, p. 144. It is, of course, Innstetten's social identity as a civil servant and not his class background which is the factor. Mittenzwei is too quick to speak of a nobleman. Leslie Miller offers an interesting analysis of Innstetten and a plea for understanding his character: Leslie L. Miller, "Fontane's *Effi Briest.* Innstetten's Decision: In Defense of the Gentleman," *German Studies Review,* 4-3 (October, 1981), pp. 383-402.

33 Such an interpretation of the function of conversation, monologue, and dialogue disagrees with Gilbert's analysis of the place of conversation in *Effi Briest* as contributing to the "Abgeschlossenheit des Romanverlaufs." Gilbert, *Das Gespräch,* pp. 35-39. Elsbeth Hamann has published two books on *Effi Briest,* and portions of the sections on conversation as a narrative tech-

nique are identical. Although she states that it is not the plot, but the dialogue which creates "den epischen Zusammenhang," she categorizes the conversational scenes according to their function for the plot: "vorantreiben," "verzögern," "verdichten," "ausweiten." Elsbeth Hamann, *Theodor Fontane. Effi Briest* (Munich: Oldenbourg, 1981), pp. 88-93; E. Hamann, *Theodor Fontanes "Effi Briest" aus erzähltheoretischer Sicht* (Bonn: Bouvier, 1984), pp. 337-390.

34   Wandrey, p. 285. The reference ("größte Sprechszene des deutschen Romans") is invariably cited in studies of *Effi Briest*. Reuter's statement that the dialogue remains an intermezzo (Reuter, II, p. 685) because it is Effi's story and not Innstetten's is somewhat misleading. In the constitution of the field of reference of the text, Innstetten's belated insights are extremely important because, as Reuter himself points out, Innstetten reaches a level of recognition which Effi does not attain (Reuter, II, p. 683).

35   The imagery in this passage and its connection to Effi's character and to a thematic complex within the novel is well analyzed by Demetz in the section "Symbolische Motive: Flug und Flocke." Demetz: *Formen*, pp. 179-189, esp. 184-189. Thum's comment that Demetz merely "mentions" swing and sled in the novel is curious, considering the extent of the analysis in *Formen des Realismus:* Thum, p. 124, notes 2 and 10. Bindokat's study of the novel devotes a chapter to the motif of "Tochter der Luft": Karla Bindokat, *Effi Briest: Erzählstoff und Erzählinhalt* (Bern: Lang, 1984), pp. 149-165.

36   Müller-Seidel's commentary assigns a central role to the phenomenon of *Angst*. He interprets it primarily in the motif of the Chinaman, which he links to the significance of Bismarck in the novel. Müller-Seidel, *Theodor Fontane*, pp. 363-365. Effi's anxiety at the end of Chapter 4 precedes the introduction of the Chinaman motif, but it can be connected to the same thematic complex. Her fear of Innstetten ("Ich fürchte mich vor ihm") as a man of principles is indicative of her discomfort with the social definitions his principles represent. Jamison's interpretation of Effi's attraction to fear is not entirely convincing: Robert L. Jamison, "The Fearful Education of Effi Briest," *Monatshefte*, 74 (1982), pp. 20-32.

37   The initial scenes have received extensive commentary. The best analysis of the tension between Effi's "Unbefangenheit des Sprechens" and a clichéed "Befangenheit der Sprache im durchaus Gängigen und Herkömmlichen" is Mittenzwei's interpretation. Mittenzwei, pp. 135-137.

38   The play was written by Ernst Wichert and first performed in 1873. As in the minor historical details of *Schach von Wuthenow*, acquaintance with the play might enhance a reading of the novel, but the narrative function does not rest upon the literary qualities or upon Fontane's attitude to the play in other writings. Similarly, the actual incident of the affair of Frau von

Ardenne, which forms the basis for Spielhagen's *Zeitvertreib* as well, is peripheral to an understanding of the novel. Müller-Seidel gives detailed background on the incident, as does the Reclam volume of materials for analysis. Müller-Seidel, *Theodor Fontane,* pp. 325-357; Walter Schafarschik ed., *Theodor Fontane. "Effi Briest:" Erläuterungen und Dokumente* (Stuttgart: Reclam, 1972), pp. 83-100. Anna Maria Gilbert also argues for not overestimating the role of the Ardenne affair in the genesis of *Effi Briest* and illuminates the contribution of Kleist's *Käthchen von Heilbronn* and Roderick Benedix' play *Aschenbrödel* to Fontane's concept. Anna Maria Gilbert, "A New Look at *Effi Briest.* Genesis and Interpretation," *Deutsche Vierteljahrsschrift für Literaturwissenschaft und Geistesgeschichte,* 53-1 (1979), pp. 96-114.

39 Martini tends to overemphasize the psychological dimension to the novel, and his designation of moral catharsis in the face of death and resignation in the face of the inexplicable as the final themes diminishes somewhat the force of the novel. Martini, pp. 790-794. Schillemeit follows a similar thesis in positing a circular movement in the work which restores Effi to her origins. He grants the significance of the final sentence but finds the end characteristic for the "Frieden" and "Trost" which always round off a Fontane novel. Schillemeit, p. 82.

40 Briest's refrain has been duly noted in most studies of the novel. Perhaps the most succinct comment on the sentence is that of Mittenzwei, who finds it a "listiger Satz," "der, so sehr er nach außen Formel ist, inhaltlich gerade das Gegenteil, nämlich eine Infragestellung, eine Absage an alles zur Formel Verfestigte, bedeutet." Mittenzwei, p. 145. Her interpretation supports my analysis of the tension between the conventional, logical level of the narrative and an underlying ambiguity.

41 A comparison to the function of the dialogues between Anton Wohlfart and Schröter in *Soll und Haben* is enlightening. In Freytag's novel, the conversations serve to reinforce the legitimacy of the narrated action. See my Chapter 2.

42 Berger and Luckmann, p. 44.

43 Müller-Seidel, *Theodor Fontane,* p. 362. Ohl, 210 ff. Ohl uses a very carefully defined concept of symbolism in his analysis of Fontane's prose. Reuter's attempt to retain a modified concept of symbolism for Fontane, specifically in the analysis of *Schach von Wuthenow,* is less successful. Reuter, II, pp. 602-608. Brackert and Schuller emphasize the pared-down plot and the "Substituierung der Erzählung der Handlung durch symbolische Metaphorisierung" (p. 156), which is taken as a manifestation of an aesthetic conservatism corresponding to a resignative understanding of the relative passivity of the individual in the historical-social situation: Helmut Brackert and Marianne Schuller, "Theodor Fontane, *Effi Briest,*" in *Literaturwissen-*

schaft. Grundkurs 1, ed. H. Brackert and J. Stückrath, v. I (Reinbek bei Hamburg: Rowohlt, 1981), pp. 153-172.

44 Ferdinand de Saussure, *Course in General Linguistics,* trans. W. Baskin (New York: McGraw-Hill, 1959), pp. 122-127. For various adaptations of the terms: Robert Scholes, *Structuralism in Literature: An Introduction* (New Haven: Yale Univ. Press, 1974), pp. 18-19, 149, 161 f, 187; Terence Hawkes, *Structuralism and Semiotics* (Los Angeles: Univ. of California Press, 1977), pp. 26-7, 65; Culler, *Structuralist Poetics,* pp. 13, 36-7.

45 Effi is not the only figure deserving of reader sympathy. Reuter points out that Innstetten's own personal tragedy is often neglected, and Demetz correctly assesses the probable reader attitude by stating that it would be understandable but misleading to find sympathy only for the title figure. Reuter, II, pp. 683-4; Peter Demetz, *Kitsch, Belletristik, Kunst: Theodor Fontane* (Berlin: Akademie der Künste, 1970), p. 18.

46 Reuter, II, pp. 680-682. Reuter writes of the "Souveränität und heiteren Schwerelosigkeit des Erzählflusses," and the contrast "zwischen dieser Leichtigkeit und dem Gewicht des Geschehens." See also: M.C. Devine, "Erzähldistanz in Fontanes *Effi Briest,"* in *Formen realistischer Erzählkunst,* pp. 544-549.

47 Martini points out a dominant tenor of sentimentality in the obvious sympathy of the narrator in the final chapter of the novel, which he regards as a break in style. Martini, p. 790.

48 Fassbinder's film casts an interesting focus on this passage. His voice-over narration presents the sentence as it stands, but the visual scene shows Gieshübler merely sitting with Effi. The lack of congruence between narrated action and filmed action emphasizes the presence of the narrator and the significance of the passage.

49 Demetz, *Kitsch, Belletristik, Kunst,* pp. 20-21.

50 Reinhard Thum's article discussing the complex pattern of symbols, motifs, and leitmotifs in *Effi Briest* states that this aspect of the novel has been neglected. The assessment is misleading, as he doesn't consider the studies by Ohl, Mittenzwei, and Schillemeit, among others. Nevertheless, his essay, although reductive in its rigid attempts at categorization, does illuminate some previously unanalyzed aspects of the work, such as the Graf von Strahl motif and the pagan rituals of the "Hertasee." Thum, *passim.* See note 30 above for his typology of blonds and brunettes in the work. Analyses of the Chinaman and other motifs in addition to works already cited are: T.E. Carter, "A Leitmotif in Fontane's 'Effi Briest'," *German Life and Letters,* 10 (1956-7), pp. 38-42; Joseph Thanner, "Symbol and Function of the Symbol in Theodor Fontane's 'Effi Briest'," *Monatshefte,* 57 (1965), pp. 187-192;

Ulrike Rainer, "Effi Briest und das Motiv des Chinesen: Rolle und Darstellung in Fontanes Roman," *Zeitschrift für deutsche Philologie,* 101 (1982), pp. 545-561; Ingrid Schuster, "Erotik als Chiffre: Zum Chinesen in *Effi Briest," Wirkendes Wort,* 33 (1983), pp. 115-125; Peter Utz, "Effi Briest, der Chinese und der Imperialismus: eine 'Geschichte' im geschichtlichen Kontext," *Zeitschrift für deutsche Philologie,* 103 (1984), pp. 212-225.

51 In a letter to Joseph Viktor Widmann from November 19, 1895. The phrase is quoted almost invariably in interpretations of *Effi Briest.* The section of the letter is accessible in the Reclam volume of commentary: Schafarschik, p. 112. J.P. Stern appears to be one of the few to discount the device, and his comment is also invariably quoted. He finds the motif of the Chinaman a "blemish in the novel," "a piece of bric-à-brac left over by 'poetic realism'." Stern, p. 319.

52 Müller-Seidel, *Theodor Fontane,* p. 426. Josef Hofmiller, " 'Stechlin'-Probleme," in his *Ausgewählte Werke* (Rosenheim: Rosenheimer Verlagshaus, 1975), p. 224. Alan Bance quotes Flaubert's phrase *le roman sur rien* and finds that "its essence is unpretentiousness." Alan Bance, *Theodor Fontane: The Major Novels* (Cambridge: Cambridge Univ. Press, 1982), p. 186. Pascal and Wandrey emphasize the apparent lack of traditional novel form: Pascal, p. 206; Wandrey, p. 301.

53 Quoted in: Julius Petersen, "Theodor Fontanes Altersroman," *Euphorion,* 29 (1928), p. 13. The same phrase appears in the outline of a letter to Adolf Hoffmann printed in the Reclam collection of materials on *Der Stechlin,* taken from the Aufbau edition of Fontane's letters, edited by G. Erler: Hugo Aust, ed., *Theodor Fontane: "Der Stechlin": Erläuterungen und Dokumente* (Stuttgart: Reclam, 1978), p. 85. The novel first appeared in "Über Land und Meer."

54 One of the most fitting contemporaneous comments is the following answer by Ernst Heilborn to those critics reproaching the work for not being a true novel: "Aber es giebt so viel Romane und so wenig gute Bücher, daß ich's dem alten Fontane verzeihen möchte, daß er diesmal 'nur' ein gutes Buch gegeben." Review of "Der Stechlin" in *Das litterarische Echo,* I (1898/99), column 58 f. Quoted from: *Theodor Fontane 1819-1969: Stationen seines Werkes — Eine Ausstellung des Deutschen Literaturarchivs im Schiller-Nationalmuseum Marbach a.N.,* ed. W. Migge (Munich: Kösel, 1969), p. 212. More extensive documentation of the initial reception of the work is found in the Reclam volume of commentary: Aust, *Theodor Fontane: "Der Stechlin,"* pp. 89-149. The term "Vermächtnis" occurs frequently and is still used in current studies of the novel. The work is also often compared with Fontane's first novel *Vor dem Sturm,* a connection which cannot be pursued in the context of my investigation of reading patterns.

55 Gilbert, *Das Gespräch*, p. 43; Demetz, *Formen*, pp. 158-159, 161-162. Demetz contrasts the work to the dialectical structure of other Fontane novels. Müller-Seidel's interpretations stress the importance of the underlying *Gesinnung*, an assessment in which Hugo Aust concurs. Müller-Seidel is careful to emphasize the manner in which the *form* of the conversations, with its scepticism and ambiguity, works against reading the *content* of the conversations as fixed: Müller-Seidel, in *Der deutsche Roman*, esp. p. 177, also in *Theodor Fontane*, pp. 426-456. Hugo Aust, *Theodor Fontane: "Verklärung": Eine Untersuchung zum Ideengehalt seiner Werke* (Bonn: Bouvier, 1974), pp. 322, 325.

56 E.M. Forster, *Aspects of the Novel*, p. 28. For the applicability of his statement to all of the works I am considering, see my first chapter. Fontane's comment is found in notes for a letter to Adolf Hoffmann, quoted in Aust, *Theodor Fontane: "Der Stechlin,"* p. 86.

57 The first three sections of the novel ("Schloß Stechlin," "Kloster Wutz," "Nach dem Eierhäuschen") introduce the reader to the main spheres of the novel, as outlined by Demetz, *Formen*, p. 159.

58 Theodor Fontane, *Sämtliche Werke* (Munich: Nymphenburger Verlag, 1959) v. VIII, p. 251. All further references to the novel will be to this edition and will be given in parentheses in the text. Martini gives an interesting insight into the phrase "Zusammenhang der Dinge," which he connects to the idealist philosopher Hermann Lotze: Martini, 43-4, 672-3.

59 A good study of Dubslav's conscious juxtaposition of "old and new" vocabulary items is Hermann Meyer's volume: Hermann Meyer, *Das Zitat in der Erzählkunst: Zur Geschichte und Poetik des europäischen Romans* (Stuttgart: Metzler, 1961), on *Der Stechlin*, pp. 174-186, esp. p. 176.

60 Heiko Stech bases his entire interpretation of *Der Stechlin*, which he views as the summation of Fontane's works, on the thematic complex of the old and the new: Heiko Stech, *Theodor Fontane: Die Synthese von Alt und Neu: "Der Stechlin" als Summe des Gesamtwerkes* (Berlin: Erich Schmidt Verlag, 1970). Richter also analyzes the theme at length and reaches the conclusion that the final result is not a "Synthese" but an enduring "Anspannung," an observation which I find applicable to the narrative structure as well: Richter, *Resignation*, p. 106.

61 It is a misreading of the thematic complex of the old and the new to interpret the novel as portraying a culture in decline as Barlow does. In overlooking the ambivalence of both positions he foreshortens the work by a central dimension. The result is such one-sided interpretations as that designating the boulders ("Findlinge") as "a permanent symbol of the useless and the grotesque," and "like Dubslav and the class which he represents, a strange and ludicrous survival from a bygone era." He also reads the story of the

Siamese princess as illustrating the fact that only a miracle can save the Junkers. D. Barlow, "Symbolism in Fontane's 'Der Stechlin'," *German Life and Letters*, 12 (1958-9), pp. 282-286.

62 For Fontane's continued fascination with the mermaid figure and an interpretation of her inner affinity with the essence of nature see Renate Schäfer, "Fontanes Melusine-Motiv," *Euphorion*, 56 (1962), pp. 69-104; Hubert Ohl, "Melusine als Mythos bei Theodor Fontane," in *Mythos und Mythologie in der Literatur des 19. Jahrhunderts*, ed. H. Koopmann (Frankfurt am Main: Vittorio Klostermann, 1979), pp. 289-305; Ursula Schmalbruch, "Zum Melusine-Motiv in Fontanes *Cécile*," *Text und Kontext*, 8 (1980), pp. 127-44.

63 Demetz, *Formen*, p. 195.

64 In an otherwise disappointingly impressionistic study, Guido Vincenz offers an interesting defense of the figure of Adelheid, concentrating especially on her chiding of Woldemar for attaching importance to the regimental hierarchy and her fondness for the museum models of the mills. Guido Vincenz, *Fontanes Welt. Eine Interpretation des Stechlin*, Diss. Zürich 1966 (Zürich: Juris Druck und Verlag, 1966), pp. 11-12.

65 Demetz, *Formen*, p. 167.

66 Max Rychner terms *Der Stechlin* "eines der weisesten Spiele, die mit der deutschen Sprache gespielt wurden." Max Rychner, "Theodor Fontane: Der Stechlin," *Deutsche Romane von Grimmelshausen bis Musil*, ed. J. Schillemeit (Frankfurt am Main: Fischer. 1966), p. 218. See also Hans-Martin Gauger, "Sprachbewußtsein im 'Stechlin'," in *Bild und Gedanke: Festschrift für Gerhart Baumann zum 60. Geburtstag*, ed. G. Schnitzler (Munich: Fink, 1980), pp. 311-323; Katharina Mommsen, "Vom 'Bamme-Ton' zum 'Bummel-Ton': Fontanes Kunst der Sprechweisen," in *Formen realistischer Erzählkunst*, pp. 325-334.

67 The verbal signs which foreshadow Woldemar's choice of the younger Barby sister are as important as the fact that Armgard and Woldemar join hands. The Baron asks if an engagement has perchance been declared; and the description of João de Deus as saintly, "weil er für die Armen gelebt hatte und *nicht für sich*" (p. 145, original emphasis) finds a direct verbal echo in Armgard's explanation of her preference for Elisabeth von Thüringen: "Anderen leben und der Armut das Brot geben – darin allein ruht das Glück" (226).

68 The narrative function of England is to open the horizons of the novel. A comparison with the "narrowing" effect of Poland in Freytag's work, which functions only as the negative contrast to German middle-class values, is productive.

69 In connection with Cujacius, Hermann Meyer's excellent analysis of the use of "Bildung" in *Der Stechlin* should be mentioned. His conclusion that

Woldemar's open admission of his confusion of Millet and Millais is "gebildeter" than Cujacius' pedantry reinforces my analysis of the tone of discourse prevalent in the novel. Meyer, pp. 175-6.

70 The positioning of the initial appearance of Agnes and Buschen is also significant. In Chapter 23, Dubslav receives a letter from Woldemar with the news of the latter's departure for England. In the following conversation with Lorenzen, Dubslav's conservative Russophilia leaves the pastor feeling uneasy. After his departure, Dubslav ponders the course of his own life while looking out over the lake. A variety of central themes coalesce in the segment: the horizon of England, the tradition-bound side of the *Junker*, and the balanced moment of pause and reflection on the interchange of "Altes und Neues" (209), which shaped the course of his life. The appearance of Agnes and Buschen at this juncture and Dubslav's tolerant, gentle manner of talking with them lend the incident and the figures significance.

71 Preisendanz, *Humor*, 232. His analysis of the conversation between Baruch and Isidor Hirschfeld early in the novel is a good illustration of what he means.

72 Vincenz has a short section on "Das Heldische," and Aust has a more thorough treatment of the question. Vincenz, pp. 80-85, Aust, *Theodor Fontane: "Verklärung,"* pp. 302-307. See also: A. Bance, "The Heroic and the Unheroic in Fontane," in *Formen realistischer Erzählkunst*, pp. 404-416.

73 I can't agree with Brinkmann's reading of the passage, which establishes clear agreement of Lorenzen, Dubslav, narrator, author and reader on the issue. Brinkmann, *Theodor Fontane*, p. 110.

74 Müller-Seidel, *Theodor Fontane*, p. 451. Preisendanz, *Humor*, p. 238. See also note 43 above.

75 Schäfer, p. 96.

76 Bruno Hildebrandt, "Fontane's Altersstil in seinem Roman 'Der Stechlin'," *German Quarterly*, 38 (1965), pp. 139-156, here 150-152. Meyer and Petersen also treat the stylistic use of parenthetical asides in the novel. Meyer, p. 176; Petersen, pp. 69-70.

Chapter IV: The Elusive Center

1 In his study of "Eigentum" as a central concept for Raabe, Peter Sprengel assigns *Alte Nester* thematically to the earliest phase of Raabe's works, separating it distinctly from the companion volumes of the trilogy. Peter

Sprengel, "Interieur und Eigentum. Zur Soziologie bürgerlicher Subjektivität bei Wilhelm Raabe," *Jahrbuch der Jean-Paul Gesellschaft,* 9 (1974), pp. 127-176. Hermann Helmers has a comparative study of all three works. Hermann Helmers, *Die bildenden Mächte in den Romanen Wilhelm Raabes* (Weinheim: Julius Beetz, 1960), pp. 53-95.

2 Berger and Luckmann, pp. 106-7, 120 ff. The term refers more specifically to groups and not to individuals, as in my adaptation. The analysis of a challenge or disruption is parallel.

3 Hubert Ohl, "Eduards Heimkehr oder Le Vaillant und das Riesenfaultier: Zu Wilhelm Raabes 'Stopfkuchen' " (1964), in *Raabe in neuer Sicht,* ed. H. Helmers (Stuttgart: Kohlhammer, 1968), p. 275.

4 Wilhelm Raabe, *Sämtliche Werke,* v. 19 (Freiburg and Braunschweig: Klemm, 1957), p. 220. Further page references to *Die Akten des Vogelsangs* will be to this volume of the Braunschweig edition and will appear in parentheses in the text.

5 Ulf Eisele, *Der Dichter und sein Detektiv: Raabes 'Stopfkuchen' und die Frage des Realismus* (Tübingen: Max Niemeyer Verlag, 1979), p. 14.

6 Martini, *Deutsche Literatur im bürgerlichen Realismus 1848-1898,* pp. 680-681. In a separate essay, Martini designates Raabe as the realist who draws the reader most carefully as "mitdenkender und mitwirkender Partner." It is necessary to amend the statement to specify particular texts by Raabe, whose *oeuvre* includes distressingly mediocre as well as intriguingly complex narratives. Fritz Martini, "Wilhelm Raabe," in *Deutsche Dichter des 19. Jahrhunderts,* ed. B. von Wiese (Berlin: Erich Schmidt, 1969), p. 540.

7 Further temporal dimensions are opened up by the motif of the Seven Years' War connected with the Rote Schanze and by the fossils which Schaumann has unearthed. A good study of the temporal structure is Hermann Meyer, "Raum und Zeit in Wilhelm Raabes Erzählkunst" (1953), in *Raabe in neuer Sicht,* pp. 98-129. Also in the same volume is a somewhat less perceptive essay by Hans Oppermann, "Zum Problem der Zeit bei Wilhelm Raabe" (1964), pp. 294-311. Peter Detroy offers a schematic representation of the time levels of *Stopfkuchen*: Peter Detroy, *Wilhelm Raabe: Der Humor als Gestaltungsprinzip im 'Stopfkuchen'* (Bonn: Bouvier, 1970), p. 33. The basic study of Raabe's retrospective mode of narration is still Pascal's: Roy Pascal, "The Reminiscence-Technique in Raabe," *Modern Language Review,* 49 (1954), pp. 339-384.

8 Ohl has also pointed out that the letter immediately introduces another perspective and is therefore already indicative of the polyperspectival narration which works to undermine Krumhardt's authority: Ohl, *Bild und Wirklichkeit,* pp. 107-108.

9 Claude David, "Über Wilhelm Raabes Stopfkuchen," in *Lebendige Form: Interpretationen zur deutschen Literatur. Festschrift für Heinrich Henel,* ed. J.L. Sammons and E. Schürer (Munich: Fink, 1970), p. 263.

10 Barker Fairley, *Wilhelm Raabe: An Introduction to his Novels* (Oxford: At the Clarendon Press, 1961), p. 12.

11 Eisele, p. 1. The same issue is raised in much less complex form by William Webster, who considers the central question of the novel to be the relationship of perception, reality, and illusion. William Webster, "Idealisierung oder Ironie? Verstehen und Mißverstehen in Wilhelm Raabes 'Stopfkuchen'," tr. R. Becker, *Jahrbuch der Raabe-Gesellschaft* (1978), pp. 146-170. See also his "Der 'Hinhocker' und der 'Weltwanderer.' Zur Bedeutung der Reise bei Wilhelm Raabe," *Jahrbuch der Raabe-Gesellschaft* (1982), pp. 26-39.

12 To cite a few of the positive assessments of Heinrich Schaumann: David, p. 267: "ein durchaus positiv zu wertender Ausbund der Tugend"; on pages 260-261 he offers a comparison with Goethe's Iphigenie. Martini, *Deutsche Literatur im bürgerlichen Realismus,* p. 728, stresses the humanity. Günther Matschke points to Schaumann as a symbol of a humane, superior form of existence: Günther Matschke, *Die Isolation als Mittel der Gesellschaftskritik bei Wilhelm Raabe* (Bonn: Bouvier, 1975), p. 81. Mayer, "Raum und Zeit ...," p. 121: "Stopfkuchen will haltbare, dauerhafte Lebenslehre vermitteln." Paul Derks answers David's argument and has a more negative view of the figure, using psychoanalytical categories: Paul Derks, "Vom Kap der Guten Hoffnung: Zu Wilhelm Raabes 'Stopfkuchen'," in his *Raabe-Studien: Beiträge zur Anwendung psychoanalytischer Interpretationsmodelle: 'Stopfkuchen' und 'Das Odfeld'* (Bonn: Bouvier, 1976), pp. 5-95.

13 Helmers consistently analyzes a bipolar structure in the Braunschweig trilogy which results in the confrontation of two worlds: Hermann Helmers, "Die Figur des Erzählers bei Raabe" (1965), in *Raabe in neuer Sicht,* pp. 317-337. See also Helmers. *Die bildenden Mächte,* p. 87 ff and Hans Kolbe, *Wilhelm Raabe. Vom Entwicklungs- zum Desillusionierungsroman* (Berlin/DDR: Akademie Verlag, 1981), p. 181.

14 Erich Weniger, "Wilhelm Raabe und das bürgerliche Leben" (1951), in *Raabe in neuer Sicht,* pp. 74-97.

15 Meyer designates the shift in Raabe's "outsider" figures from Stopfkuchen, who directs his own fate, to Andres, who can only follow his, as proof, "daß der Sonderling im Werke Raabes immer mehr der wesentliche Mensch schlechthin wurde," Hermann Meyer, *Der Sonderling in der deutschen Dichtung* (Munich: Carl Hanser Verlag, 1963), p. 287.

16 Raabe himself spoke of the work as his best novel, and Guardini concurs in the basic study which attempted to deal with the complexities at an early date (1932): Romano Guardini, "Über Wilhelm Raabes 'Stopfkuchen'," in

Raabe in neuer Sicht, p. 13. Karl Hoppe designates it as his most puzzling work, and Meyer twice terms it the most inaccessible: Karl Hoppe, *Wilhelm Raabe: Beiträge zum Verständnis seiner Person und seines Werkes* (Göttingen: Vandenhoeck and Ruprecht, 1967), p. 209; Meyer, "Raum und Zeit ...," p. 108; Meyer, *Der Sonderling,* p. 276. Martini calls it his most personal book, and Lukács, following the author's own description of it as "ein subjektives Buch," describes it as his most subjective: Martini, *Deutsche Literatur im bürgerlichen Realismus,* p. 727; Lukács, *Die Grablegung,* p. 99. Fairley chooses the term Bildungsroman, with some reservations, and Pascal emphasizes the humor: Fairley, p. 3; Pascal, *The German Novel,* p. 172.

17 Wilhelm Raabe, *Sämtliche Werke,* v. 18 (Göttingen: Vandenhoeck and Ruprecht, 1963), p. 117. I shall use this volume of the Braunschweig edition of *Stopfkuchen,* and further page references will be given in parentheses in the text.

18 Ohl, "Eduards Heimkehr ...," pp. 253-4. Dierkes expands the Schopenhauer connection into a total interpretation of the work. Hans Dierkes, "Der 'Zauber des Gegensatzes': Schopenhauer und Wilhelm Raabes 'Stopfkuchen'," *Schopenhauer Jahrbuch,* 54 (1973), pp. 93-107. Eisele doesn't draw on the Schopenhauer association but provides an analysis congruent with his basic epistemological model as described in his *Realismus und Ideologie,* which I discussed in conjunction with the programmatic realism at mid-century in my second chapter. It is questionable whether such a model, entirely applicable at mid-century, is appropriate for all German Realism, as Eisele claims.

19 David, p. 264; Gisela Warnke, "Das 'Sünder'-Motiv in Wilhelm Raabes 'Stopfkuchen'," *DVjs,* 50 (1976), pp. 465-476.

20 Martini, *Deutsche Literatur im bürgerlichen Realismus,* p. 727.

21 For a strictly structuralist analysis of the narrative system which does not consider the import of the content see Jean-Charles Margotton, "Stopfkuchen de W. Raabe. À propos de la structure narrative du roman," *Études Germaniques* 36 (1981), pp. 291-305.

22 Webster, "Idealisierung oder Ironie," p. 152; Detroy, p. 17; Jeffrey Sammons, "Wilhelm Raabe's *Stopfkuchen* pro and contra," in *Wilhelm Raabe, Studien zu seinem Leben und Werk,* ed. L. Lensing and H.-W. Peter (Braunschweig: pp-Verlag, 1981), p. 283; Philip J. Brewster, "Onkel Ketschwayo in Neuteutoburg. Zeitgeschichtliche Anspielungen in Raabes 'Stopfkuchen'," *Jahrbuch der Raabe-Gesellschaft* (1983), p. 107. Brewster's essay on the anti-colonial perspective of the novel in its original context of German colonial enthusiasm is very persuasively argued. On the beginning of *Stopfkuchen* see especially pp. 109-110.

23 For a detailed interpretation of the Platen allusion see Derks, pp. 33-95.

24 For Matschke, the Rote Schanze is the symbol of a superior form of existence and the archimedian point of the novel: Matschke, p. 81. Meyer, "Raum und Zeit ...," p. 111, views the hedge as the central leitmotif. In his *Der Sonderling*, p. 279, he designates the Rote Schanze as the main symbol of fate in the novel. His article on temporal and spatial questions in Raabe also has an excellent analysis of the spatial constellation in the work, granting the Rote Schanze a central position. Webster has a good section on the implications of the phrase "unter der Hecke" as signifying exclusion, isolation, and the ability to reflect: Webster, "Idealisierung oder Ironie," p. 163. Bange has a similar interpretation of the phrase as encompassing the negative "exclusion" and the positive "élection." He finds the conquest of the Rote Schanze the central metaphor of the novel: Pierre Bange, " 'Stopfkuchen': Le Solipsisme de l'original et l'humour," *Études Germaniques*, 24 (1969), pp. 1-15.

25 Günter Witschel, *Raabe-Integrationen: 'Die Innerste,' 'Das Odfeld,' 'Stopfkuchen'* (Bonn: Bouvier, 1969), p. 31.

26 Berger and Luckmann, p. 65.

27 Brewster fittingly designates Störzer and Le Vaillant as Eduard's Achilles' heel: Brewster, p. 104.

28 Theodor Fontane, *Sämtliche Werke*, v. 8, p. 20.

29 Fairley, p. 2.

30 Guardini, p. 13.

31 Meyer, "Raum und Zeit ...," p. 122.

32 Eisele, *Der Dichter und sein Detektiv*, p. 21.

33 Dierkes' study points to the "Satz von zureichendem Grunde" as the oppositional epistemological principle to Schaumann's contemplative "Anschauung." The opposition is a basis of his interpretation of the connection to the philosophy of Schopenhauer. Dierkes, *passim*. Sammons has a perceptive interpretation of Eduard's "pattern of avoidance": Sammons, p. 284.

34 "Jener dialektische Umschlag ...von der apologetischen und selbstbestätigenden Verklärung zur unbestechlichen und oft melancholischen Selbstkritik." Widhammer, *Realismus und klassizistische Tradition*, p. 71. See also the related discussion in my first chapter.

35 Berger and Luckmann, pp. 24-5.

36 Felix Wassermann, " 'Die Akten des Vogelsangs' und das Problem der bürgerlichen Existenz im Neuen Reich," *German Quarterly*, 36 (1963), p. 421.

37 Fairley, pp. 251-2; Pascal, *The German Novel,* p. 174. Preisendanz correctly points out, however, that the narrator's concerns are much more central in the story in Raabe: Wolfgang Preisendanz, "Die Erzählstruktur als Bedeutungskomplex der 'Akten des Vogelsangs'," *Jahrbuch der Raabe-Gesellschaft* (1981), p. 220.

38 Wassermann, p. 421.

39 Helmers, *Die bildenden Mächte,* p. 87. Meyer gives a similar analysis of the mutual exclusivity of Velten Andres' and Karl Krumhardt's modes of existence: "zwei in sich geschlossene, und, wie wir sehen werden, in sich berechtigte Welten stehen sich gegenüber." Meyer, *Der Sonderling,* p. 282; also Kolbe, p. 181.

40 Studies such as those by Emrich or Webster which hypostatize "das Geheimnis der Person" or insecurity as "a universal human condition" do not do justice to the historical character of such terminology itself. Ohl forms an exception in expressly recognizing Velten Andres as an element of bourgeois self-realization which he traces back to the Enlightenment. Hubert Ohl, "Der Bürger und das Unbedingte bei Wilhelm Raabe," *Jahrbuch der Raabe-Gesellschaft* (1979), pp. 7-26; Wilhelm Emrich, "Personalität und Zivilisation in Wilhelm Raabes 'Die Akten des Vogelsangs'." *Jahrbuch der Raabe-Gesellschaft* (1982), pp. 7-25; William Webster, "Social Change and Personal Insecurity in the Late Novels of Wilhelm Raabe," in *Formen realistischer Erzählkunst,* pp. 233-243.

41 Born, p. 35. Also Bramstedt's characterization of the ascendant period of the middle classes. Bramstedt, pp. 118-19. See also my first chapter.

42 A comparison of the passage with a related statement from *Alte Nester* reveals the intensification of the theme in the last novel of the Braunschweig trilogy. In *Alte Nester,* the initial volume (1879), disorientation can have a decidedly beneficial result: "es ist manchmal dem Menschen nichts dienlicher, als daß er mal so recht vollständig umgekehrt wird! Wenn das Allerinnerste nach außen kommt, dann erfährt er erst, was eigentlich alles in ihm gesteckt hat und was ihm nur angeflogen war." W. Raabe, *Sämtliche Werke,* v. 14, p. 99.

43 In a biographical aside, it should be noted that Raabe had just lost his youngest daughter the year before beginning work on the novel.

44 The conclusion by Hartwig Schultz that Helene Trotzendorff is the only figure to attain a degree of inner balance and to live the life which Raabe valued for his characters is rather surprising and hardly tenable. Wischniewski's dismissal of her figure in the novel as "bloße Staffage" is equally exaggerated. Hartwig Schultz, "Werk- und Autorintention in Raabes 'Alten Nestern' und 'Akten des Vogelsangs'," *Jahrbuch der Raabe-Gesellschaft* (1979), p. 151; Horst Wischniewski, " 'Die Akten des Vogelsangs.' Freiheit in Wilhelm Raabes Roman," *Jahrbuch der Raabe-Gesellschaft* (1974), p. 99.

45 Rolf-Dieter Koll's analysis of Velten's wishes and the repeated, extensive reference to them in a later conversation with Krumhardt (351) reads the wish to set Persepolis on fire as having been rescinded when Velten states on the later occasion; "Auf das Vergnügen, Persepolis in Brand zu stecken, verzichtet man, wenn man sein letztes Schulheft in den Ofen gesteckt hat." I read the passage as an equivalency, as a fulfillment of the wish in the personal autodafé. Koll's interpretation of the fairy-tale components of "Heckepfennig," "Däumling," and "Tellertuch des Rolandsknappen" as instruments to free their owner from reality is a valid insight. Rolf-Dieter Koll, *Raumgestaltung bei Wilhelm Raabe* (Bonn: Bouvier, 1977), pp. 70-71.

46 Ohl, "Der Bürger und das Unbedingte," p. 23.

47 Peter Sprengel traces the concept throughout Raabe's works and establishes the social-historical context. See the first footnote to this chapter and also Gernot Folkes, *Besitz und Sicherheit. Zur Soziologie einer bürgerlichen Illusion am Beispiel Goethes und Raabes* (Kronberg/Cz.: Scriptor, 1976).

48 Joachim Müller, "Das Zitat im epischen Gefüge. Die Goethe-Verse in Raabes Erzählung 'Die Akten des Vogelsangs'," *Jahrbuch der Raabe-Gesellschaft* (1964), pp. 7-23; rpt. in *Raabe in neuer Sicht*, pp. 179-193.

49 One of the earliest studies of the novel traces this motif, or as she terms it, symbol: Margarete Bönneken, *Wilhelm Raabes Roman "Die Akten des Vogelsangs"* (Marburg: N.G. Elwert'sche Verlagsbuchhandlung, 1918), pp. 84-86.

50 Pascal, "The Reminiscence-Technique in Raabe."

51 Hermann Meyer and Hans Oppermann seem to imply that the complex admixture of time, in connection with the careful manipulation of place, conveys the sense of a timeless essence. Meyer's analysis of the unity in *Die Chronik der Sperlingsgasse* is appropriate, but his comments on the later novels sometimes neglect the manner in which the effect of time on familiar places emphasizes the vulnerability of "das Bleibende." Meyer, "Raum und Zeit in Wilhelm Raabes Erzählkunst;" Hans Oppermann, "Zum Problem der Zeit bei Wilhelm Raabe."

52 An essay by Geisler on the theme of Herzensmuseum in the novel skillfully analyzes the function of the des Beaux family. Eberhard Geisler, "Abschied vom Herzensmuseum. Die Auflösung des Poetischen Realismus in Wilhelm Raabes *Akten des Vogelsangs*," in *Wilhelm Raabe. Studien zu seinem Leben und Werk*, pp. 365-380.

53 Wassermann points to the significance of the names of Leon's children as opposed to the connection of his own and his sister Leonie's names to their heritage. The new generation of the family des Beaux carries the respectable and timely (for the new Reich) names of Friedrich and Victoria. Wassermann, p. 432.

54 Lukács appropriately chose Mutter Andres to illustrate the dilemma of "Die Relativität gesellschaftlich wurzellos gewordener Ideale." His analysis agrees with Geisler's connection of the fate of the des Beaux family with the historical situation in Germany at the end of the century. Georg Lukács, "Wilhelm Raabe," (originally published in 1940), in *Raabe in neuer Sicht*, pp. 62-3.

55 Wassermann has an interesting insight into the connection of Frau Fechtmeisterin Feucht to the university of Jena with its liberal tradition of the *Burschenschaften*. Wassermann, p. 430. In 1892 the university was again a center of attention, as Bismarck gave a speech to students there.

56 Wilhelm Raabe, *Sämtliche Werke*, v. 19, p. 468. The motto is not the sole reference to Chamisso, as Velten's wish alludes to the poem "Salas y Gomez" by Chamisso.

Chapter V: The Extended Perspective

1 Ulf Eisele, "Realismus-Problematik: Überlegungen zur Forschungssituation," *DVjs*, 51 (1977), pp. 148-174.

2 Theodor Fontane, *Sämtliche Werke* v. XXI:1 (Munich: Nymphenburger Verlagshandlung, 1963), p. 247.

3 E.M. Forster, pp. 28-9.

SELECTED BIBLIOGRAPHY

I. Cultural and Historical Background of the Nineteenth Century
II. Literary Realism
III. Narrative and Textual Analysis
IV. Gustav Freytag and Berthold Auerbach
V. Theodor Fontane
VI. Wilhelm Raabe

Works of importance for more than one author will be listed in section II. The editions cited are specified at the beginning of sections IV, V, VI.

I. Cultural and Historical Background of the Nineteenth Century

Böhme, Helmut. *Deutschlands Weg zur Großmacht 1848-1881.* Cologne: Kiepenheuer and Witsch, 1966.

-.- *Probleme der Reichsgründungszeit 1848-1879.* Cologne: Kiepenheuer and Witsch, 1968.

-.- *Prolegomena zu einer Sozial- und Wirtschaftsgeschichte Deutschlands im 19. und 20. Jahrhundert.* Frankfurt/Main: Suhrkamp, 1978.

Bramstedt, Ernest K. *Aristocracy and the Middle-Classes in Germany: Social Types in German Literature 1830-1900.* 1937; rpt. Chicago: University of Chicago Press, 1964.

Craig, Gordon A. *Germany 1866-1945.* New York: Oxford University Press, 1978.

Deutsche Sozialgeschichte: Dokumente und Skizzen. Vols. I, II. Munich: C.H. Beck, 1973-4.

Hamerow, Theodore S. *Social Foundations of German Unification 1858-1871: Ideas and Institutions.* Princeton: Princeton University Press, 1969.

-.- *The Social Foundations of German Unification 1858-1871: Struggles and Accomplishments.* Princeton: Princeton University Press, 1972.

-.- *Restoration, Revolution, Reaction: Economics and Politics in Germany, 1815-1871.* Princeton: Princeton University Press, 1958.

Holborn, Hajo. *A History of Modern Germany.* Vol. III. New York: A. Knopf, 1969.

Motteck, Hans. *Wirtschaftsgeschichte Deutschlands.* 2nd. ed. v. II. Berlin/GDR: VEB Deutscher Verlag der Wissenschaften, 1969.

Peschken, Bernd, and Claus-Dieter Krohn, eds. *Literaturwissenschaft und Sozialwissenschaft 7: Der liberale Roman und der preußische Verfassungskonflikt: Analyseskizzen und Materialien.* Stuttgart: Metzler, 1976.

Sagarra, Eda. *Tradition and Revolution: German Literature and Society 1830-1890.* New York: Basic Books, 1971.

Sheehan, James S., ed. *Imperial Germany.* New York: New Viewpoints (Franklin Watts), 1976.

Stern, Fritz. *The Failure of Illiberalism: Essays on the Political Culture of Modern Germany.* New York: A Knopf, 1972.

II. Literary Realism

Auerbach, Erich. *Mimesis.* Trans. W. Trask. Princeton: Princeton University Press, 1968.

Aust, Hugo. *Literatur des Realismus.* Sammlung Metzler, 157. Stuttgart: Metzler, 1981.

-.- "Bürgerlicher Realismus. Forschungsbericht." *Wirkendes Wort,* 6 (1980), pp. 427-447.

Boeschenstein, Hermann. *German Literature of the Nineteenth Century.* London: Edward Arnold, 1969.

Brinkmann, Richard, ed. *Begriffsbestimmung des literarischen Realismus.* Wege der Forschung, 212. Darmstadt: Wissenschaftliche Buchgesellschaft, 1969.

-.- *Wirklichkeit und Illusion. Studien über Gehalt und Grenzen des Begriffs Realismus für die erzählende Dichtung des neunzehnten Jahrhunderts.* 2nd ed. Tübingen: Max Niemeyer, 1966.

Demetz, Peter. "Defenses of Dutch Painting and the Theory of Realism." *Comparative Literature,* 15 (1963), pp. 97-115.

-.- "Über die Fiktionen des Realismus." *Neue Rundschau,* 88 (1977), pp. 554-567.

-.- "Zur Definition des Realismus." *Literatur und Kritik,* 16-17 (1967), pp. 333-345.

Eisele, Ulf. "Realismus Problematik: Überlegungen zur Forschungssituation." *DVjs,* 51 (1977), pp. 148-174.

Hahl, Werner. *Reflexion und Erzählung: Ein Problem der Romantheorie von der Spätaufklärung bis zum programmatischen Realismus.* Stuttgart: Kohlhammer, 1971.

Jakobson, Roman. "Über den Realismus in der Kunst." (1921). Rpt. in *Russischer Formalismus.* Ed. Jurij Striedter. Munich: Fink, 1975, pp. 373-391.

Kahn, Ludwig. "Fortschrittsglaube und Kulturkritik im bürgerlichen Roman: Gustav Freytag und Wilhelm Raabe." In *Corona: Festschrift Singer.* Ed. A. Schirokauer and W. Paulsen. Durham: Duke University Press, 1941.

Kaiser, Gerhard. "Realismusforschung ohne Realismusbegriff." Rev. of *Bild und Wirklichkeit,* by H. Ohl. *DVjs,* 43 (1969), pp. 147-160.

Killy, Walter. *Wirklichkeit und Kunstcharacter: Neun Romane des 19. Jahrhunderts.* Munich, 1963; rpt. Göttingen: Vandenhoeck und Ruprecht, 1967.

Kohl, Stephan. *Realismus: Theorie und Geschichte.* UTB 643. Munich: Fink, 1977.

Lukács, Georg. *Die Grablegung des alten Deutschland.* Reinbek bei Hamburg: Rowohlt, 1967.

Martini, Fritz. *Deutsche Literatur im bürgerlichen Realismus 1848-1898.* 4th ed. Stuttgart: Metzler, 1981.

-.- "Ironischer Realismus: Keller, Raabe und Fontane." In *Ironie und Dichtung.* Ed. A. Schaefer. Munich: C.H. Beck, 1970.

Müller, Klaus-Detlev, ed. *Bürgerlicher Realismus. Grundlagen und Interpretationen.* Königstein/Cz.: Athenäum, 1981.

Ohl, Hubert. *Bild und Wirklichkeit: Studien zur Romankunst Raabes und Fontanes.* Heidelberg: Lothar Stiehm, 1968.

Preisendanz, Wolfgang. "Das Problem der Realität in der Dichtung." *Bogawus,* 9 (1968), pp. 3-9.

-.- *Humor als dichterische Einbildungskraft.* 2nd. ed. Munich: Fink, 1976.

-.- "Voraussetzungen des poetischen Realismus in der deutschen Erzählkunst des 19. Jahrhunderts." In *Formkräfte der deutschen Dichtung.* Ed. H. Steffen. Göttingen: Vandenhoeck und Ruprecht, 1963, pp. 187-210. Also in Brinkmann. *Begriffsbestimmung,* pp. 453-479.

-.- *Wege des Realismus.* Munich: Fink, 1977.

Realismus und Gründerzeit: Manifeste und Dokumente zur deutschen Literatur 1848-1880. 2 vols. Ed. M. Bucher, W. Hahl, G. Jäger, R. Wittmann. Stuttgart: Metzler, 1976.

Steinmetz, Horst. "Der vergessene Leser. Provokatorische Bemerkungen zum Realismusproblem." In *Dichtung und Leser*. Ed. F. van Ingen, E. Kunne-Ibsch, H. de Leeuwe, F. Maatje. Groningen: Wolters Noordhoff, 1972. pp. 113-133.

Wellek, René. "The Concept of Realism in Literary Scholarship." (1961). Rpt. in his *Concepts of Criticism*. New Haven: Yale University Press, 1963.

Widhammer, Helmuth. *Die Literaturtheorie des deutschen Realismus (1848-1860)*. Sammlung Metzler, 152. Stuttgart: Metzler, 1977.

-.- and Hans-Joachim Ruckhäberle, eds. *Roman und Romantheorie des deutschen Realismus*. Kronberg/Cz.: Athenäum, 1977.

III. Narrative and Textual Analysis

Anderegg, Johannes. *Fiktion und Kommunikation: Ein Beitrag zur Theorie der Prosa*. Göttingen: Vandenhoeck und Ruprecht, 1973.

Barthes, Roland. *Writing Degree Zero/Elements of Semiology*. Trans. A. Lavers and C. Smith. Ed. S. Sonntag. Boston: Beacon, 1970.

-.- *Image, Music, Text*. Trans. and ed. S. Heath. New York: Hill and Wang, 1977.

-.- *S/Z*. Trans. R. Miller. Ed. R. Howard. New York: Hill and Wang, 1974.

Chatman, Seymour. "New Ways of Analyzing Narrative Structure, with an Example from Joyce's *Dubliners*." *Language and Style*, 2 (1969), pp. 3-36.

-.- "Towards a Theory of Narrative." *New Literary History*, 6 (1975), pp. 295-318.

Culler, Jonathan. "Defining Narrative Units." In *Style and Structure in Literature: Essays in the New Stylistics*. Ed. R. Fowler. Oxford: Basil Blackwell, 1975, pp. 123-142.

-.- *Structuralist Poetics*. 2nd. ed. New York: Cornell University Press, 1976.

Eco, Umberto. *The Role of the Reader: Explorations in the Semiotics of Texts*. Bloomington: Indiana University Press, 1979.

Fokkema, D.W. and E. Kunne-Ibsch. *Theories of Literature in the Twentieth Century: Structuralism, Marxism, Aesthetics of Reception, Semiotics*. London: C. Hurst and Co., 1977.

Funktionen des Fiktiven. Ed. D. Henrich and W. Iser. Poetik und Hermeneutik, 10. Munich: Fink, 1983.

Forster, E.M. *Aspects of the Novel*. New York: Harcourt, Brace and World, 1927.

Goldmann, Lucien. *Towards a Sociology of the Novel.* Trans. A. Sheridan. London: Tavistock, 1975.

Grimm, Gunter, ed. *Literatur und Leser: Theorien und Modelle zur Rezeption literarischer Werke.* Stuttgart: Reclam, 1975.

Gülich, Elisabeth und Wolfgang Raible. *Linguistische Textmodelle: Grundlagen und Möglichkeiten.* Munich: Fink, 1977.

-.- eds. *Textsorten.* Frankfurt/Main: Athenäum, 1972.

Hawkes, Terence. *Structuralism and Semiotics.* Berkeley: University of California Press, 1977.

Holub, Robert C. *Reception Theory: A Critical Introduction.* London: Methuen, 1984.

Iser, Wolfgang. *Der Akt des Lesens: Theorie ästhetischer Wirkung.* Munich: Fink, 1976.

-.- *Die Appellstruktur der Texte.* Constance: Universitätsverlag, 1971.

-.- *Der implizierte Leser.* 2nd. ed. Munich: Fink, 1976.

-.- "Interaction between Text and Reader." In *The Reader in the Text. Essays on Audience and Interpretation.* Princeton: Princeton Univ. Press, 1980.

-.- "The Reading Process: A Phenomenological Approach." *New Literary History,* 3 (1971-2), pp. 270-299.

Jauß, Hans-Robert. *Ästhetische Erfahrung und literarische Hermeneutik I.* Munich: Fink, 1977.

-.- *Literaturgeschichte als Provokation.* Edition Suhrkamp, 418. Frankfurt am Main: Suhrkamp, 1970.

-.- "Nachahmungsprinzip und Wirklichkeitsbegriff in der Theorie des Romans von Diderot bis Stendahl." In *Nachahmung und Illusion.* Ed. H.-R. Jauß. Poetik und Hermeneutik, 1. Munich: Fink, 1969.

Lange, Viktor. "The Reader in the Strategy of Fiction." In *Expression, Communication and Experience in Literature and Language.* Ed. R. G. Popperwell. London: Modern Humanities Research Association, 1973, pp. 86-102.

Mukařovský, Jan. *Kapitel aus der Ästhetik.* Frankfurt/Main: Suhrkamp, 1970.

-.- *Structure, Sign and Function.* Trans. J. Burbank and P. Steiner. New Haven: Yale University Press, 1978.

-.- *The Word and Verbal Art.* Trans. J. Burbank and P. Steiner. New Haven: Yale University Press, 1977.

Pfeiffer, K. Ludwig. "The Novel and Society: Reflections on the Interaction of Literary and Cultural Paradigms." *Poetics and Theory of Literature,* 3 (1978), pp. 45-69.

Plett, Heinrich. *Textwissenschaft und Textanalyse.* Heidelberg: Quelle and Meyer, 1975.

The Reader in the Text. Essays on Audience and Interpretation. Ed. S. Suleiman and I. Crosman. Princeton: Princeton Univ. Press, 1980.

Schmidt, Henry J. "Text-Adequate Concretizations and Real Readers: Reception Theory and Its Applications." *New German Critique,* 17 (1979), pp. 157-169.

Schmidt, Siegfried J. *Elemente einer Textpoetik: Theorie und Anwendung.* Munich: Bayerischer Schulbuchverlag, 1974.

-.- "Fictionality in literary and non-literary discourses." *Poetics,* 9 (1980), pp. 525-546.

-.- *Text, Bedeutung, Ästhetik.* Munich: Bayerischer Schulbuchverlag, 1970.

-.- *Texttheorie: Probleme einer Linguistik der sprachlichen Kommunikation.* 2nd ed. Munich: Fink, 1976.

Searle, John. "The Logical Status of Fictional Discourse." *New Literary History,* 6 (1975), pp. 319-332.

Warning, Rainer, ed. *Rezeptionsästhetik: Theorie und Praxis.* Munich: Fink, 1975.

Watt, Ian. *The Rise of the Novel.* Berkeley, University of California Press, 1957.

Weimann, Robert. *Structure and Society in Literary History: Studies in the History and Theory of Historical Criticism.* Charlottesville: University of Virginia Press, 1976.

Wellek, René. "The Literary Theory and Aesthetics of the Prague School." In his *Discriminations.* New Haven: Yale University Press, 1970, pp. 275-303.

Weinold, Götz. "Probleme der linguistischen Analyse des Romans: Zugleich eine Studie zu Kriminalromanen Patricia Highsmiths." *Jahrbuch für internationale Germanistik,* 1 (1969), pp. 108-128.

-.- *Semiotik der Literatur.* Frankfurt/Main: Athenäum, 1972.

Zéraffa, Michel. *Fictions: The Novel and Social Reality.* Trans. C. and T. Burns. New York: Penguin, 1976.

IV. Gustav Freytag and Berthold Auerbach

Auerbach, Berthold. *Gesammelte Schriften.* Vols. I, XX. Stuttgart/Augsburg: Cotta, 1857-8.

Freytag, Gustav. *Soll und Haben.* Ed. Hans Mayer. Munich/Vienna: Hanser, 1977.

Améry, Jean. "Schlecht klingt das Lied vom braven Mann." *Neue Rundschau,* 89 (1978), pp. 84-93.

Baur, Uwe. *Dorfgeschichte – Zur Entstehung und gesellschaftlichen Funktion einer literarischen Gattung im Vormärz.* Munich: Fink, 1978.

Beaton, K.B. "Gustav Freytag, Julian Schmidt und die Romantheorie nach der Revolution von 1848." *Jahrbuch der Raabe-Gesellschaft* (1976), pp. 7-32.

Bettelheim, Anton. *Berthold Auerbach: Der Mann – Sein Werk – Sein Nachlaß.* Stuttgart/Berlin: Cotta'sche Buchhandlung Nachfolger, 1907.

-.- *Biographenwege: Reden und Aufsätze.* Berlin: Verlag von Gebrüder Paetel, 1913.

Carter, T.E. "Freytag's *Soll und Haben*: A Liberal National Manifesto as a Best-Seller." *German Life and Letters,* 21 (1967-8), pp. 321-329.

Eisele, Ulf. *Realismus und Ideologie: Zur Kritik der literarischen Theorie nach 1848 am Beispiel des Deutschen Museums.* Stuttgart: Metzler, 1976.

Gelber, Mark. "An Alternate Reading of the Role of the Jewish Scholar in Gustav Freytag's *Soll und Haben.*" *Germanic Review,* 58 (1983), pp. 83-88.

-.- "Die literarische Umwelt zu Gustav Freytags *Soll und Haben* und die Realismustheorie der *Grenzboten.*" *Orbis Litterarum,* 39 (1984), pp. 38-53.

-.- "Teaching 'Literary Anti-Semitism': Dickens' *Oliver Twist* and Freytag's *Soll und Haben.*" *Comparative Literature Studies,* 16, No. 1 (1979), pp. 1-11.

Hahl, Werner. "Gesellschaftlicher Konservativismus und literarischer Realismus. Das Modell einer deutschen Sozialverfassung in den Dorfgeschichten." In *Realismus und Gründerzeit.* Vol. I. Ed. M. Bucher, W. Hahl, G. Jäger and R. Wittmann. Stuttgart: Metzler, 1976.

Hein, Jürgen. *Dorfgeschichte.* Sammlung Metzler, 145. Stuttgart: Metzler, 1976.

Hubrich, Peter Heinz. *Gustav Freytags 'Deutsche Ideologie' in 'Soll und Haben.'* Scriptor Hochschulschriften, 3. Kronberg/Cz.: Scriptor, 1974.

Jäger, Hans-Wolf. "Gesellschaftliche Aspekte des bürgerlichen Realismus und seiner Theorie. Bemerkungen zu Julian Schmidt und Gustav Freytag." *Text und Kontext,* 2, Heft 3 (1974), pp. 7-32.

Kafitz, Dieter. *Figurenkonstellation als Mittel der Wirklichkeitserfassung: dargestellt an Romanen der 2. Hälfte des 19. Jahrhunderts.* Kronberg/Cz.: Athenäum, 1978.

Kaiser, Herbert. *Studien zum deutschen Roman nach 1848.* Duisburger Hochschulbeiträge 8. Duisburg: Walter Braun, 1977.

Kaiser, Nancy A. "Berthold Auerbach: The Dilemma of the Jewish Humanist from *Vormärz* to Empire." *German Studies Review,* 6 (1983), pp. 399-420.

Kienzle, Michael. *Der Erfolgsroman: Zur Kritik seiner politischen Ökonomie bei Gustav Freytag und Eugenie Marlitt.* Stuttgart: Metzler, 1975.

Kinder, Hermann. *Poesie als Synthese: Ausbreitung eines deutschen Realismusverständnisses in der Mitte des 19. Jahrhunderts.* Frankfurt am Main: Athenäum, 1973.

Kockjoy, Wolfgang. *Der Deutsche Kaufmannsroman: Versuch einer kultur- und geistesgeschichtlichen genetischen Darstellung.* Strassburg: Universitätsbuchdruckerei Heitz & Co., 1932.

Kreuzer, Helmut. "Zur Theorie des deutschen Realismus zwischen Märzrevolution und Naturalismus." In *Realismustheorien in Literatur, Malerei, Musik und Politik.* Ed. R. Grimm and J. Hermand. Stuttgart: Kohlhammer, 1975, pp. 48-67.

Lindau, Hans. *Gustav Freytag.* Leipzig: Hirzel, 1907.

Löwenthal, Leo. "Gustav Freytag." In *Festschrift zum 80. Geburtstag von Georg Lukács.* Ed. F. Benseler. Neuwied/Berlin: Luchterhand, 1965, pp. 392-401. Rpt. L. Löwenthal. *Erzählkunst und Gesellschaft.* Neuwied/Berlin: Luchterhand, 1971.

McHale, John L. *Die Form der Novellen "Die Leute von Seldwyla" von Gottfried Keller und der "Schwarzwälder Dorfgeschichten" von Berthold Auerbach.* Bern: Paul Haupt, 1957.

McInnes, E. " 'Die Poesie des Geschäfts'. Social Analysis and Polemic in Freytag's *Soll und Haben."* In *Formen realistischer Erzählkunst. Festschrift für Charlotte Jolles.* Ed. J. Thunecke. Nottingham: Sherwood Agencies, 1979, pp. 99-107.

Mettenleitner, Peter. *Destruktion der Heimatdichtung: Typologische Untersuchungen zu Gotthelf – Auerbach – Ganghofer.* Tübingen: Tübinger Vereinigung für Volkskunde E.V. Tübingen Schloß, 1974.

Mosse, Georg L. "The Image of the Jew in German Popular Culture: Felix Dahn and Gustav Freytag." *Publications of the Leo Baeck Institute,* 2 (1957), pp. 218-227.

Nothmann, Karl-Heinz. *Erziehung und Werdegang des Kaufmanns im Spiegel deutscher Romane des 19. Jahrhunderts.* Diss. Hamburg 1970. Hamburg, 1970.

Pazi, Margarita. "Berthold Auerbach und Moritz Hartmann." In *Leo Baeck Institute Yearbook* 1973, pp. 201-218.

-.- "Berthold Auerbach — dem jüdischen Autor der deutschen Dorfgeschichte zum 100. Todestag." *Neue Deutsche Hefte,* 173 (1982), pp. 95-109.

-.- "Revolution und Demokratie im Leben und Werk von Berthold Auerbach." In *Revolution und Demokratie in Geschichte und Literatur. Festschrift für Walter Grab zum 60. Geburtstag.* Ed. J.H. Schoeps and I. Geiss. Duisburg: Walter Braun, 1979, pp. 355-374.

Rhöse, Franz. *Konflikt und Versöhnung: Untersuchungen zur Theorie des Romans von Hegel bis zum Naturalismus.* Stuttgart: Metzler, 1978.

Richter, Claus. "Freytags *Soll und Haben.*" In C. Richter. *Leiden an der Gesellschaft. Vom literarischen Liberalismus zum poetischen Realismus.* Königstein/Cz.: Athenäum, 1978, pp. 209-244.

Sammons, J.L. "The Evaluation of Freytag's *Soll und Haben.*" *German Life and Letters,* 22 (1968-9), pp. 315-324.

Schneider, Michael. "Apologie des Bürgers. Zur Problematik von Rassismus und Antisemitismus in Gustav Freytags Roman 'Soll und Haben'." *Jahrbuch der deutschen Schillergesellschaft,* 25 (1981), pp. 385-413.

-.- *Geschichte als Gestalt. Formen der Wirklichkeit und Wirklichkeit der Form in Gustav Freytags Roman "Soll und Haben."* Stuttgart: Akademischer Verlag Hans-Dieter Heinz, 1980.

Schwitzgebel, Helmut. "Gustav Freytags 'Soll und Haben' in der Tradition des deutschen Kaufmannsromans." *Gustav-Freytag-Blätter,* 24 (1980), pp. 3-12; 25 (1981), pp. 3-11; 26 (1982), pp. 3-13.

Seuffert, Bernard. "Betrachtungen über dichterische Komposition." *Germanisch-Romanische Monatsschrift,* 1 (1909), pp. 599-617.

Steinecke, Hartmut. "Gustav Freytags *Soll und Haben* — ein realistischer Roman?" In *Formen realistischer Erzählkunst. Festschrift für Charlotte Jolles.* Ed. J. Thunecke. Nottingham: Sherwood Agencies, 1979, pp. 108-119.

-.- "Gustav Freytag: *Soll und Haben* (1855). Weltbild und Wirkung eines deutschen Bestsellers." In *Romane und Erzählungen des bürgerlichen Realismus. Neue Interpretationen.* Ed. H. Denkler. Stuttgart: Reclam, 1980, pp. 138-152.

-.- *Romantheorie und Romankritik in Deutschland: Die Entwicklung des Gattungsverständnisses von der Scott-Rezeption bis zum programmatischen Realismus,* 2. vol. Stuttgart: Metzler, 1975-6.

Stockinger, Ludwig. "Realpolitik, Realismus und das Ende des bürgerlichen Wahrheitsanspruchs. Überlegungen zur Funktion des programmatischen Realismus am Beispiel von Gustav Freytags 'Soll und Haben'." In *Bürgerlicher Realismus. Grundlagen und Interpretationen.* Ed. Klaus-Detlev Müller. Königstein/Cz.: Athenäum, 1981, pp. 174-202.

Ulrich, Paul. *Gustav Freytags Romantechnik.* Marburg: N.G. Elwert'sche Verlagsbuchhandlung, 1907.

Widhammer, Helmuth. *Realismus und klassizistische Tradition: Zur Theorie der Literatur in Deutschland 1848-1860.* Tübingen: Max Niemeyer, 1972.

Winterscheidt, Friedrich. *Deutsche Unterhaltungsliteratur der Jahre 1850-1860.* Bonn: Bouvier, 1970.

Worthmann, Joachim. *Probleme des Zeitromans: Studien zur Geschichte des deutschen Romans im 19. Jahrhundert.* Heidelberg: Carl Winter Universitätsverlag, 1974.

Zimmermann, Peter. *Der Bauernroman: Antifeudalismus – Konservativismus – Faschismus.* Stuttgart: Metzler, 1975.

Zwick, M.J. *Berthold Auerbachs sozialpolitischer und ethischer Liberalismus.* Stuttgart: Kohlhammer, 1933.

V. Theodor Fontane

Fontane, Theodor. *Sämtliche Werke.* Vols. II, VII, VIII. Munich: Nymphenburger Verlag, 1959.

Aust, Hugo, ed. *Theodor Fontane: Der Stechlin: Erläuterungen und Dokumente,* Stuttgart: Reclam, 1978.

-.- *Theodor Fontane: "Verklärung": Eine Untersuchung zum Ideengehalt seiner Werke.* Bonn: Bouvier, 1974.

Bance, Alan. *Theodor Fontane: The Major Novels.* Cambridge: Cambridge University Press, 1982.

Bange, Pierre. "Humor und Ironie in 'Effi Briest'." In *Fontanes Realismus,* pp. 143-148.

-.- "Motifs imaginaires dans les romans de Th. Fontane. Essai de sémantique discursive." *Recherches Germaniques,* 11 (1981), pp. 87-104.

Barlow, D. "Symbolism in Fontanes 'Der Stechlin'." *German Life and Letters,* 12 (1958-9), pp. 282-286.

Berend, Eduard. "Die historische Grundlage von Theodor Fontanes Erzählung 'Schach von Wuthenow'." *Deutsche Rundschau,* 50 (1924), pp. 168-182.

Betz, Frederick. "Fontane Scholarship, Literary Sociology, and *Trivialliteraturforschung.*" In *Internationales Archiv für Sozialgeschichte der deutschen Literatur,* 8 (1983), pp. 200-220.

Biener, Joachim. "Zur Aneignung von Fontanes Epik durch Film und Fernsehen." *Fontane-Blätter,* Bd. 4, Heft 8 (1981), pp. 713-728.

Bindokat, Karla. *Effi Briest: Erzählstoff und Erzählinhalt.* Bern: Peter Lang, 1984.

Brackert, Helmut und Marianne Schuller. "Theodor Fontane, *Effi Briest.*" In *Literaturwissenschaft. Grundkurs 1.* Ed. H. Brackert and J. Stückrath. Reinbek bei Hamburg: Rowohlt, 1981, pp. 153-172.

Brinkmann, Richard. *Theodor Fontane: Über die Verbindlichkeit des Unverbindlichen.* Munich, 1967; rpt. Tübingen: Max Niemeyer, 1977.

Buck, Theo. "Zwei Apotheker-Figuren in 'Madame Bovary' und 'Effi Briest'. Anmerkungen zur realistischen Schreibweise bei Flaubert und Fontane." *Jahrbuch der Raabe-Gesellschaft* (1976), pp. 35-59.

Carter, T.E. "A Leitmotif in Fontane's 'Effi Briest'." *German Life and Letters,* 10 (1956-7), pp. 38-42.

Cartland, Harry E. "The 'Old' and the 'New' in Fontane's *Stechlin.*" *Germanic Review,* 54-1 (Winter, 1979), pp. 20-28.

Chambers, Helen Elizabeth. *Supernatural and Irrational Elements in the Works of Theodor Fontane.* Stuttgart: Akademischer Verlag Hans-Dieter Heinz, 1980.

Davis, Gabriele A. Wittig. *Novel Associations: Theodor Fontane and George Eliot within the Context of Nineteenth-Century Realism.* Bern: Peter Lang, 1983.

Degering, Thomas. *Das Verhältnis von Individuum und Gesellschaft in Fontanes 'Effi Briest' und Flauberts 'Madame Bovary'.* Bonn: Bouvier, 1978.

Demetz, Peter. *Formen des Realismus: Theodor Fontane: Kritische Untersuchungen.* Munich, 1964; rpt. Frankfurt: Ullstein, 1973.

-.- *Kitsch, Belletristik, Kunst: Theodor Fontane.* Berlin: Akademie der Künste, 1970.

-.- "Über Fontanes Realismus." *Orbis Litterarum,* 16 (1961), pp. 34-47; rpt. in *Bürgerlicher Realismus.* Ed. K.-D. Müller, pp. 203-213.

Devine, M.C. "Erzähldistanz in Fontanes *Effi Briest.*" In *Formen realistischer Erzählkunst,* pp. 544-549.

Fontane aus heutiger Sicht. Ed. H. Aust. Munich: Nymphenburger Verlag, 1980.

Fontanes Realismus: Wissenschaftliche Konferenz zum 105. Geburtstag Theodor Fontanes in Potsdam: Vorträge und Berichte. Berlin: Akademie Verlag, 1972.

Formen realistischer Erzählkunst. Festschrift for Charlotte Jolles in Honour of her 70th Birthday. Ed. J. Thunecke. Nottingham: Sherwood Agencies, 1979.

Garland, Henry. *The Berlin Novels of Theodor Fontane.* Oxford: Clarendon Press, 1980.

Gauger, Hans-Martin. "Sprachbewußtsein im 'Stechlin'." In *Bild und Gedanke. Festschrift für Gerhard Baumann zum 60. Geburtstag.* Ed. G. Schnitzler. Munich: Fink, 1980, pp. 311-323.

Gilbert, Anna Maria. "A New Look at *Effi Briest*: Genesis und Interpretation." *Deutsche Vierteljahrsschrift für Literatur und Geistesgeschichte,* 53 (1979), pp. 96-114.

Gilbert, Mary-Enole. *Das Gespräch in Fontanes Gesellschaftsroman.* Palaestra, 174. Leipzig: Mayer und Müller, 1930.

-.- "Fontanes 'Effi Briest'." *Deutschunterricht,* 11, Heft 4 (1959), pp. 63-75.

Grawe, Christian. "Wuthenow oder Venedig. Analyse von Schachs reisefantasie im fontaneschen kontext." *Wirkendes Wort,* 30 (1980), pp. 258-267.

Guidry, Glenn. "Myth and Ritual in Fontane's *Effi Briest*." *Germanic Review,* 59-1 (Winter, 1984), pp. 18-25.

Guthke, Karl S. "Fontane's Craft of Fiction: Art or Artifice." In *Essays in Honor of James Edward Walsh.* Cambridge: Goethe Institute of Boston and The Houghton Library, 1983, pp. 67-94.

Hamann, Elsbeth. *Theodor Fontane. Effi Briest.* Munich: Oldenbourg, 1981.

-.- *Theodor Fontanes "Effi Briest" aus erzähltheoretischer Sicht unter besonderer Berücksichtigung der Interdependenzen zwischen Autor, Erzählwerk und Leser.* Bonn: Bouvier, 1984.

Harrigan, Renny. "The Portrayal of the Lower Classes and the Petty Bourgeoisie in Theodor Fontane's Social Novels." Diss. Brown 1973.

Hauschild, Brigitte. *Gesellschaftsformen und Erzählstruktur. Die Darstellung von Geselligkeit und Naturbegegnung bei Gottfried Keller und Theodor Fontane.* Bern: Peter Lang, 1981.

Hildebrandt, Bruno. "Fontane's Altersstil in seinem Roman 'Der Stechlin'." *German Quarterly,* 38 (1965), pp. 139-156.

Hillman, Roger. "Theodor Fontane: *Der Stechlin*." In his *Zeitroman: The Novel and Society in Germany 1830-1900.* Bern: Peter Lang, 1983, pp. 87-116.

Hoeltz, Nikola. "Fontane – mediengerecht?" *Kürbiskern*, 2/79 (1979), pp. 91-104.

Hofmiller, Josef. " 'Stechlin'-Probleme." In his *Die Bücher und wir.* Ed. Hulda Hofmiller. Zürich: Im Verlag der Arche, 1950; rpt. "Fontane: 'Stechlin'-Probleme." In his *Ausgewählte Werke.* Rosenheim: Rosenheimer Verlagshaus, 1975, pp. 224-229.

Jamison, Robert. "The Fearful Education of Effi Briest." *Monatshefte*, 74 (1982), pp. 20-32.

Jolles, Charlotte. " 'Der Stechlin': Fontanes Zaubersee." In *Fontane aus heutiger Sicht*, pp. 239-257.

-.- *Theodor Fontane.* Sammlung Metzler, 114. 3rd edition. Stuttgart: Metzler, 1983.

Koc, Richard A. *The German Gesellschaftsroman at the Turn of the Century: A Comparison of the Works of Theodor Fontane and Eduard von Keyserling.* Bern: Peter Lang, 1982.

Lützen, Wolf-Dieter and W.H. Pott. "Stechlin für viele. Zur historisierenden Bearbeitung einer literarischen Vorlage." In *Literatur in den Massenmedien. Demontage von Dichtung?* Ed. F. Knille, K. Hickethier, and W.D. Lützen. Munich: Hanser, 1976, pp. 103-130.

Lukács, Georg. "Der alte Fontane." In his *Die Grablegung des alten Deutschland*, Reinbek bei Hamburg: Rowohlt, 1967, pp. 120-159.

Magretta, William R. "Reading the Writerly Film: Fassbinder's *Effi Briest* (1974)." In *Modern European Filmmakers and the Art of Adaptation.* Ed. A. Horton and J. Magretta. New York: Frederick Ungar, 1981, pp. 248-262.

Mann, Thomas. "Der alte Fontane." In *Theodor Fontane.* Ed. W. Preisendanz. pp. 1-24.

Martini, Fritz. "Ironischer Realismus: Keller, Raabe und Fontane." In *Ironie und Dichtung.* Ed. A. Schaefer. Munich: Beck, 1970, pp. 113-141.

Meyer, Hermann. *Das Zitat in der Erzählkunst: Zur Geschichte und Poetik des europäischen Romans.* Stuttgart: Metzler, 1961.

Miller, Leslie L. "Fontane's *Effi Briest.* Innstetten's Decision: In Defense of the Gentleman." *German Studies Review,* 4-3 (October, 1981), pp. 383-402.

Minden, Michael. " 'Effi Briest' and 'Die historische Stunde des Takts'." *Modern Language Review,* 76 (1981), pp. 869-879.

Mittelmann, Hanni. *Die Utopie des weiblichen Glücks in den Romanen Theodor Fontanes.* Bern: Peter Lang, 1980.

Mittenzwei, Ingrid. *Die Sprache als Thema. Untersuchungen zu Fontanes Gesellschaftsromanen.* Bad Homburg v.d.H.: Gehlen, 1970.

-.- "Theorie und Roman bei Theodor Fontane." In *Deutsche Romantheorien.* Vol. II. Ed. R. Grimm. 1968; rpt. Frankfurt/Main: Fischer, 1974, pp. 277-294.

Mommsen, Katharina. "Vom 'Bamme-Ton' zum 'Bummel-Ton'. Fontanes Kunst der Sprechweisen." In *Formen realistischer Erzählkunst,* pp. 325-334.

Müller-Seidel, Walter. "Fontane: 'Der Stechlin'." In *Der deutsche Roman.* Vol. II. Ed. B. von Wiese. Düsseldorf: Bagel, 1963, pp. 146-189.

-.- "Gesellschaft und Menschlichkeit im Roman Theodor Fontanes." In *Theodor Fontane.* Ed. W. Preisendanz, pp. 169-200.

-.- *Theodor Fontane: Soziale Romankunst in Deutschland.* Stuttgart: Metzler, 1975.

Ohl, Hubert. "Melusine als Mythos bei Theodor Fontane." In *Mythos und Mythologie in der Literatur des 19. Jahrhunderts.* Ed. H. Koopmann. Frankfurt/Main: Vittorio Klostermann, 1979, pp. 289-305.

Pascal, Roy. *The German Novel.* Toronto: University of Toronto Press, 1956.

Paulsen, Wolfgang. "Zum Stand der heutigen Fontane-Forschung." *Jahrbuch der deutschen Schillergesellschaft,* 25 (1981), pp. 474-508.

Petersen, Julius. "Theodor Fontanes Altersroman." *Euphorion,* 29 (1928), pp. 1-74.

Preisendanz, Wolfgang, ed. *Theodor Fontane.* Wege der Forschung, 381. Düsseldorf: Wissenschaftliche Buchgesellschaft, 1973.

Rainer, Ulrike. "Effi Briest und das Motiv des Chinesen: Rolle und Darstellung in Fontanes Roman." *Zeitschrift für deutsche Philologie,* 101 (1982), pp. 545-561.

Remak, Joachim. *The Gentle Critic: Theodor Fontane and German Politics, 1848-1898.* Syracuse: Syracuse University Press, 1964.

Reuter, Hans-Heinrich. *Fontane.* 2 vols. Munich: Nymphenburger Verlag, 1968.

Richert, Hans-Georg. "Über eine andere Randfigur bei Fontane: Wüllersdorf." *Colloquia Germanica,* 13 (1980), pp. 246-252.

Rychner, Max. "Theodor Fontane: 'Der Stechlin'." In *Deutsche Romane von Grimmelshausen bis Musil.* Ed. J. Schillemeit. Interpretationen, III. Frankfurt/Main: Fischer, 1966, pp. 218-230.

Sagave, Pierre-Paul, ed. *Schach von Wuthenow*. By Theodor Fontane. Frankfurt/ Main: Ullstein, 1966.

-.- " 'Schach von Wuthenow' als politischer Roman." In *Fontanes Realismus*, pp. 87-94.

Schäfer, Renate. "Fontanes Melusine-Motiv." *Euphorion*, 56 (1962), pp. 69-104.

Schafarschik, Walter, ed. *Theodor Fontane: 'Effi Briest': Erläuterungen und Dokumente*. Stuttgart: Reclam, 1972.

Schanze, Helmut. "Fontane Effi Briest: Bemerkungen zu einem Drehbuch von Rainer Werner Fassbinder." In *Literatur in den Massenmedien. Demontage von Dichtung?* Ed. F. Knilli, K. Hickethier, and W.-D. Lützen. Reihe Hanser, 221. Munich: Hanser, 1976, pp. 131-138.

Schillemeit, Jost. *Theodor Fontane: Geist und Kunst seines Alterswerkes*. Zürcher Beiträge, 19. Zürich: Atlantis, 1961.

Schlaffer, H. "Das Schicksalsmodell in Fontanes Romanwerk." *Germanisch-Romanische Monatsschrift*, 16 (1966), pp. 392-409.

Schmalbruch, Ursula. "Zum Melusine-Motiv in Fontanes 'Cécile'." *Text und Kontext*, 8 (1980), pp. 127-144.

Schuster, Ingrid. "Exotik als Chiffre: Zum Chinesen in *Effi Briest*." *Wirkendes Wort*, 33 (1983), pp. 115-125.

Schwan, Werner. "Fontanes 'Stechlin' als Roman einer sozialen Lebensweise." *Text und Kontext*, 12 (1984), pp. 64-100.

Škreb, Zdenko. "Fragen zum deutschen Realismus: Fontane." *Jahrbuch der Raabe-Gesellschaft* (1979), pp. 155-185.

Stern, J.P. "Realism and Tolerance: Theodor Fontane." In his *Re-interpretations: Seven Studies in Nineteenth-Century German Literature*. New York: Basic Books, 1964, pp. 301-347.

Strech, Heiko. *Theodor Fontane: Die Synthese von Alt und Neu. 'Der Stechlin' als Summe des Gesamtwerks*. Berlin: Erich Schmidt Verlag, 1970.

Swales, Erika. "Private Mythologies and Public Unease: On Fontane's *Effi Briest*." *Modern Language Review*, 75 (1980), pp. 114-123.

Thanner, Josef. "Symbol and Function of the Symbol in Theodor Fontane's 'Effi Briest'." *Monatshefte*, 57 (1965), pp. 187-192.

Thum, Reinhard. "Symbol, Motif and Leitmotif in Fontane's 'Effi Briest'." *Germanic Review*, 54 (1979), pp. 115-124.

Tontsch, Ulrike. *Der 'Klassiker' Fontane: Ein Rezeptionsprozeß*. Bonn: Bouvier, 1977.

Utz, Peter. "Effi Briest, der Chinese und der Imperialismus: eine 'Geschichte' im geschichtlichen Kontext." *Zeitschrift für deutsche Philologie.* 103 (1984), pp. 212-225.

Vaget, H. R. "Schach von Wuthenow: 'Psychographie' und 'Spiegelung' im 14. Kapitel von Fontanes 'Schach von Wuthenow'." *Monatshefte,* 61 (1969), pp. 1-14.

Verchau, Ekkhard. *Theodor Fontane. Individuum und Gesellschaft.* Frankfurt/ Main: Ullstein, 1983.

Vincenz, Guido. *Fontanes Welt. Eine Interpretation des Stechlin.* Diss. Zürich 1966. Zürich: Juris Druck und Verlag, 1966.

von Wiese, Benno. "Theodor Fontane: 'Schach von Wuthenow'." In *Die deutsche Novelle von Goethe bis Kafka: Interpretationen.* Vol. II. Ed. B. von Wiese. Düsseldorf: Bagel, 1963, pp. 236-260.

Wagner, Walter. *Theodor Fontane: Schach von Wuthenow: Erläuterungen und Dokumente.* Stuttgart: Reclam, 1980.

Wandrey, Conrad. *Theodor Fontane.* Munich: Beck, 1919.

Waniek, Erdmann. "Beim zweiten Lesen: der Beginn von Fontanes *Effi Briest* als verdinglichtes *tableau vivant.*" *German Quarterly,* 55 (1982), pp. 164-174.

Wittkowski, Wolfgang. "Theodor Fontane und der Gesellschaftsroman." In *Handbuch des deutschen Romans.* Ed. H. Koopmann. Düsseldorf: Bagel, 1983, pp. 418-433.

Wolff, Jürgen. "Verfahren der Literaturrezeption im Film, dargestellt am Beispiel der Effi-Briest-Verfilmungen von Luderer und Fassbinder." *Der Deutschunterricht,* 33 (1981), pp. 47-75.

VI. Wilhelm Raabe

Raabe, Wilhelm. *Sämtliche Werke,* Vols. XVIII (Göttingen: Vandenhoeck and Ruprecht, 1963), XIX (Freiburg/Braunschweig: Klemm, 1957).

Bange, Pierre. "Stopfkuchen. Le solipsisme de l'original et l'humour." *Études Germaniques,* 24 (1969), pp. 1-15.

Brewster, Philip J. "Onkel Ketschwayo in Neuteutoburg. Zeitgeschichtliche Anspielungen in Raabes 'Stopfkuchen'." *Jahrbuch der Raabe-Gesellschaft* (1983), pp. 96-118.

Bullivant, Keith. "Wilhelm Raabe and the European Novel." *Orbis Litterarum,* 31 (1976), pp. 263-281.

Daemmrich, Horst. *Wilhelm Raabe*. Boston: Twayne, 1981.

David, Claude. "Über Wilhelm Raabes Stopfkuchen." In *Lebendige Form: Festschrift für Heinrich Henel*. Ed. J. Sammons and E. Schürer. Munich: Fink, 1970.

Derks, Paul. *Raabe-Studien: Beiträge zur Anwendung psychoanalytischer Interpretationsmodelle: 'Stopfkuchen' und 'Das Odfeld'*. Bonn: Bouvier, 1976.

-.- "Eduard als Kunstfigur. Zu Wilhelm Raabes 'Stopfkuchen'." In *Jahrbuch der Raabe-Gesellschaft* (1976), pp. 60-68.

Detroy, Peter. *Wilhelm Raabe: Der Humor als Gestaltungsprinzip im 'Stopfkuchen'*. Bonn: Bouvier, 1970.

Dierkes, Hans. "Der 'Zauber des Gegensatzes': Schopenhauer und Wilhelm Raabes Stopfkuchen." In *Schopenhauer-Jahrbuch,* 54 (1973), pp. 93-107.

Eisele, Ulf. *Der Dichter und sein Detektiv: Raabes 'Stopfkuchen' und die Frage des Realismus*. Tübingen: Max Niemeyer, 1979.

Emrich, Wilhelm. "Personalität und Zivilisation in Wilhelm Raabes 'Die Akten des Vogelsangs'." *Jahrbuch der Raabe-Gesellschaft* (1982), pp. 7-25.

Fairley, Barker. *Wilhelm Raabe: An Introduction to his Novels*. Oxford: At the Clarendon Press, 1961.

-.- "The Modernity of Wilhelm Raabe." In *German Studies*. Oxford: Basil Blackwell, 1952.

Folkes, Gernot. *Besitz und Sicherheit. Über Entstehung und Zerfall einer bürgerlichen Illusion am Beispiel Goethes und Raabes*. Kronberg/Cz.: Scriptor, 1976.

Guardini, Romano. "Über Wilhelm Raabes 'Stopfkuchen'." 1932. Rpt. in *Raabe in neuer Sicht*. Ed. H. Helmers. Stuttgart: Kohlhammer, 1968, pp. 12-43.

Hahn, Walther L. "Zum Erzählvorgang in Raabes 'Akten des Vogelsangs'." In *Jahrbuch der Raabe-Gesellschaft* (1972), pp. 61-71.

Helmers, Hermann. *Die bildenden Mächte in den Romanen Wilhelm Raabes*. Weinheim: Julius Beetz, 1960.

-.- ed. *Raabe in neuer Sicht*. Stuttgart: Kohlhammer, 1968.

-.- *Wilhelm Raabe*. Sammlung Metzler, 71. 2nd. ed. Stuttgart: Metzler, 1978.

Hoppe, Karl. *Wilhelm Raabe: Beiträge zum Verständnis seiner Person und seines Werkes*. Göttingen: Vandenhoeck und Ruprecht, 1967.

Kolbe, Hans. *Wilhelm Raabe. Vom Entwicklungs- zum Desillusionierungsroman*. Berlin/GDR: Akademie Verlag, 1981.

Koll, Rolf-Dieter. *Raumgestaltung bei Wilhelm Raabe*. Bonn: Bouvier, 1977.

Margotton, Jean-Charles. "Stopfkuchen, de W. Raabe. À propos de la structure narrative du roman." *Études Germaniques,* 36 (1981), pp. 291-305.

Martini, Fritz. "Wilhelm Raabe." In *Deutsche Dichter des 19. Jahrhunderts.* Ed. B. von Wiese. Berlin: Erich Schmidt, 1969, pp. 528-556.

Matschke, Günther. *Die Isolation als Mittel der Gesellschaftskritik bei Wilhelm Raabe.* Bonn: Bouvier, 1975.

Meyer, Hermann. *Der Sonderling in der deutschen Dichtung.* Munich: Hanser, 1963.

Ohl, Hubert. "Der Bürger und das Unbedingte bei Wilhelm Raabe." In *Jahrbuch der Raabe-Gesellschaft* (1979), pp. 7-26.

Pascal, Roy. "The Reminiscence-Technique in Raabe." *Modern Language Review,* 49 (1954), pp. 339-384.

Pongs, Hermann. "Wilhelm Raabes Roman 'Stopfkuchen'." In his *Das Bild in der deutschen Dichtung.* Vol. III. Marburg: N.G. Elwert, 1969, pp. 361-383.

Preisendanz, Wolfgang. "Die Erzählstruktur als Bedeutungskomplex der 'Akten des Vogelsangs'." *Jahrbuch der Raabe-Gesellschaft* (1981), pp. 210-224.

Richter, Helmut. "Erinnerung an einen alten Dichter." *Sinn und Form,* 12 (1960), pp. 869-894.

Sammons, Jeffrey L. "Wilhelm Raabe's *Stopfkuchen.* Pro and Contra." In *Wilhelm Raabe. Studien zu seinem Leben und Werk.* Ed. L.A. Lensing and H.-W. Peter. Braunschweig: pp-Verlag, 1981, pp. 281-298.

Sander, Volkmar. "Corviniana non leguntur. Gedanken zur Raabe-Rezeption in Amerika und England." *Jahrbuch der Raabe-Gesellschaft* (1981), pp. 118-127.

-.- "Illusionszerstörung und Wirklichkeitserfassung im Roman Raabes." In *Deutsche Romantheorien.* Ed. R. Grimm. Vol. II. Frankfurt: Fischer, Athenäum, 1974, pp. 262-276.

Schmidt-Stotz, Regina. *Von Finkenrode nach Altershausen. Das Motiv der Heimkehr im Werk Wilhelm Raabes als Ausdruck einer sich wandelnden Lebenseinstellung, dargestellt an fünf Romanen aus fünf Lebensabschnitten.* Bern: Lang, 1984.

Schomerus, Hans. "Salas y Gomez und die Rote Schanze: Von der Einsamkeit des Menschen." In *Jahrbuch der Raabe-Gesellschaft* (1968), pp. 41-48.

Schultz, Hartwig. "Werk- und Autorintention in Raabes 'Alten Nestern' und 'Akten des Vogelsangs'." In *Jahrbuch der Raabe-Gesellschaft* (1979), pp. 132-154.

Schweckendiek, Adolf. "Wilhelm Raabes 'Stopfkuchen'. Eine ketzerische Betrachtung." In *Jahrbuch der Raabe-Gesellschaft* (1974), pp. 75-97.

Sorg, Bernard. "Realismus und Resignation: Wilhelm Raabe." In his *Zur literarischen Schopenhauer-Rezeption im 19. Jahrhundert.* Heidelberg: Winter, 1975, pp. 159-184.

Sprengel, Peter. "Interieur und Eigentum. Zur Soziologie bürgerlicher Subjektivität bei Wilhelm Raabe." In *Jahrbuch der Jean-Paul-Gesellschaft*, 9 (1974), pp. 127-176.

Warnke, Gisela. "Das 'Sünder'-Motiv in Wilhelm Raabes 'Stopfkuchen'." *DVjs*, 50 (1976), pp. 465-476.

Wassermann, Felix. " 'Die Akten des Vogelsangs' und das Problem der bürgerlichen Existenz im Neuen Reich." *German Quarterly*, 36 (1963), pp. 421-433.

Webster, William T. "Der 'Hinhocker' und der 'Weltwanderer'. Zur Bedeutung der Reise bei Wilhelm Raabe." *Jahrbuch der Raabe-Gesellschaft* (1982), pp. 26-39.

-.- "Idealisierung oder Ironie? Verstehen und Mißverstehen in Wilhelm Raabes 'Stopfkuchen'." *Jahrbuch der Raabe-Gesellschaft* (1978), pp. 146-170.

-.- "Social Change and Personal Insecurity in the Late Novels of Wilhelm Raabe." In *Formen realistischer Erzählkunst*, pp. 233-243.

Wilhelm Raabe. Studien zu seinem Leben und Werk. Ed. L.A. Lensing and H.-W. Peter. Braunschweig: pp-Verlag, 1981.

Wischniewski, Horst. " 'Die Akten des Vogelsangs' Freiheit in Wilhelm Raabes Roman." *Jahrbuch der Raabe-Gesellschaft* (1974), pp. 98-101.

Witschel, Günter. *Raabe-Integrationen: 'Die Innerste', 'Das Odfeld', 'Stopfkuchen'.* Bonn: Bouvier, 1969.

Zwilgmeyer, Franz. "Archetypische Bewußtseinsstufen in Raabes Werken insbesondere in den 'Akten des Vogelsangs'." *Jahrbuch der Raabe-Gesellschaft* (1984), pp. 99-120.

NEW YORK UNIVERSITY OTTENDORFER SERIES. NEUE FOLGE

Bd. 1   Rosenbauer, Brecht und der Behaviorismus. 102 Seiten, 1970.
Bd. 2   Zipes, The Great Refusal, Studies of the Romantic Hero in German and American Literature. 158 Seiten, 1970.
Bd. 3   Hughes, Mythos und Geschichtsoptimismus in Thomas Manns Joseph Romanen. 116 Seiten, 1975.
Bd. 4   Salloch, Peter Weiss' «Die Ermittlung». Zur Struktur des Dokumentartheaters. 170 Seiten, 1972.
Bd. 5   Peter/Grathoff/Hayes/Loose, Ideologiekritische Studien zur Literatur, Essays I. 260 Seiten, 1972.
Bd. 6   Seitz, Johann Fischarts Geschichtsklitterung zur Prosastruktur und zum grobianischen Motivkomplex. 252 Seiten, 1974.
Bd. 7   Vaget/Barnouw, Thomas Mann-Studien zu Fragen der Rezeption. 158 Seiten, 1975.
Bd. 8   Baron/Mühsam/Heidesieck/Grimm/Theisz, Ideologiekritische Studien zur Literatur. Essays II. 158 Seiten, 1975.
Bd. 9   Silbermann, Literature of the Working World. A Study of the Industrial Novel in East Germany. 118 Seiten, 1976.
Bd. 10 Rosellini, Thomas Müntzer im deutschen Drama. Verteufelung. Apotheose und Kritik. 176 Seiten, 1978.
Bd. 11 Antosik, The Question of Elites. An Essay on the Cultural Elitism of Nietzsche, George and Hesse. 204 Seiten, 1978.
Bd. 12 Becker, A War of Fools. The Letters of Obscure Men: A Study of the Satire and the Satirized. 190 Seiten, 1981.
Bd. 13 Van Cleve, Herlequin Besieged. The Reception of Comedy in Germany during the Early Enlightenment. 203 Seiten, 1980.
Bd. 14 McKnight, The Novels of Johann Karl Wezel. Satire. Realism and Social Criticism in Late 18th Century Literature. 311 Seiten, 1981.
Bd. 15 Stern, Gegenbild, Reihenfolge, Sprung. An Essay on Related Figures of Argument in Walter Benjamin. 121 Seiten, 1982.
Bd. 16 Poore, German-American Socialist Literature, 1865–1900. 225 Seiten, 1982.
Bd. 17 Berman, Between Fontane and Tucholsky: Literary Criticism and the Public Sphere in Imperial Germany. 175 Seiten, 1983.
Bd. 18 Blevins, Franz Xaver Kroetz: The Emergence of a Political Playwright. 295 Seiten, 1983.
Bd. 19 Grimm, Texturen – Essays und anderes zu Hans Magnus Enzensberger. 236 Seiten, 1984.
Bd. 20 Reutershan, Clara Zetkin und Brot und Rosen... Literaturpolitische Konflikte zwischen Partei und Frauenbewegung in der deutschen Vorkriegssozialdemokratie. 264 Seiten, 1985.
Bd. 21 Teraoka, The Silence of Entropy or Universal Discourse. The Postmodernist Poetics of Heiner Müller. 240 Seiten, 1985.
Bd. 22 Kirchberger, Franz Kafka's Use of Law in Fiction. A New Interpretation of «In der Strafkolonie», «Der Prozess», and «Das Schloss». 212 Seiten, 1986.
Bd. 23 Kaiser, Social Integration and Narrative Structure. Patterns of Realism in Auerbach, Freytag, Fontane, and Raabe. 230 Seiten, 1986.

Die Bände 1, 2, 4, 5 und 6 sind direkt beim Athenäum-Verlag in Frankfurt/M. zu beziehen. Alle übrigen, sowie die später erscheinenden Bände werden durch den Verlag Peter Lang AG, Bern hergestellt und ausgeliefert.